Regional Development in Communist Yugoslavia

Regional Development in Communist Yugoslavia

Success, Failure, and Consequences

Dijana Pleština

Routledge
Taylor & Francis Group
LONDON AND NEW YORK

First published 1992 by Westview Press, Inc.

Published 2019 by Routledge
52 Vanderbilt Avenue, New York, NY 10017
2 Park Square, Milton Park, Abingdon, Oxon OX14 4RN

Routledge is an imprint of the Taylor & Francis Group, an informa business

Library of Congress Cataloging-in-Publication Data
Pleština, Dijana.
Regional development in Communist Yugoslavia : success, failure, and consequences / by Dijana Pleština.
p. cm.
Includes bibliographical references and index.
ISBN 0-8133-8186-X
1. Yugoslavia—Economic conditions—1945- —Regional disparities.
2. Yugoslavia—Economic policy—1945- I. Title.
HC407.P57 1992
330.9497'02—dc20 92-32259
CIP

ISBN 13: 978-0-367-28544-9 (hbk)

ISBN 13: 978-0-367-30090-6 (pbk)

To Pat, Felix and D. J.

Contents

Tables

Acronyms and Abbreviations

BiH	Bosnia-Hercegovina
BOAL	Basic Organization of Associated Labor
CPY	Communist Party of Yugoslavia
Development Fund/The Fund	Fund for the Accelerated Development of the Insufficiently Developed Republics and the Autonomous Province of Kosovo
DR	Developed Region
FEC	Federal Executive Council
FNRJ	Federalna Narodna Republika Jugoslavije (Federal Peoples' Republic of Yugoslavia)
GIF	General Investment Fund
GMP	Gross Material Product
LCY	League of Communists of Yugoslavia
LDR	Less Developed Region
SFRY	Socialist Federative Republic of Yugoslavia

Acknowledgments

The research for this book was first undertaken in fall 1982 thanks to the Canada-Yugoslavia Exchange Fellowship. The University of California, Berkeley, provided additional support for research in Yugoslavia as well as for the early stages of the writing through the U. C. Chancellor's Fellowship, the Robert A. Braden Fellowship and the Andrew W. Mellon Fellowship. For the latter two, I thank the Department of Political Science and the Center for Slavic and East European Studies. I also thank Andrew Janos, Kenneth Jowitt and Laura D'Andrea Tyson for their early guidance on the dissertation on which this book is based. Three institutions provided the support necessary to complete the project. The Social Science Research Council organized a Workshop on Soviet and East European Economics in July 1989, which was a welcome forum for a great deal of helpful discussion. The PICAS Fellowship held at the University of Michigan in Ann Arbor enabled me to begin rewriting the book in spring 1990. Finally, without the continuing support of the College of Wooster, from which I received summer research grants from 1988 to 1992, it would have been impossible to bring to date information on Yugoslav regional development policies and effects and thus to finish this book.

From September 1982 to November 1983, while holding the Canada-Yugoslavia Exchange Fellowship, I was based at the University of Belgrade. Professor Ljubislav Markovic kindly arranged access to various libraries and closed collections and generally proved helpful in the early orientation in Belgrade. During those fifteen months I travelled extensively throughout Yugoslavia. While the travelling and the work load on the trips were often gruelling, the courtesy and unfailing helpfulness of my respondents, especially in the less developed regions, provided that extra push when my stamina and energy faltered. Their surprise and genuine delight that I was Croatian, and as such "theirs," showed in their frequent exclamations of *"a, pa ti si nasa!"* (well, you're [one] of *ours!*); their pleasure that though now living in America I still wanted to find out about them made me indeed feel Yugoslav, in the best sense of the word. The time and effort they spent in the exchange of information and ideas cannot be overemphasized. For that I thank each person named in Appendix III.

Additionally, there are a few individuals whose endless patience in repeated and/or particularly long and exhaustive interviews I wish to especially acknowledge: Milovan Djilas, Bosko Gluscevic, Hasan Zolic, Misa Jandric, Marjan Korosic, Sulejman Kamenica, Ljubislav Markovic, Kosta Mihailovic, Mihailo Mladenovic, Jovan Radovanovic, Maurice Romano and Rudi Supek were particularly generous with their time and energy and helpful in explaining the broader socio-political context in which regional development occurred.

Various parts of the manuscript were read by friends and colleagues to whom I remain indebted. Many of their helpful remarks and incisive comments have been incorporated into the book. For this I thank Ellen Elias-Bursac, Aleksandar Bogunovic, Ognjen Caldarovic, Bogomil Ferfila, Gregory Grossman, Thomas Hellie, David Ost, Stjepan Plestina, Jan Svejnar and Mark Weaver.

Without my family in Croatia and Canada, who provided love and support, this project would have been far more difficult to carry out. In particular, I thank my family in Zagreb and Novska, who have continued through the years to provide me with a bed and a place for my suitcase even though I come so often and often stay for so long.

The assistance provided by Sarah Choudhury, Kimberly Niezgoda and Teresa Wilson was most helpful in the completion of the manuscript. Kim's library research kept me supplied with the books that I needed. Terry and Sarah did an excellent job typing and preparing the manuscript for camera-ready copy. The skill, good humor and encouragement of all three lightened my work considerably. In addition, Sarah undertook the task of indexing as well as of seeing the project through to completion. I am immensely grateful to her for her excellent work.

Finally, there are a number of individuals who, through the years, directly or indirectly contributed a great deal to this book. Richard Lowenthal, who in his own life so successfully combined social and political involvement with intellectual concerns, has been an inspiration. Patricia Walker has helped me to find a voice without which it would have been impossible to write. The friendship and the shared conversations with Gary Bonham and Christine Paige have been important throughout this project. Issues of social equity and social justice, which form the background of this project, were first explored many years ago with Atul Kohli. Those times of shared concerns and mutual support I continue to cherish. Marina Gozze-Gucetic and Branislav Pujevic have for years provided me with my home in Belgrade. Jovan Radovanovic has been a friend and a colleague for a decade. Our long conversations have helped me to understand a great deal of the "Yugoslav" realities, perceptions and self-perceptions. In Zagreb, I can always count on a well-informed, intelligent and thoughtful perspective thanks to my friend and cousin Mario Weisser.

To the above-mentioned, this acknowledgment is a small expression of my gratitude.

Dijana Pleština

Introduction

I feel compelled to begin by acknowledging that my interest in Yugoslav politics in general and in the politics of regional development in particular is not that of a supposedly neutral observer; nor is it a recent development based upon the savage war currently being waged on its soil. I was born in Zagreb. My experiences of the 1950s, filtered through the memory of childhood were, like those of most small children, shaped by the prism of family life. One *Jaffa* orange carefully wrapped in tissue paper, brought to my sister's birthday party as the present; certain friends coming to our house every few weeks for a bath; visiting our *kumove*[1] and walking self-consciously through their once-large apartment, now subdivided among several families, until we were in the one room that remained theirs. Later, after my parents left Yugoslavia, and my sister and I went to live with our grandparents on their farm, I became part of a still different world. Peasant women walking barefoot on the dusty, dirt-packed road, one hand steadying the baskets of cheese and *kajmak*[2] perched on their heads, in the other carrying their town-shoes, meant market days and excitement if we too were going to buy piglets or sell a cow; a marker on the side of the road where a partisan had been killed by the *ustase* was the half-way point to a friend's house; a tin of orange marmalade, left-over from food packages dropped by Americans during the war, was the prize found in the pantry one cleaning day; and daily card games with my dear grandfather who, crushed by the helplessness of watching his once-prosperous flour mill nationalized then left empty to crumble before his eyes, would be briefly assuaged by a high-spirited and blissfully happy granddaughter.

Two decades later, when I began my graduate work at U.C., Berkeley, those childhood memories reemerged and gave substance and color to the study of modernizing peasant societies. Problems of rapid urbanization and shortages of consumer goods, aggravated by the "socialist" framework which decreed discriminatory policies against agriculture, especially that of the private sector, and which, in its zeal

1 The closest English translation of *kumove* in this case is godparents.

2 *Kajmak* is an unprocessed dairy product not unlike whey or crème fraîche.

for egalitarianism, first nationalized and then so often destroyed through incompetence the small enterprises in their charge, were already familiar to me. But that came later. In 1957, the orchards, fields and gardens, all immense and beautiful, were mine to roam at will. The interruption to this happiness was sudden, swift and, to a child, horribly final. The exit visas arrived, and my sister and I were taken first to Germany to join our parents, and, henceforth, to Canada.

I first returned to Yugoslavia in the summer of 1968 and again in 1969. My grandfather had died, my aunt and two uncles had married, and four little cousins stared shyly as we met for the first time. Much had changed in Yugoslavia in the intervening decade, all of it for the better. The country was more open; foreigners came to holiday on the Adriatic and those Yugoslavs who could afford to were now free to travel to the West. In the house, wood cooking stoves had been replaced or supplemented by small gas stoves, and the urban middle class in the supposedly classless society was acquiring modern conveniences; transistor radios, telephones and even waist-high refrigerators were not uncommon, especially in the cities, nor were cars, the ultimate symbol of freedom. One uncle, who had worked on Yugoslav-run projects in the Middle East and had earned foreign currency, had bought a German-made Opel; the other uncle had the more common, tiny, Yugoslav-made Fiat. But with a car and more or less open borders, they, like so many others, felt that the gap with the West was beginning to close.

By 1973 the feeling had grown. Although political retrenchment following the purge of the liberal-nationalists in Croatia and Serbia in 1971 and 1972 showed that, even in Yugoslavia, free speech and dissent had definite limits, living conditions continued to improve. Now, even relatives who still lived in small towns and on farms scattered throughout Slavonia had refrigerators, and at least one person in every family had bought the small Fiat; the city relatives now owned washing machines and, at least once a year, travelled to Italy to buy jeans and other fashionable clothing.

I spent six months in Yugoslavia in 1973, living on my own and for a time working as an interpreter for an import-export firm specializing in lumber and wood products. As a natural extension of my life there, I took out a Yugoslav identity card and passport. It was a logical step given that I had desperately not wanted to leave as a child, that I loved the country (what I knew of it) and that I *felt* Yugoslav; that step was also to prove extremely helpful nine years later when I began my doctoral research.

When I returned to Yugoslavia in the spring of 1974 after a month of travel through Turkey, Iran, Afghanistan and Pakistan and a four-month stay in India and Nepal, Yugoslavia seemed like the proverbial land of milk and honey. The sheer amount and the nature of the poverty I had seen during those five months of travel by trains and buses were staggering. The economic disparities, class-based ones so visible in cities like Istanbul, Teheran and Delhi (or, as an earlier trip around the North American continent had disclosed, in Los Angeles, Mexico and Washington), as well as more regional ones, were conspicuously absent in what I had seen of Yugoslavia. The Yugoslav way of life and the system that made it possible seemed far better, certainly far more equitable and humane, than what I had seen elsewhere.

In 1978 I returned for another semester-long stay. This time I travelled beyond the Croatian areas of Slavonia and Dalmatia, where I had family, to Montenegro, Bosnia-Hercegovina and Serbia. The differences between what I had known of Yugoslavia from travelling in the "north" and these areas in the "south" were visually striking. A skyline of minarets and steeples, the latter both Orthodox and Catholic, peasant dress so varied and so colorful, the foods--*burek* and *pljeskavica* as common as the ubiquitous *snicl* in the "north"--and, of course, the music . . . and the traditional arts . . . ; the variety was extraordinary and marvellous.

However, the disparities in development and in lifestyle between the Slovenia and Croatia that I knew and the areas I was travelling through and discovering, were also striking--and troubling. Often what I saw in these regions reminded me of what I remembered of Yugoslavia of the 1950s and at times even of what I had seen while travelling to and in India. Dirt roads, ragged children, open sewers or peasants who would get off the bus in the middle of nowhere to take a path which led across mountains to a hamlet on the other side--all these were a stark contrast to life in the "north." There, by 1978, Volkswagens had replaced the tiny Fiats and major cities could boast occasional traffic congestion, shopping trips to Italy had become *de rigueur* for the growing middle class, and the yearning, and to some extent the accessibility, for the "exotic" could be seen in such things as the proliferation of new and modified dessert recipes substituting bananas, kiwis and pineapples for apples, cherries and strawberries.

The previous year I had returned to graduate school in order to explore more systematically phenomena I had seen or experienced as a result of my own background and my continuing links to Yugoslavia, as well as of living and travelling in North America, Europe and India. The questions that interested me the most were related to poverty and conditions which create, perpetuate or alleviate it, the role of governments in these and the effects of development-oriented policies and plans. By 1982 these broad concerns had crystallized around the topic of regional development in communist Yugoslavia. For, by 1982, the Yugoslav economy was in crisis and regional differences over the allocation of shrinking resources to the less developed regions (LDRs) had led to a government impasse, one result of which was the year-and-a-half delay in passing the 1981-1985 Five-Year Plan. Clearly, regional development was a critical issue in Yugoslav domestic politics if differences over it could delay the five-year plan at a time of economic crisis. Yet I could find no comprehensive study of the subject.

Furthermore, I wasn't sure myself whether economic inequalities between republics and regions in Yugoslavia had increased or decreased, and how significantly, under communist rule. The perusal of Yugoslav literature revealed a debate of sorts, which seemed to indicate that inequalities had increased, although the conclusion varied according to the indicators used, the regions examined and, most of all, who was presenting the argument: the developed regions (DRs) or the less developed regions (LDRs). The Western studies which discussed briefly the problem of Yugoslav regional development generally indicated that the disparities had grown. That was both curious and somewhat counterintuitive despite what I had seen while travelling in the LDRs in 1978.

For although regional disparities between the "north" and the "south" in the international arena were widening as were those within most capitalist countries, Yugoslavia's circumstances were different. First, unlike liberal democracies, both developing and developed, independence from a sometimes fickle electorate freed the Yugoslav regime to pursue economic policies which could be painful in the short run but which might be necessary for long-term development. At the same time, unlike other communist states of East Europe, Yugoslavia was free to pursue a development model best suited to its capacity and needs with no fear of Soviet intervention. Indeed, throughout the postwar period it benefited from a long and rare period of international political stability, certainly an asset to economic development. Furthermore, throughout this period of international stability, there was also domestic stability and leadership continuity. Tito, who had assumed leadership of the CPY in 1937 and of Yugoslavia in 1945, continued to rule the country until his death in May 1980. And although his rule was punctuated by periods of political turmoil, these periods were always brief, localized and, most importantly, successfully contained.

Finally, during this time of international and domestic stability and leadership continuity, Yugoslavia's political system had undergone dramatic changes. The highly centralized, Soviet-patterned Yugoslavia of the early days was a very different country from the self-managed, decentralized and relatively open Yugoslavia of the post-1965 Reform. Yet, in both centralized and decentralized periods, despite the reiteration in every five-year plan that "development . . . through industrialization so that the developed states continue to develop, but the less developed are enabled to catch up in 'revolutionary jumps'"[3] would remain one of the priorities of the regime, it seemed that economic inequalities between the developed and less developed had continued to increase. In a reportedly socialist state, where for both pragmatic and ideological reasons the narrowing of economic inequalities between republics and regions should have been and, according to every formal pronouncement made by the regime, was a priority, the increase in inequalities was problematic. Furthermore, since in mutinational Yugoslavia the politicization of economic inequalities along ethnonational lines, especially as these corresponded to the political and national boundaries, was likely, this increase in inequalities was also dangerous. Thus, if economic inequalities had increased, how could one explain it? That's what I wanted to find out.

More specifically, I wanted to know first how the regime had performed in one area, that of regional development, which, after all, for a socialist state was crucial since the claim to narrowing economic inequalities was at the core of its *raison d'être.* For that I needed to find out if economic inequalities between the DRs and the LDRs really did increase as was usually claimed and, if they did, if that increase occurred across the board, for all LDRs and according to all indicators of development or, if the results were more differentiated with inequalities increasing according to certain indicators and/or in some regions though decreasing in others. Second, I wanted to know how those most closely associated with the regime viewed and explained their performance. For that I sought to find out how the Yugoslavs judged their effort and their record on regional development and, if the disparities had increased, how they explained that increase.

[3]Boris Kidric, *Privredni problemi FNRJ* [*Economic Problems of FSRY*] (Belgrade: Kultura, 1948). Kidric, who was also part of Tito's close entourage from 1937, became Chairman of the Economic Council and Minister of Industry in 1946 and architect of Yugoslavia's highly ambitious First Five-Year Plan, inaugurated in April 1947. As a member of the Politburo and Chairman of the State Planning Commission, he was responsible for passing the first reforms of the economic system. He died in 1953 of leukemia.

To answer these questions I examined each of the four postwar decades in terms of policies pursued and their effects on regional development as well as the "Yugoslav" respondents' perceptions of their effort and its results. The decades were further subdivided into the five-year plan periods, and although there is some overlapping between the planning period and the decade, these are minimal and of no consequence to the argument. The interviews were first conducted from fall 1982 to winter 1983 and subsequently yearly from 1988 to 1992. They were conducted in all the republics and regions of Yugoslavia, and the respondents were drawn from a wide cross section of academics, bureaucrats and politicians who were involved in the advising, planning or implementation of regional development policies.[4] The four chapters, Chapter 2 through Chapter 5, which examine and assess regional development policies and effects from 1950 to 1990 as well as the Yugoslav perceptions and explanations of these, form the core of the study. Chapter 6 summarizes the various explanations given by the Yugoslavs for the regime's failure to abolish regional economic inequalities by aggregating the various explanations into three categories. This classification is useful for providing some theoretical underpinning to the discussion as well as for clarifying the arguments and positions of the Yugoslav decision-makers. It also illustrates how the Yugoslavs' perception and position on regional inequalities (1) varied according to their region of origin and (2) changed over time.

The three categories which encompass the explanations are: (1) the lack of a *coherent plan of development;* (2) the explanations which center on *external politics,* notably the geopolitical argument according to which international tensions forced a shift in goal priority, relegating regional development for the first fifteen to twenty years to a low rank on the list of regime priorities and the economic argument, which holds that lack of economic resources prevented the Yugoslav Communist regime from actively pursuing development of the LDRs before 1960 or even 1965; and (3) the explanations based on the imperatives of *domestic politics,* which, in addition to the economic argument, consider the role of ideology, the ethnic-national conflict and the power of interest groups as decisive after 1965 in forcing a displacement of the goal of faster development of the LDRs from its place of priority.

[4]For more on the conceptual and methodological difficulties encountered, as well as on the research method used, please see Appendix I. For a list of the formal questions posed to the respondents in the first phase of the interview process, 1982-1983, see Appendix II. For a complete list of those interviewed, see Appendix III.

Although the various explanations for regional development which characterized certain periods are not exclusive of each other, they were chosen on the basis of their importance in determining the policies pursued in that specific period. Thus, as we shall see in Chapter 2, explanations for the Yugoslavs' failure to abolish regional inequality in the 1950s are based on *external* factors, notably on the Yugoslav geopolitical and economic situations. Chapter 3 will examine the impact of the rise of *domestic politics*, specifically of the rise of ethnonationalism and of economic cycles on regional development in the 1960s; in addition to the continuing influence of these two, the shift in ideology to permit the pursuit of economic interests in the 1970s will be examined in Chapter 4.

Because there is so much current discussion of "nationalism" and "ethnic-nationalism," it is important to note how I use these terms. I have chosen to use *ethnonationalism* (or *ethnic-nationalism* when stylistic considerations warrant it) to differentiate what James Kellas calls the "'exclusive nationalism', since it excludes from membership of the nation those people who do not share a common ethnicity, which usually means a common descent," from "official nationalism of the state, encompassing all those legally entitled to be citizens, irrespective of their ethnicity, national identity or culture."[5] Thus, it was nationalism *tout court* (what Kellas calls "official nationalism") which rallied the Yugoslav population behind Tito and the CPY at the time of the Cominform resolution in 1948 and which they tried to further promote through the policy of *Jugosloventsvo*. But it was ethnonationalism (or ethnic-nationalism), the "divisive nationalism"[6] both of the officially recognized nations of the former Yugoslavia (Slovenes, Croats, Serbs, Montenegrins, Macedonians and, after 1968, Bosnian Moslems) as well as of the unrecognized Albanians of Kosovo, each of which inhabited its own distinct political unit--a republic or, in the case of Kosovo, a region--which played such a critical role in

[5]For an excellent discussion on nationalism and ethnicity see James G. Kellas, *The Politics of Nationalism and Ethnicity* (New York: St. Martin's Press, 1971), pp. 51-52; see also Paul R. Brass, *Ethnicity and Nationalism* (New Delhi: Sage Publications, 1991), Paul S. Shoup, ed., *Problems of Balkan Security; Southeastern Europe in the 1990s* (Washington: The Wilson Center Press, 1990), and Dennison Rusinow, "Nationality Policy and the 'National Question,'" in *Yugoslavia in the 1980s*, Pedro Ramet, ed. (Boulder: Westview Press, 1985).

[6]The term is taken from Eric Hobsbawm in *Nations and Nationalism since 1780* (New York: Cambridge University Press, 1990).

Yugoslav postwar development and eventually led to its disintegration.

In addition, the term "less developed republics and regions" needs to be specified since the definition of the LDRs changed over time. In the First Five-Year Plan (1947-1952) and in the yearly plans until 1957, the LDRs consisted of Bosnia-Hercegovina, Macedonia and Montenegro, although Macedonia was virtually ignored in terms of investments. In 1957 Bosnia-Hercegovina was taken off the list and Kosovo-Metohija (later changed to Kosovo) was added, though it received minimal investments, and even those were controlled by Serbia. In 1961, BiH was readmitted to the list of the LDRs as were the less developed areas of the developed republics, which were kept on until 1970, that is even after the Development Fund began to operate in 1965. From 1965, Bosnia-Hercegovina, Kosovo, Macedonia and Montenegro were defined as the LDRs.

Among the various explanations given by the Yugoslavs for the failure to decrease regional economic disparities, one, which was rarely mentioned overtly and never publicly, stands out by its glaring omission. *Economic regionalism,* the regional pursuit of economic interests, was never formally acknowledged by the regime. Yet evidence shows and interviews corroborate that protection and enhancement of one's region's economic interests, present throughout the postwar period, were the most salient determinants of policy promulgation and implementation. In the deteriorating situation of the 1980s, as will be shown in Chapter 5, this protection of one's region's interests led to a more open and explicit struggle among the regional political elites for the decreasing resources.

It is this acute awareness of regional economic interests and their staunch defense by means of a variety of purportedly "objective proofs" put forth by all the republics and regions, and often by the communes as well, which accounts for the Yugoslavs' failure to arrive at a "coherent plan of development." That is, fundamentally different and often opposing economic interests of the constituent republics and regions of the Yugoslav federation prevented the formulation of a consensus regarding a "coherent plan of development," since in such a heterogeneous country, any one plan would almost by definition be seen to favor some regional interest(s) at the expense of other(s).

Whereas the initial federalization of Yugoslavia was the answer to the age-old yearning for self-rule in the face of both historical and inter-war domination, the further devolution of power which occurred between 1965 and 1975 was an attempt, first, to counteract the increase in ethnonationalism by divorcing it from the belief that a still dominant center promoted the economic interests of some at the expense of others; second, it sought to overcome the economic inefficiency that ensued from a meddling center and the resultant lack of autonomy and therefore of responsibility for one's actions in the economic sphere. By shifting power from the center to the republics and regions, the Belgrade leaders aimed to free themselves from charges of discrimination, while enhancing economic rationality in the production process as well as regime legitimacy and political stability. All this was to be accomplished by giving republics and regions what they had most wanted, power to determine their own social and economic destinies.

Yet, while decision-making was to proceed henceforth by mutual agreements of the republics and regions based on their harmonization of interests, as has been pointed out by Burg, Comisso, Milenkovitch, Ramet, Tyson and others,[7] decision-making by consensus works only when consensus can be arrived at. Given the historical legacy and the often divergent views and interests of the republics and regions, consensus was very difficult to achieve.

Although this lack of consensus was typically manifested as ethnonationalism, it is important to note that most often the primary cause was not ethnonationalism per se, but economic interest. In the words of Saljic, head of the section for Regional Development at the Serbian Planning Ministry and member of the Krajger Commission for the Economic Stabilization of Yugoslavia: "Economic localism of republics and regions leads to increased nationalism."[8] That both the defense and the promotion of economic interests in Yugoslavia often took on an ethnic-nationalist form is not surprising considering that major ethnic and national groups largely corresponded to republic/regional boundaries, while economic structure, type and level of development, and therefore economic interests, also tended to be regionally dependent and defined.

Because regional economic inequalities could pose grave problems for the Yugoslav regime, it carefully avoided public confrontation over the issue. Fearing that the multiplicity of interests affected by both

[7] Steven Burg, *Conflict and Cohesion in Socialist Yugoslavia* (Princeton: Princeton University Press, 1983). Ellen Turkish Comisso, *Workers Control Under Plan and Market* (New Haven & London: Yale University Press, 1979). Laura D'Andrea Tyson, *The Yugoslav Economic System and Its Performance in the 1970s* (Berkeley: Institute of International Studies, University of California, 1980). Pedro Ramet, *Nationalism and Federalism in Yugoslavia, 1963-1988* (Bloomington: Indiana University Press, 1970). Deborah Milenkovitch, *Plan and Market in Yugoslav Economic Thought* (New Haven: Yale University Press, 1971).

[8] Saljic, Interview, Planning Ministry of Serbia, Belgrade, September 16, 1983.

the problem and its potential solutions would be so divisive as to threaten the political stability of the regime, the central government insistently attempted to divorce regional inequalities from "politics." Yet, in a nation where ethnic and national identity coincided with regional (political) boundaries, the problem of regional economic disparities was bound to become politicized.

The politicization of economic inequalities along ethnic-national lines, especially likely as they corresponded to the political boundaries, had long been one of the greatest fears of the regime. For by bringing forth both the specter of the 1941-1945 civil war atrocities, as well as the postwar brewing of ethnic-nationalist outbursts, such politicization could potentially transform almost any regional issue into a threat to the survival of Yugoslavia. It is for this very reason that the Yugoslav regime publicly insisted on treating the problem of regional inequalities solely as an economic problem.

This, of course, is not to say that all issues or disagreements were economic. The point made here is: first, that economic disagreements occurred the most frequently; second, that they could be used to mobilize support and turned into more volatile and destabilizing ethnic-national manifestations; and third and most importantly, that the regional leaders' pursuit of their (regional) economic interests, which remained unacknowledged and thus unaddressed, best explains the displacement and eventual subversion of the goal of regional equalization.

As a result, contrary to the CPY stated goal, forty years of development effort did not lead to a narrowing of inequalities between the DRs and the LDRs. Certainly all the LDRs improved their position in an absolute sense. This is especially evident when comparing a broader series of development indices such as life expectancy, live births, literacy and others (Table 6.1). Furthermore, there was a general consensus among the decision-makers, academics, bureaucrats and politicians that very real and substantial progress in terms of regional development had been achieved, although by the mid-1980s that had been halted and a slow regression had begun.

Nevertheless, according to the regime's own indicators of development--GMP per capita,[9] fixed assets per worker and social

[9] "Gross Material Product or Gross Social Product in Yugoslavia includes production and services in industry, agriculture, construction, transport, commerce, tourism and crafts. It does not include services of government, defence, health and welfare insurance and scientific, cultural, political and professional organizations. Consequently, Yugoslav Social Product is from 10 to 15% lower and national income is about 3% lower than GNP - Gross National Product - calculated by Western Methods." This explanation is given by

sector--employment per thousand--the results of the Yugoslav policies of regional equalization through faster development of the LDRs were far less satisfactory. That is, only Montenegro, which managed throughout the postwar period to secure far more than its share of resources, succeeded in narrowing the gap with the DRs. For Macedonia, the gap narrowed in terms of employment, stayed the same in fixed assets and increased in GMP per capita. For both Bosnia-Hercegovina and Kosovo, the disparity increased across the board (Table 5.3). This is especially true for Kosovo, which in terms of GMP per capita had fallen behind the Yugoslav average from its position of 1:2 in 1950 to 1:4 in 1990.

It is a tragic irony that the regime was unwilling to confront the political aspect of regional inequalities for fear of inciting ethnonationalism. For as a result, development policies continued to be partial and somewhat haphazard and economic inequalities between the DRs and the LDRs continued to increase. In the context of the rapidly deteriorating Yugoslav economy of the 1980s, this increase in regional economic inequalities took on an overtly political expression. The correspondence of the major ethnic-national groups with republic and regional boundaries exacerbated ethnic-national tensions, as each group sought to preserve its own republic/regional interests. These tensions and divisions were further exacerbated by the appearance of Slobodan Milosevic, the populist leader whose ascendance was predicated on finding scapegoats for Serbia's economic decline.

The conflation of economic mismanagement resulting in economic decline with the closet boogeyman of ethnic-national discrimination increased the dormant suspicions among the republics and regions. Three years of provocation through staged ethnic-national incidents, organized "meetings of truths," populist, quasi-democratic mob action, economic boycotts, armed insurrections and illegal political blockades,[10] eventually led to the civil war and to the bloody disintegration of the second Yugoslavia.

Albert Waterston, *Planning in Yugoslavia: Organization and Implementation* (Baltimore: The Johns Hopkins University Press, 1962).

[10]For an explanation and discussion of the above please refer to Chapter 5.

Map of Yugoslavia

1

Historical Antecedents of Regional Inequality

Introduction

One of the most striking features of the former Yugoslavia was the extent of the country's diversity. With eight political units, seven borders, six republics--one for each of the six recognized nations--and a population speaking four main languages, following three religions and using two different alphabets, further subdivided between the wealthier, historically more industrialized, Catholic, European-oriented and influenced northwest (Slovenia, Croatia and Vojvodina) and the poorer, peasant, Orthodox or Islamic southeast (Serbia, Bosnia-Hercegovina, Macedonia, Montenegro and Kosovo), Yugoslavia was easily the most heterogeneous country in Europe.

This heterogeneity can be seen by other indicators as well. With a population of 23,559,000 Yugoslavia was comprised of twelve officially recognized nationalities inhabiting an area of 255,804 square kilometers,[1] approximately the size of the state of Wyoming. Politically and administratively it was divided into six republics and two autonomous regions which varied a great deal in size and only roughly corresponded to the ethnic and national divisions of the population.[2] These were, starting in the northwest and moving southeast, Slovenia, Croatia, Vojvodina, Bosnia-Hercegovina, Serbia, Montenegro, Kosovo

[1] Savezni Zavod za Statistiku (SZZS), *Statisticki godisnjak Jugoslavije, 1989,* Beograd, 1989 [Statistical Yearbook of Yugoslavia, Belgrade, 1989].

[2] This "rough" correspondence of political boundaries with the majority nation inhabiting it meant that the six republics and the two regions were taken as national homelands, although all except Slovenia had significant national minorities within their boundaries. Though intermittent flare-ups of tensions between the majority nation and the national minorities within most of the republics and regions occurred at some time during the post-World War II period, until the 1980s, these were contained through a combination of repression and elite co-optation.

and Macedonia.[3] A further division, an economic one, cut across the ethnic, national, linguistic, religious and cultural differences and bifurcated the country between a wealthier, historically more industrialized and relatively developed northwest and a poor, peasant, "Balkan" southeast. But this "north-south" division, which corresponded to the former boundaries of the Austro-Hungarian and Ottoman Empires that ruled over much of this area from the twelfth and fifteenth centuries to the twentieth, should not obstruct the fact that development in Yugoslavia was highly uneven, not only along this primary axis, but also along republic and regional lines, as well as within the republics and regions.

This chapter will examine the impact of the diverse geography and history of the republics and regions which comprised the Federative People's Republic of Yugoslavia (FNRJ), at its creation in 1945. It will focus on the centuries-long foreign domination and the different values, cultures and institutions which resulted at all levels of societal interaction--social, political and economic. In addition, it will examine how, during the inter-war period, nationalist suspicion and distrust were added to this historical legacy of differentiated development and overall backwardness as one nation sought to politically dominate all others in the newly created Kingdom of Yugoslavia. The discussion will turn briefly to the ways in which this political repression and economic immiseration, along with the devastation of World War II and the civil war which raged simultaneously throughout, further set back the underdeveloped country. It will conclude with the formation of the second Yugoslavia, the initial obstacles faced by the communist regime and the first steps taken to create a developed socialist society.

Geography and Its Effects [4]

Running the full length of the coastline in a narrow stretch is the *Adriatic Littoral* with the typical Mediterranean climate of mild winters, hot summers and a heavy rainfall. Tourism has become the major "industry" in the economy of the littoral, though shipping, ship-

[3] Here denotes Serbia proper; greater Serbia includes the two autonomous regions of Vojvodina and Kosovo.

[4] The following characterization of geographical and climatic regions is based on the work of George Hoffman and Fred Warner Neal, 1962, as well as the works of Fred Singleton, *Twentieth Century Yugoslavia* (New York: Columbia University Press, 1976); Jozo Tomasevich, *Peasants, Politics and Economic Change in Yugoslavia* (Stanford: Stanford University Press, 1955); and talks with Milorad Lecic of The Agricultural Institute in Belgrade, held in the fall of 1983.

building, cement making, canning and aluminum plants remain significant. Meanwhile, the historic sources of income (fishing and crops such as olives, vines, figs, almonds and citrus fruit), though retaining some importance, have been declining.

Parallel to the littoral and extending in a triangular shape across much of Bosnia-Hercegovina, all of Montenegro, southwest Serbia and northern Kosovo is the *Mountainous Heartland* of the country. Comprising about 25% of the total area of Yugoslavia and corresponding roughly to the Dinaric mountain range, this area is relatively sparsely populated and, because of the inaccessibility of much of the terrain, has been underused economically. Where accessibility permits, forestry, mining and stockbreeding have been the main occupations through the centuries. Some agriculture is found in the fields and valleys between the mountains; in the northeast, cereals like barley, oats, rye and buckwheat are grown, while in the southwest, vineyards, tobacco, almond trees and maize predominate. Droughts, poor drainage and an inadequate transportation system, as well as the scarcity of land suitable for agriculture, however, limit their commercial value. In more recent times (since 1945), the development of mineral resources (both ferrous and non-ferrous metals like copper, gold, silver, lead and zinc), as well as the channeling of water power for electricity, has meant rapid modernization for selected parts of the area.[5] Historically isolated and backward, the mountainous area has been a source of some seasonal out-migration within the country, like the Serbian *pecalba,* and more importantly of permanent migration outside the country, notably to America. With the rapid industrialization in the post-World War II period, migration gravitated to the urban center(s) within republics and regions, with both the positive and negative effects that very rapid urbanization entails.

Adjoining the Dinaric range of the mountainous heartland are the outliners of the *Rhodope Massif*[6] which form Central Serbia. The varied relief and climate of this area, which is transitional to the neighboring regions, is reflected in the diversity and distribution of crops. Wheat and maize are grown predominantly in the north and wheat, tobacco and some cotton in the south. Fruits, especially plums, are found everywhere. Cattle in the west, sheep in the south and east and pigs in the north and center round out the agricultural importance of this region. Large deposits of non-ferrous metals, chromite, magnesium, asbestos, as well as the historically important copper mines of Bor and

[5] Because the building of dams for electricity is a capital intensive low labor industry, its impact or spread effect on the rest of the economy of the region has been minimal.

[6] The Rhodope Massif is the original core of the Balkan peninsula.

Majdanpek, form the base of many of the industries established in the aftermath of World War II.

To the south of central Serbia is the *Kosovo and Vardar Region* which encompasses all of the former republic of Macedonia and autonomous region of Kosovo. A hilly area consisting of a series of basins interconnected by low mountain passes, it has relatively little land suitable for agriculture. The diversity of this region is seen by the varied climate and vegetation which range from subtropical in southeast Macedonia (where, with the help of irrigation, cotton, rice, tobacco, ground nuts and fruit-growing predominate) to the more continental climate in the northern part of the region; here cattle and stock-breeding as well as mining remain the base of the economy today as they have for centuries. Lignite, lead, zinc, silver, chrome, manganese, uranium and some low-grade brown coal are all mined throughout the region, while the lead-zinc ores of Trepce in Kosovo are among the largest deposits in Europe. It is ironic that this region, rich in the mineral deposits which form the backbone of Yugoslav industry, was and remained the least economically developed region in Yugoslavia.

To the north and east of central Serbia is the *Plain of Vojvodina,* the "bread basket" of the former Yugoslavia. Once the Pannonian sea, subsequently filled with alluvial deposits from rivers in the surrounding mountains, it is now, along with adjoining Slavonia (in Croatia), the richest agricultural area of the region. Wheat and maize are the main cereals, though viticulture, the raising of poultry and geese and freshwater fishing are also of importance. New industries, as well as those built up during the Hungarian rule and greatly enlarged since 1945, also center on agriculture. Processing of agricultural products --canning, sugar refining, alcohol distilling and flour milling--and the production of fertilizers, agricultural machinery and building materials round out the economy, while the excellent transportation and communications network and the natural proximity to the major markets enhance their commercial value.

To the west and north of Vojvodina are *The Croatian-Slovenian Hill Lands,* the oldest and still the most important industrial region of Yugoslavia. Ironworks, machinery, textiles, furniture, electrical appliances, building materials and food processing are some of the major industries which thrive in this area. The fertile loess-covered valleys and the mostly continental climate of this para-Panonian region are suitable for agriculture. With the modernization of the latter from the mid-1960s, this region assumed a position of importance in the Yugoslav economy. The overall combination of skilled labor, industrial tradition and excellent rail and road connections to all parts of Yugoslavia, including to the ports on the Adriatic, as well as to neighboring

European capitals, made the *Croatian-Slovenian Hill Lands* the most important and, as we shall see, the most developed region of the country.

Finally, *Isolated Mountain Regions* are located in a number of areas along the former Yugoslav frontier, notably separating Slovenia from Italy and Austria, Macedonia from Albania and Bulgaria and Serbia from Romania and Bulgaria. Though generally poor and a source of out-migration, they typically took on the characteristics of the neighboring region. Thus, the Slovenian Alps, historically the most developed mountain region, is indistinguishable from other areas in the developed regions partly as a result of the development of tourism. In contrast, the mountain regions in southeast Serbia and those of northeast and western Macedonia have become almost depopulated, as city jobs, inevitably easier and better paying by comparison, have attracted the young and able-bodied. From the late 1970s, the regime did for strategic and security reasons make some effort at reversing this trend by facilitating work in these areas, such as setting up knitting cooperatives using wool from local sheep and starting the wool mill in Tetovo. Nevertheless, both the overall attraction of life in the city, on the one hand, and the psychological and material hardships associated with living in isolated mountain areas, on the other, limited the success of government intervention.

By isolating the mountain people while exposing those of the lowlands to easy conquest, geography had obstructed the possibility of their union. Simultaneously, as will be shown below, history had ensured that the various conquests that did take place over the centuries resulted in further fragmentation into widely differentiated patterns of socio-political rule, as well as great differences in the manner and extent of their economic development.

The Impact of History[7]

The Slavic tribes which came from trans-Carpathia to the Balkans between the sixth and tenth centuries A.D. were the last migratory wave to settle into the territory that became known as Yugoslavia. By the time of their arrival the Roman Empire had been overrun by the Lombards, and the area had already been divided for three centuries between Rome and Byzantium. The original dividing line traced by the Roman Emperor Diocletian in 285 A.D. still forms the boundary between the Western-oriented, Roman Catholic Slovenes and Croats in the

[7] The following is based on the works of Hoffman and Neal, 1962, Singleton, 1976, and Tomasevich, 1955.

northwest and the Orthodox Serbs, Macedonians and Montenegrins of the southeast.

As various Slav tribes migrated into different regions, they established their own systems of rule, beginning with tribal communism, some progressing to larger political units which achieved periods of prominence under later near-mythologized leaders. During the four to six centuries of political independence, a number of these units developed their own cultural characteristics, political and economic institutions and national identity. These periods of political independence and expansionist greatness, which have survived in the respective collective national memory, have sporadically reappeared either in the form of a nostalgic glance backward or as political demands for the restoration to the past position of independence or even dominance.[8] Thus, each of the six republics has had its period of greatness to look back to. For the Slovenes, this was the kingdom of Samo, circa 650 A.D., which encompassed Slovenia and parts of Austria, Czechoslovakia and southern Germany; the Serbs looked back to Tsar Dusan, who in 1345 extended the Serbian Empire to include Macedonia, Albania, Montenegro, northern Greece and Bulgaria; Macedonia was at its greatest under Tsar Samuilo around 1000 A.D., Bosnia-Hercegovina under the Kotromani dynasty of the late fourteenth century; and an active and independent state of Croatia flourished from the tenth to the twelfth centuries, reaching its zenith with King Tomislav in 924 A.D.

For all, however, the period of independence was relatively shortlived. The Slovenes came under the rule of Charlemagne by the eighth century and remained under Germanic domination until World War I. The Croatians, who first came willingly under Hungarian rule in 1102,[9] elected the Habsburgs as their kings in 1526 following the Hungarian defeat by the Turks. Thereafter they remained under Germanic rule, first under the Habsburgs until 1806, then as part of the "Austrian Empire" until 1867 and, finally, under the Austro-Hungarian monarchy until 1918. The battle of Kosovo Polje in 1389 established the Ottoman Empire in the southern part, with Serbia, Macedonia and Bosnia-

[8] More precisely, as Ivo Banac points out, for Croats and Serbs national identity was acquired long before the development of modern nationalism and survived centuries of foreign rule, while for Slovenes it is a product of the nineteenth century and for Macedonians, Montenegrins and Muslims from BiH, it is still in the process of formation. Ivo Banac, *The National Question in Yugoslavia* (Ithaca: Cornell University Press, 1984).

[9] When the last Croatian king lost his life without leaving an heir, the Croatian nobility invited the Hungarian king to assume the Croatian crown. Croatia was to be allowed internal autonomy and a separate administrative system; the degree of these, however, varied over time.

Hercegovina falling under Turkish rule in 1463.[10] Dalmatia, the original seat of the Croatian kingdom, also came under various rules including the Byzantine, Hungarian, Turk and, for a short time, Napoleonic, though the Venetian control which lasted from 1420 to 1797 was predominant.[11]

One other distinct area, which emerged as a result of the invasions was the *military frontier*. Established in the sixteenth century by the Habsburgs, it consisted of a narrow belt which stretched from the north Dalmatian coastline, along northern Bosnia-Hercegovina, to Belgrade. Here, Serbs fleeing from Turkish rule settled as free peasants, their emancipation an exchange for defending the Habsburg frontier against Turkish incursions. Later incorporated mostly into Bosnia-Hercegovina, though a part of it went to Croatia, the military frontier has left as its permanent legacy settlements of Serbs in both Bosnia-Hercegovina and Croatia, adding a potentially volatile political factor which could be used to exacerbate the nationality conflicts within the two republics as well as between them and Serbia. These conflicts climaxed during the civil war which raged throughout Yugoslavia during World War II, as the documented atrocities committed by both sides testify. It subsequently also made the task of consolidation and state-building more difficult for the Communist regime.[12]

Only two areas remained unconquered during this turbulent thousand-year history. The first was the city-state of Ragusa (Dubrovnik), an important trading center linking the East with the West, where medieval culture flourished and early "democratic" political institutions developed. Ragusa preserved its independence, except for a few years under Napoleon, through skillful use of diplomacy. The second area which remained unconquered was the tiny state of Montenegro, which emerged as a separate political unit in the fifteenth century. Settled by Serbs who fled Turkish rule in 1389, relatively protected from invasions by the inaccessibility of the

10 It is interesting to note that Bosnia-Hercegovina, inhabited by both Serbs and Croats, developed a native Slav Moslem aristocracy from the members of the former Bogomil heretics, the Slavs who had rebelled against both the Western and the Eastern variants of Catholicism. It is this group which was recognized as the sixth nation in Yugoslavia.

11 In this process Croatia itself was divided between two empires, with the Dalmatian coast under Venetian rule, while Slavonia was part of the Austrian and later Austro-Hungarian Empire.

12 More recently, this volatile political factor has been activated by the Serbian leadership of Slobodan Milosevic, on a crusade to "free their brethren" in the *krajina* and other areas of Croatia, as well as elsewhere in Yugoslavia, especially in Bosnia-Hercegovina, Kosovo and Macedonia. The war launched first against Slovenia and Croatia in July 1991 has led to the bloody disintegration of the Yugoslav state.

terrain, Montenegro developed into a society of closed, clannish, fiercely proud and independent guerrillas and outlaws (*hajduk*), whose occupation and mission in life became fighting the Turks. It is by virtue of this historical independence from foreign rule, as well as acknowledgment of their war effort in the Partisan Resistance, that Montenegrins acquired the status of a separate nation and, with it, their own republic after World War II.

As a result of these various conquests, by the beginning of the nineteenth century, the age of the rise of national consciousness and the formation of modern nation-states, the people living in what later became Yugoslavia had spent between four and eight hundred years politically and culturally suppressed and economically exploited. Furthermore, their experiences varied greatly depending on whose rule they had been under, as was reflected in the legacy of different values, culture and institutions at all levels of societal interaction--social, political and economic. The major division was, as mentioned, between the wealthier, somewhat industrialized, Catholic, European-oriented and influenced northwest (Slovenia, Croatia and Vojvodina), with a legacy of Roman Law, Latin alphabet and Western institutions, and the poor, peasant, Orthodox or Islamic southeast, where Ottoman rule, Cyrillic alphabet and Middle-Eastern culture and institutions were predominant.

In view of the above, it is not surprising that the rising national consciousness and the movement for unification of all south Slavs which began to develop in the early nineteenth century reflected these two major divisions within the country. In the north, Croatia, Dalmatia, Slavonia (later incorporated into Croatia) and parts of Slovenia (notably Istria and Trieste) were united for the first time under Napoleon's rule in 1809. Spurred on by this unification, as well as by the ideas and ideals of the French Revolution, which were gaining prominence in the early nineteenth century across Eastern Europe and Russia, and by the influence of a new breed of nationalist poets, folklorists and philologists, feelings of solidarity against the Austrian and Hungarian rule gained prominence. The so-called Illyrian Movement that developed,[13] which aimed primarily at a linguistic and cultural unification of the Slavs, was not received with equal enthusiasm in Serbia; its socio-political implications, particularly the concretized yearning for national independence, were increasingly

[13] The Illyrian movement, which arose in Croatia in the 1830s, was originally a literary and a cultural movement which held that the Slav peoples are basically one people with different names. (For more on the Illyrian movement see Banac, 1984, and Tomasevich, 1955.)

visible in all parts of the country.

As the nineteenth century progressed, the Slovenes turned their energies from the Pan-Slav Illyrian movement to a push for Slovene autonomy within the Austrian Monarchy. In Croatia itself, the earlier romanticized aspects of the Illyrian movement steadily gave way to more practical demands for a semi-independent, self-ruled greater Croatia within the Austrian Empire.

This belief in the betterment of their situation through reform of the Empire was shattered when, after supporting the Austrian Emperor against the Magyar rebellion of 1849,[14] the Croats were not only denied self-rule by the Austrians but in 1868 were returned to the more oppressive Hungarian rule. It was after this disappointment that the Croats began to think in terms of a Yugoslav solution outside the boundary of the Empire. Under the advocacy of Bishop Strossmayer (1815-1905), who believed in a union of all south Slavs, including the reconciliation between Serbs and Croats, the idea of a broader union steadily gained prominence in Croatia.

In contrast to the idea of a peaceable, constitutionally derived democratic union of south Slavs, which was making headway in the "North," the people in the "South" sought to gain independence by armed revolt. Beginning with the 1804 revolt led by Karadjordje,[15] the nineteenth-century history of Serbia is, on the one hand, a series of intrigues, murders and coups in the struggle for the throne between two Serbian dynasties, the Karadjordjevic and the Obrenovic; on the other, it is an attempt by the Serbs, rulers and people alike, to cast off the Ottoman rule. This they succeeded in doing with the help of Russia, Romania and Bulgaria in 1877, and the following year at the Congress of Berlin, both Serbia and Montenegro, with enlarged frontiers, gained independence.

Proud of their success and their new-won independence, Serb nationalists shifted their ideals of Pan-Slavism in the direction of Pan-Serbianism in the hope of recreating Tsar Dusan's medieval

[14] Josip Jelacic, the newly appointed governor of Croatia, led 40,000 Croatian troops against the Hungarians. The Croatians who expected in return to be granted an autonomous Croatia within the Austrian Empire were not only denied self-rule but in 1868 were returned to Hungary. [For more on these events, see Singleton, 1976, pp. 55 and 64.]

[15] Djordje Petrovic, known as Karadjordje (Black George), who led the first revolt against Ottoman rule in 1804, was the founder of one of the two houses which, throughout the nineteenth century, vied for the Serbian throne, the Karadjordjevic dynasty. The other dynasty was founded by Milos Obrenovic, a village headsman, who had also participated in the first revolt. The Obrenovic dynasty died out with the murder of the king and queen in 1903. The Karadjordjevics continued to rule Serbia and later the kingdom of Yugoslavia until 1941 when King Alexander fled, or formally until 1945 when the Federative People's Republic of Yugoslavia was proclaimed.

Empire which had included Macedonia, Bosnia-Hercegovina, as well as Vojvodina. With Macedonia freed from Ottoman rule by the first Balkan war of 1912 and incorporated into the Serbian kingdom in 1913 and with Bosnia's shifting position between the Ottoman Empire up to the nineteenth century and the Austrian military occupation from 1878, certain possibilities presented themselves.

As noted earlier, Bosnia-Hercegovina is inhabited by three major distinct national groups. The largest, comprising more than 40% of the population, is that of the Moslems, Slav descendents of the Bogomil heretics who were converted to Sunni Islam after the Turkish occupation in the fifteenth century. The second largest national group is that of Serbs who comprise some 32% of the population of Bosnia-Hercegovina. The third largest is that of Croats, who account for approximately 18% of the inhabitants.[16] Preferential treatment of Croats was part of the Austrian policy of creating hostility among the Bosnians to discourage a potentially united Slav separatist movement, especially after Serbia achieved independence in 1878. As a result, Bosnian Serbs increasingly saw their future in terms of a Yugoslavia led by Serbs; aspirations of Bosnian Croats similarly turned to Croatia. In both Vojvodina under Hungarian rule and Dalmatia under the Habsburgs, the Yugoslav movement also gained momentum; again, we should note the difference in the direction of that movement. In Vojvodina, it tended to be more pro-Serbian; in Dalmatia, the all-Yugoslav cooperation was the major characteristic.

The First Yugoslavia: Political and Economic Aspects

With the beginning of World War I, both the Austro-Hungarian Monarchy and the Ottoman Empire had ceased to exist. The Yugoslav idea, which had been gaining prominence with all the nations in Yugoslavia both before and during World War I, was also seen by the Allies as the solution to the "Balkan problem." As a result, on December 1, 1918, the Kingdom of Serbs, Croats and Slovenes, a "constitutional, democratic and parliamentary monarchy" guaranteeing equality to all peoples within its boundaries, was proclaimed.

But while the new state was the realization of an age-old dream of independence from foreign rule, it also had its precarious side. For not only did the many centuries spent under Hungarian, Austrian, Venetian and Ottoman rule result in different values, cultures and institutions, but in addition, the formation of the new political unit meant different

[16] Based on the 1981 census. SZZS, *Jugoslavija 1918-1988, statisticki godisnjak* [Yugoslavia 1918-1988, Statistical Yearbook] (Belgrade, February 1989), p. 45.

things to different people. To Croats and Slovenes, the new state was to have been a federation, or minimally a state in which all nationalities would be autonomous, though formally under the Serbian monarchy. Yet, over a period of time, political power came to be held almost exclusively by Serbs with other nationalities living in what was effectively a greater Serbia, as the Serbian capital, Serbian prime ministers during the inter-war period, Serb dominance of the bureaucracy and the police and, finally, the imposition of the Serbian royal dictatorship in January, 1929, all testified.[17]

Economically, also, the formation of the new state affected different regions in different ways. Slovenia and Croatia, which had been part of the Austro-Hungarian monarchy, had enjoyed a higher living standard and possessed most of whatever existed of modern industry, communication and transportation. With the new state, their market was reduced in absolute size from a population of 59 million to 12 million, while Serbia had its market increased from 1.9 million to 12 million. The creation of a customs frontier further separated the north from their traditional markets, resulting in important losses to the most advanced regions. The result of these differences in outcome brought about by the unification, according to Rudolf Bicanic, has been at the root of the subsequent tensions between the two conceptions of development. That is, for Slovenia and Croatia, who lost their vast markets of central Europe, the belief that for the development of the country the economy needed to be outwardly oriented continued to prevail. For Serbia, content with the initial expansion of its market, the orientation was to preserve what it acquired; it, therefore, sought to create a self-contained national market. This struggle, argues Bicanic, continued through the inter-war period into the postwar period of communist rule.[18]

One of the key tasks of the new regime was to devise an economic policy which, by creating a national market, would bolster the formation of national capital.[19] Consequently, the policies followed were, first, rapid expansion of some branches of industry largely financed by foreign capital and highly protected industrialization at the expense of the average consumer; second, a general neglect of agriculture including the 1918 Land Reform which, while benefitting some of the landless, was more a political act than a sound economic

[17] Dennison Rusinow, *The Yugoslav Experiment 1948-1974* (Berkeley: University of California Press, 1977), pp. xiii-xviii, and Hoffman and Neal, 1977, pp. 55-65.

[18] Rudolf Bicanic, *Economic Policy in Socialist Yugoslavia* (Cambridge: Cambridge University Press, 1973), pp. 1-4.

[19] Bicanic, 1973, p. 17.

proposition; and third, almost total neglect of transportation. Their cumulative effect was a general fall in the standard of living, a decline in real wages of workers and government employees and an opening of the scissors crisis which by 1926 had grown to a full-blown agricultural crisis, with peasants, who comprised 76.3% of the population, paying an estimated 50% of their cash income in taxes.[20] The general economic situation was aggravated by the bureaucratic mentality of civil servants who viewed the state as a means for private accumulation and by the existence of a quasi-capitalist class relying on state contracts, rather than on the dynamic, self-propelled capitalist entrepreneur whose drive for industrialization might have alleviated peasant poverty through industrial (urban) employment.

The increasing economic stagnation and dependency of inter-war Yugoslavia was echoed in the growing political chauvinism and chaos. A month after the elections to the Constituent Assembly in 1920, the Communist Party, the third largest party of fifteen, was outlawed and a few months later its deputies were deprived of their Parliamentary mandates. Then, beginning with the highly centralized constitution proclaimed in 1921, despite the absence of Croat, Slovene and Communist delegates protesting the centralist character of the constitution, conflicts between Serbs and Croats increased. By 1924 the Croat Peasant Party, the leading political party of Croatia, was outlawed and its leader and founder, Stjepan Radic, briefly imprisoned.[21] When Radic was fatally shot by a Serb delegate during a debate in parliament in 1928, the king suspended the constitution and proclaimed a royal dictatorship. Thereafter, Yugoslavia became increasingly a police state under Serbian rule. Political repression and increasing economic immiseration, which followed the dashed hopes in the new state, created a revolutionary potential in inter-war Yugoslavia, a widespread if vague sympathy with "Communism,"[22] as well as some mass following of right-wing ultra-nationalist organizations, notably the *Cetnici* in Serbia and the *Ustase* in Croatia.

On April 6, 1941, Germany invaded Yugoslavia. The "provocation"

[20] The so-called scissors crisis, created by the widening gap in prices between agricultural and manufactured goods to the detriment of agriculture, left the peasantry choking in debt. Tomasevich, 1955, p. 702.

[21] In effect, this meant that one-quarter of the representatives elected to the Constituent Assembly in 1920 had, by 1924, been suspended by the king—that is, the Communist Party in 1920-1921 with 59 members and the Croat Peasant Party in 1924 with 51 members. It also meant that the Constitution, which had been passed by 223 votes to 35, with 160 absent in protest, was opposed by almost 40% of the deputies and had full support of less than 45%.

[22] Hugh Seton-Watson, *Eastern Europe Between the Wars, 1918-1941*, third edition, (Hamden: Archon Books, 1962), pp. 256 -267.

was the *coup d'état* by a group of young officers in Belgrade deposing the regent and the Prime Minister for signing the Axis Tripartite Pact on March 25, 1941. Within two weeks of the invasion, the Yugoslav army was defeated, the new king fled into exile, and Yugoslavia was dismembered with various parts annexed by Italy, Hungary, Bulgaria and Albania. Serbia was granted a separate status under German control, and an enlarged Croatia was granted independence, though it remained a de facto puppet state of the Axis powers.

Thus, even before the great destruction of the war years, Yugoslavia was an underdeveloped country with the general configuration of a poor peasant society. Although it had small enclaves of wealth and culture scattered in a few cities, mostly in the north, 76.5% of the population was still peasant.[23] Furthermore, the high birth-rate and slow industrialization process of the inter-war years had resulted in an actual deterioration of the peasant-land ratios, with the result that there was a decreasing amount of food for the growing population as well as a decrease in the surplus of food available for export. Not surprisingly, the per capita national income in the inter-war period grew at only 0.7% per annum.[24]

In terms of industrialization, foreign-owned or foreign-dominated industry,[25] with emphasis on extraction of raw materials in the "south" and processing industry in the "north," both relying on cheap local labor, continued the legacy of differentiated development of the "north" and the "south" within the framework of underdevelopment of the country as a whole. This overall underdevelopment is reflected in the illiteracy rate, which on the eve of World War II was 44.6%,[26] with a mere 1.3% of the population having secondary education and a miniscule 0.15%, university.[27] It is also seen in the national income, which for 1938 has been estimated at between $60 and $70.[28]

[23] Todorovic et al., *Ekonomska politika FNRJ* [Economic Policy of FPRY] (Beograd: Rad, 1958), p. 188.

[24] Branko Colanovic, *Razvoj nerazvijenih pokrajina Jugoslavije* [Development of the Underdeveloped Areas of Yugoslavia] (Beograd: Medunarodna Politika 1966, no. 9).

[25] According to Hoffman and Neal, approximately 46% of all industrial production was owned by foreign companies, mostly British, 46%, and French, 41%. (Hoffman and Neal, 1962, p. 87).

[26] Rusinow, 1977, p. xviii.

[27] Martin Schrenk, Cyrus Ardalan and Nawal A. El Tatawy, *Yugoslavia: Self-management Socialism and the Challenges of Development*, A World Bank Country Economic Report (Baltimore: The Johns Hopkins University Press, 1979), p. 13.

[28] Rusinow, 1977, p. xviii.

World War II and the Formation of the Second Yugoslavia

For an already underdeveloped country, the cumulative effects of World War II, the foreign occupation and the civil war were devastating. It has been estimated that as many as 1.7 million people or 11% of the total prewar population lost their lives.[29] Of these, a disproportionate number were young (average age 22) and better educated, those whose energy and skills were most needed in the reconstruction. Another 23% of the population was left homeless.[30]

In the economy, the destruction was even greater. The production in the textile industry in December 1945 was only 30 to 40% of the prewar level, in the food processing industries 40 to 50% and in metal industries 15 to 20%. Other branches were equally hard hit. Thus, all the mines were flooded and the machinery destroyed by the retreating German army. The transportation system was in shambles; not a single railroad line was in operation at the end of the war, and 77% of locomotives and 84% of wagons had been destroyed. The merchant marine was reduced to a little more than 12% of its prewar registered tonnage. The destruction in agriculture was equally staggering: almost 300,000 farms, 50 to 70% of various draft animals and livestock, 80% of plows and harvesting machinery and 40% of peasant carts were destroyed. Another nearly 40% of vineyards and fruit-growing areas were seriously damaged.[31]

From the political point of view, both the position of the inter-war Serbian monarchist ruling group and that of the war-time Fascist-aligned Croatian state had been discredited. In contrast, the Communist Party of Yugoslavia, still fresh from its role in the national liberation struggle, drew some support from all national groups and was thus able to claim a supranational identity; as importantly, it had the support of the Soviet Union and was tolerated by the Great Powers. Furthermore, as the best organized political group in the country, it filled the vacuum by officially assuming the power that it had claimed on November 29, 1943,[32] when its leader, Josip Broz Tito, had

[29] New scholarship is revising this figure downward, approximately 1.0 or 1.1 million. See Vladimir Zerjavic, *Gubici stanovnistva Jugoslavije u drugom svjetskom ratu* [Losses of Yugoslav Population in the Second World War] (Zagreb: Jugoslavensko Viktimolosko Drustvo, 1989).

[30] Branko Horvat, *The Yugoslav Economic System* (White Plains: International Arts and Sciences Press, Inc., 1976), p. 6.

[31] For more on the following, see Hoffman and Neal, 1962, and Rusinow, 1977.

[32] At the second session of the Anti-Fascist Council for the National Liberation of Yugoslavia (*Antifasisticko Vjece Narodnog Oslobodenja Jugoslavije,* AVNOJ), held in Jajce, Bosnia, on November 29, 1943, Tito defied Stalin by proclaiming that the goal of

defied Stalin by proclaiming at the second session of the Anti-Fascist Council for the National Liberation of Yugoslavia (AVNOJ), held in Jajce, Bosnia, the formation of the de facto provisional government of Yugoslavia. Exactly two years later to the day, on November 29, 1945, the Federative People's Republic of Yugoslavia was legalized as a result of a plebiscite-like election.

According to the new Constitution adopted January 3, 1946, Yugoslavia was a federal state with six republics, one for each of the five recognized nations: these were, starting from the north, Slovenes, Croats, Serbs, Macedonians and Montenegrins. The sixth republic, Bosnia-Hercegovina was comprised of a mix of Catholic Croats, Orthodox Serbs, and Moslem Slavs, later given the status of a separate nation. In addition, two regions were attached to Serbia proper:[33] Vojvodina, newly settled mostly by Serbs and Kosovo-Metohija (Kosmet, later changed to Kosovo), inhabited mostly by Albanians.

Even though Yugoslavia was a federation, real power was concentrated at the center, though powers not specified in the Constitution as belonging to the federal government lay with the republics. And though certain aspects of Yugoslav federalism remained confusing, it was and remained significant that each of the five nations then recognized was given its own national homeland, a republic and, thus was made politically equal, despite their different historical backgrounds, levels of development and geographical and population size.

The first task of the new regime was to repair the war damage and to organize the polity along socialist principles. A combination of hard work, reparation payments from Hungary, Italy and Germany, aid from the United States (CARE) and the critical aid given by the UNRRA[34] enabled the effective restoration of war damages in a record time of two years. By 1947, when the First Five-Year Plan was launched, the

the CPY was not only to liberate Yugoslavia from foreign occupation but, also, to establish a socialist state. As the provisional government, the CPY proceeded to do this piecemeal in the liberated territories.

[33] These were attached to Serbia more by way of placating the Serbs for losing their inter-war position of dominance than as a carefully developed solution to nationality problems. It is difficult to see otherwise why Kosovo, which in 1948 had a non-Slav Albanian population of almost half a million (498,242) representing 68% of the district's total, was not granted the status of a republic, when Montenegro, with a population of just over a third of a million Montenegrins (342,009), Orthodox Slavs, many of whom considered themselves Serbs, was. As for Srem-Vojvodina, historical legacy would have made it more logical to be attached to Croatia. The 1945 solution adopted for these two areas proved unsatisfactory as the intermittent disturbances, culminating in seperatist movements, notably that of Kosovo from 1981, testified.

[34] CARE, Co-operative for American Remittance to Europe and UNRRA, United Nations Relief Rehabilitation Agency. Bicanic, 1973, p. 146.

prewar level of production in most branches of the economy had been reached;[35] furthermore, the regime no longer had to worry about opposition to its policies, as all organized opposition had been rendered ineffective.[36] Thus, the stage was set for the construction of the socialist society.

The fundamental prerequisite for a socialist society as well as for national and political equality, of prime importance in multi-national Yugoslavia, was economic equality which was to be achieved by the equalization of living and working conditions throughout Yugoslavia. This logically entailed, first, the nationalization of private property, especially the productive kind, and the equalization of income differentials to avert the re-creation or perpetuation of classes and, second, equalizing conditions between republics and regions to circumvent the possible development of a quasi-colonial relationship between a developed center and a less-developed periphery.

The nationalization of property was carried out relatively easily and quickly, much of it occurring before the Communist Party officially came to power. According to a decree issued in November 1944, all parts of the economy owned by foreign capital, as well as property owned by the Royal Government and by "enemies and collaborators," was expropriated. The Nationalization Law of December 1946 extended this to all industries of national importance as well as to mining, transport, banking and wholesale trade facilities. The agrarian equivalent of the above, the "Agrarian Reform and Colonization Law" passed in August 1945, expropriated big landowners, notably the crown, the church and foreign landowners, as well as "enemies and collaborators," distributing about one-half of the land to poor peasants and setting the limit to private ownership at 25 to 45 hectares.[37]

Thus, by 1947, the nationalization of all larger productive sectors of private property had been effectively carried out, the reconstruction of the war-damaged economy had essentially been completed, and the First Five-Year Plan, which was to lay the foundation for a developed socialist Yugoslavia was launched.

[35] Hoffman and Neal, 1962, pp. 89-91.

[36] Two kinds of opposition existed in Yugoslavia at the end of World War II. The first were the collaborators like Draza Mihailovic, leader of the Cetniks, who had actively helped the enemy. Soon however, with Stalinist-like zeal, the definition was expanded to include almost anyone who had not fought with the Partisans and who was denounced by a party member. It is people from this second group, whose arrests and convictions to long years in prisons, and occasionally to death, were by all accounts unjustified.

[37] See footnote 1; for greater detail please refer to Hoffman and Neal, 1962, p. 90, and Rusinow, 1977, pp. 19-20.

2

1950s: Centralization and the First Steps to Development

Introduction

When the Yugoslav Communist Party came to power, its avowed purpose was to create a unified egalitarian society, one in which class, ethnicity and nationality would give way to socialist "brotherhood and unity." To create this egalitarian society along Marxist-Leninist-Stalinist lines, economic development of the Soviet type was to proceed at breakneck speed. Overall "development...through industrialization so that the developed states continue to develop, but the less developed are enabled to catch up in "revolutionary jumps"[1] was the self-defined task of the new regime.

The problem of regional disparity was recognized and specifically addressed as early as 1946 by Boris Kidric, President of the Economic Council and Chairman of the Federal Planning Commission. Kidric spoke of the "unevenness of development [as] one of the difficulties of the present economic development of our country . . . [and of] aid to the underdeveloped and war-devastated states [as a] duty of the economically developed and less distressed states." He went on to add that the unevenness of development could be overcome in one of two ways: either by general levelling or through industrialization so that the developed states continue to develop but the less developed are enabled to catch up in "revolutionary jumps."[2] Indeed, the latter strategy was adopted and continued to be the official policy on development with the modification that from the early 1980s the

[1] Boris Kidric, *Privredni problemi FNRJ*, [Economic Problems of FPRY] (Belgrade: Kultura, 1948).
[2] Ibid.

LDRs were no longer expected to catch up in "revolutionary jumps." Equalization, not through levelling but through overall development via industrialization with greater emphasis on the development of the LDRs, was then to be the road to socialism.

The new regime had an additional incentive to help the LDRs in their development. As Rudolf Bicanic pointed out, there are four general motivations which can guide development policy towards less developed areas. First, there is the humanitarian or moral obligation to help the less fortunate; in Yugoslavia this was buttressed by the fact that the less developed areas bore the brunt of the liberation struggle. Second, there is the national or political motive, more acute in a multi-ethnic and multi-national state. The socialist motivation for the creation of a socialist society, the prerequisite for which is the development of the whole country, is third. And fourth, there is the economic motivation, for in the long run it is in the interest of the whole country to develop the less developed republics and regions (LDRs).[3] Since in the case of Yugoslavia all four motivations--humanitarian, national, socialist and economic--were present, one would expect that from the beginning the development of the LDRs would have been of the highest priority to the new regime.

Yet, despite the professed goal of development of the LDRs as well as the presence of all four motivations, the disparity as measured in GMP per capita between the developed and the less developed regions in Yugoslavia not only failed to narrow but had by 1960 substantially increased. This outcome will surprise us less when we note that throughout the 1950s the LDRs received less, rather than more, investment per capita than the DRs and that their products, overwhelmingly raw materials and agriculture, were grossly underpriced.

The Yugoslavs' with whom I spoke in all the republics and regions were unanimous in maintaining that the discriminatory policy towards the LDRs in the early part of their decade of development was due to the 1948 break with the Soviet Union. As they repeatedly pointed out, despite their intentions of regional equalization, faced with the geopolitical threat in a situation of acute economic scarcity, the development model of channeling resources to areas of greatest productivity "imposed itself."[4] As a result, they argued, the goal of faster development of the LDRs was put on a temporary hold until they had the means to pursue it. For some, that should have been done by the

[3] Bicanic, 1973, pp. 182-183.

[4] This was one striking area of agreement by the respondents irrespective of their ethnic-national or functional background.

mid-1950s; others maintained that the means for pursuing regional development were lacking until the late 1950s, and a few claimed until 1965.

However, as we will see in this chapter, Yugoslavia's geopolitical situation had changed dramatically for the better by 1955 as evidenced by the Yugoslav Emergency Act, the Belgrade Declaration and the Bandung Conference. Similarly, its economy, long-recovered from the war devastation, was receiving a generous boost from the West. Yet these changes did not result in a parallel reassessment and change in policy towards the development of the LDRs. While some measures of aid for the LDRs were passed, these could not offset the lack of adequate investment or the underpricing of raw materials and agriculture, their chief products.

That throughout the 1950s, faster development of the LDRs was followed more in rhetoric than in practice was neither the inevitable result of the geopolitical hostilities nor of economic scarcity and consequent need for economically rational investments. Rather, as will be argued, the faster development of the LDRs was undermined in the 1950s as a result of a competition for development projects and resources in which the three politically stronger republics--Slovenia, Montenegro and to a lesser extent Serbia proper--were successful in promoting their interests as the interests of Yugoslavia as a whole.

In order to show that both Yugoslavia's geopolitical situation and its scarcity of economic resources were, throughout most of the 1950s, constraining factors for Yugoslavia's policy of regional development rather than its determinants, we now turn to a closer examination of the actual treatment of regional development in the three sub-periods of the first decade of Yugoslavia's development: the First Five-Year Plan, 1947-1952; the First Economic Decentralization, 1952-1957; and the Second Five-Year Plan, 1957-1962.[5] In addition, a discussion focusing on detailed arguments made by the Yugoslavs concerning the continuing biased regional allocation of resources for development is included before the examination of the Second Five-Year Plan; for that is when the views of the Yugoslav decision-makers concerning the method of regional development planning first began visibly to diverge.

[5] While the strict chronology of the five-year plans and other policy decisions will occasionally overlap slightly with the decades examined, because they embody the essential character of the problems and solutions discussed by the Yugoslavs in that period, or later pertaining to that period, they are examined within the context of the decade proper.

First Five-Year Plan: 1947-1952

Because Yugoslavia as a whole was underdeveloped in 1947, the grand objective of the First Five-Year Plan was to transform the technologically backward agrarian country (Table 2.1) into an industrialized nation.[6] This was to be accomplished through a "global plan" based on the Stalinist pattern of administrative planning and centralized management. Within this framework, priority was given to the development of basic industries, such as metallurgy, steel processing and power, in order to ensure the long-term prospects for the development of Yugoslavia.[7] The distribution of these new industries was to lessen the economic differences among the various parts of the country. Accordingly, investment outlays were specified for all republics at the center, in line with the set priorities, and all investment was financed in the form of grants-in-aid, supplemented somewhat by profits from enterprises and short-term credits.[8]

The mechanism for monetary transactions was the National Bank with some 400 branches scattered throughout the country, though its role at this point was that of distributor and accountant for money received from the national budget. The main sources of revenue for the federal budget were the turnover tax[9] in the socialized sector and the income tax in the private sector. To further help in accumulating savings, wages were kept low, food and consumer items were rationed, prices on the "free market" were allowed to rise astronomically, compulsory mobilization of peasants and townspeople as well as of the prison population was utilized, and voluntary youth brigades were organized for many public projects.

[6] Bicanic, 1973, p. 61.

[7] According to Momir Cecez, Secretary of the Economic Council when the First Five-Year Plan was being drawn up, there was a great deal of dissent over the allocation between industry and agriculture with some on the Economic Council (presumably mostly from Vojvodina, Croatia and Macedonia) arguing for increased investment in agriculture. However, those arguing for industry had both the ideological argument, which equated industry with socialism, as well as political power, on their side. For more on this see Chapter 6.

[8] Nikola Cobeljic, *Privreda Jugoslavije: rast struktura i funkcionisanje, knjiga druga*, [The Economy of Yugoslavia: Growth, Structure and Functioning, Volume II] (Belgrade: Savremena administracija i institut za ekonomska istrazivanja, 1974), p. 289.

[9] The turnover tax was a tax on goods whose primary purpose was to channel excessive profits and regulate consumption of luxuries and other products containing imported or otherwise scarce raw materials. In the early period it was the primary source of revenue for the federal budget contributing to it between 29% and 43% from 1954 to 1965. The turnover tax was abolished in 1965 and replaced by a sales tax levied on the consumer goods in retail trade.

Table 2.1
Basic Economic Features of Republics and Regions of Yugoslavia

	Year	SFRJ	BiH	Montenegro	Croatia	Macedonia	Slovenia	Serbia	Serbia Proper	Vojvodina	Kosovo
Participation in Total Population	1948	100.0	16.3	2.4	23.8	7.3	8.8	41.4	26.2	10.5	4.6
	1953	100.0	16.8	2.5	23.1	7.7	8.7	41.2	26.3	10.1	4.8
Participation in Agricultural Population	1948	100.0	17.4	2.5	22.1	7.7	5.8	44.5	28.3	10.7	5.6
	1953	100.0	17.2	2.5	21.4	7.9	5.9	45.1	29.0	10.4	5.7
Participation in Working Population	1948	100.0	14.2	1.8	25.1	6.5	9.5	42.9	29.0	10.6	3.3
	1953	100.0	15.2	1.9	23.8	6.8	9.0	43.1	29.8	9.9	3.4
Participation in Working Population of Social Sector	1952	100.0	15.7	1.7	27.4	5.3	15.2	34.6	22.8	9.6	2.2
Participation in Fixed Assets of Social Sector	1952	100.0	12.7	0.8	28.5	3.7	20.8	33.5	23.4	8.3	1.8
Participation in Investments in Fixed Assets	1952	100.0	24.7	3.6	20.2	6.7	14.8	29.9	–	–	–
Participation in GMP	1947	100.0	13.0	1.9	25.0	5.2	14.1	40.7	26.2	12.2	2.3
	1953	100.0	13.8	1.7	26.4	5.3	13.3	39.5	26.0	11.2	2.3
Participation in Industrial Production	1953	100.0	11.6	0.6	30.5	3.1	22.8	31.4	20.3	8.5	2.6

(continues)

Table 2.1 *(continued)*
Basic Economic Features of Republics and Regions of Yugoslavia

	Year	SFRJ	BiH	Montenegro	Croatia	Macedonia	Slovenia	Serbia	Serbia Proper	Vojvodina	Kosovo
Participation in Agriculture Production	1953	100.0	13.7	1.7	22.3	6.1	6.9	49.3	29.6	16.7	3.0
Participation in Total Number of Illiterate	1953	100.0	25.1	2.8	15.3	10.1	0.9	45.8	31.2	5.3	9.3
Education Level of Pop/ w/3 yrs. or Less Schooling	1953	42.1	67.2	47.2	30.5	50.7	15.2	43.2	44.5	28.4	71.2
Participation in Agriculture in Total population	1948 1953	67.2 60.9	71.8 62.2	71.6 61.5	62.4 56.4	70.6 62.7	44.1 41.1	72.3 66.7	72.4 67.2	68.1 62.9	80.9 72.4
Level of Trade Per Capita	1952	100.0	84	85	108	92	175	87	–	–	–
Use of Artificial Fertilizer per Hectare (in tons)	1955	26.9	11.6	4.9	41.8	8.1	141.2	15.4	5.8	32.7	7.8
Use of Electrical Energy per Kw	1952	134.0	92	19	189.0	41	445.0	76	–	–	–
Use of Telephone/1000	1952	7	4	6	9	4	12	7	6	8	–

Source: SZZS, 1973. pp. 227-260

Although these measures can perhaps be rationalized as necessary for the development of the country, the discriminatory fiscal policies, the compulsory delivery of agricultural products and their artificially low prices to "squeeze" reserves from agriculture, as well as the low prices of raw materials and low transportation tariffs, imposed a sacrifice on a selective basis. In other words, as Yugoslav development proceeded according to a regional division of labor, the predominance of low-priced raw materials in the LDRs meant that, in the absence of offsetting transfers, the LDRs were in effect penalized for providing the raw materials necessary to industrialize the country. This sacrifice may not have been felt during the First Five-Year Plan since all profits were channeled to the central budget which then distributed them according to the investment priorities set at the center. But with the beginning of decentralization in 1952 and the first steps in the competition for investments, the negative impact of these policies on the sector of the economy to which they applied, notably agriculture, industrial raw materials and semi-finished products, electricity, transportation and communal services,[10] as well as on the republics and regions whose economy they dominated, the LDRs and Vojvodina, became more direct and obvious.

To illustrate this point, Marija Ivanovic shows that for the years 1953-1974, 100 dinars gross investment for the development of power and metallurgy yielded (in 1966 prices) a growth in GMP of 14.7 dinars; in steel processing and chemical industry, 59 dinars; in other industries, 36.7; in transportation, 17.5; and in the rest of the social sector investments, 46.1. During this same period, investments in the two least profitable branches, power/metallurgy and transportation, represented one-third of the investment of the LDRs (33.2%), while they made up only a little less than a quarter of the investment of the DRs (24%).[11] When we note that in 1952 mining represented 72.4% of Kosovo's industrial production, 37.6% of Bosnia-Hercegovina's and 16.4% of Montenegro's,[12] it is not difficult to see how, in the absence of large compensating transfers, these regions were disadvantaged. Furthermore, as Nikola Cobeljic of the Institute for Economic Research in Belgrade (in the 1950s, head of the Federal Bureau for Social Planning) has stated, "Even though the price disparities were on the whole created during the administrative period of control of the economy, they lasted much longer, so that they were carried over into

[10] Cobeljic, 1974, p. 101.

[11] Ivanovic, 1978, pp. 68-9.

[12] Savezni Zavod za Drustveno Planiranje (SZDP), *Razvoj Jugoslavije 1947-1981* [Development of Yugoslavia 1947-1981] (Belgrade, May 1982), p. 223.

the later periods when the economic system had undergone important changes."[13]

The explanation for these measures, which on the whole favored the development of the developed regions at the expense of the less developed ones, becomes clearer when we note that at this time both the Yugoslav development strategy and the means to carry it out were patterned after Soviet five-year plans. The First Five-Year Plan period had begun with the Yugoslavs, at this point still identifying with Stalin and the Soviet Union, anxious to show themselves to be ideologically the Soviets' equals. Tito's spearheading role in the Cominform, the Communist Information Bureau[14] and his general public posturing in relation to the "People's Democracies," as well as the domestic development policies pursued by Yugoslavia, all point to the preponderant influence of the Soviet model on Yugoslav early postwar development. This influence was acknowledged by virtually all those interviewed. Illustrative of the respondents' emphasis on the influence of the Soviet model is this statement by Slobodan Milic, Director of the Institute for Agricultural Economics in Belgrade:

> In the first phase of development there was a lot of influence of the Soviet Union...we had no institutions; young people came to power, 18 to 25 year olds who had fought the war and made the revolution. They wanted to change much...they were revolutionaries, Communists, with no experience (of rule), alone...emotionally tied to the Soviet Union....At first they were 'more Catholic than the Pope...' there were even some who proposed that we join the Soviet Union.[15]

The consequence of such measures, so closely patterned on the Soviet model, were that in order to stimulate certain branches of the economy in line with the overall developmental plan for a socialist society, regions with corresponding processing branches benefitted at the expense of the agricultural and raw material producing regions. In a detailed study of Yugoslav regional development, Caslav Ocic has shown that for 1952 the primary sector contribution to the GMP, valued at 24.96%, was undervalued by almost 10%; that is, its real value in 1972 prices was 34.53% of the GMP. Simultaneously, the secondary sector, which accounted for 60.56% of the GMP, was overvalued by more than 19%; its real contribution in 1972 prices was 39.4% of the GMP.

[13] Cobeljic, 1974, p. 101.

[14] Formed in 1945, this International Communist body succeeded the defunct Comintern, or Communist International.

[15] Slobodan Milic, Interview, Institute for Agricultural Economics, Belgrade, Serbia, September 8, 1983.

Thus, republics and regions whose economies were dominated by the secondary sector profited at the expense of those dominated by the primary and tertiary sectors.[16] Along with agricultural Vojvodina, the LDRs, which then and for a long time to come had mostly raw materials, extractive industry and some agriculture, were thus perhaps inadvertently, but certainly disproportionately affected.

Regional Development in the First Five-Year Plan

Having adopted the Stalinist model of development with its implicit requirement of growth maximization, the Yugoslavs found that the LDRs were quite "naturally" displaced as indicated by their low rank on the list of priority objectives.[17] Not surprisingly, the only special measure for the development of the LDRs at this point was the allocation of proportionately greater tax relief and, after 1949, of some grants-in-aid.[18]

In other words, during the period of the First Five-Year Plan, there was neither a concrete definition of LDRs nor a plan especially suited to their development needs. Rather, decisions regarding the development of the LDRs--Bosnia-Hercegovina, Macedonia and Montenegro (significantly, Kosovo was not even included until 1957)--were made at the very top level, on an ad hoc basis, following the principle of parallel and simultaneous development of all areas of Yugoslavia. The reason, as Kidric's statements throughout this period indicate, is that the development of the LDRs was to occur without slowing down the development of the more developed regions and, therefore, without impairing the development of the Yugoslav economy as a whole.

At this point, the possible incompatibility of the two strategies of development (optimal development of Yugoslavia as a whole and, parallel to it, optimal and faster development of the LDRs) was not generally recognized. It was still the immediate postwar period, and for many the revolutionary zeal and *élan* were thought sufficient to change the profile of the country almost overnight. According to Dragutin Marsenic, there was a saying which captured the enthusiasm of those days, "*Juris na nebo,*" a "charge on the heavens"; there was

16 Caslav Ocic, *Nacionalna ravnopravnost i regionalni razvoj* [National Equity and Regional Development] (Institut Ekonomskih Nauka, Belgrade, 1986), pp. 47-56.

17 *Drustveni plan razvoja Jugoslavije od 1947 do 1952 godine* [Social Plan of Development of Yugoslavia from 1947 to 1952] Sluzbeni list FNRJ br. 36/47, p. 13. "To ensure the faster tempo of development of the economically backward republics and eliminate the consequences of unequal development" (author's translation); and Bicanic, 1973, p. 61.

18 Shoup, 1968, p. 230.

also a slogan which captured the determination of the young cadre: "*sve mozemo*," "we can do it all" or "all is possible."[19]

In the meantime, even as the CPY was implementing the Stalinist model of development in Yugoslavia, its refusal to be ruled by the Soviets which dated from the 1942 meeting of AVNOJ, when Tito, contrary to Stalin's orders, proclaimed a free, independent, Socialist Federative Republic of Yugoslavia,[20] was becoming increasingly contentious. Tito's persistent defiance of Stalin's attempt at economic exploitation and political meddling in Yugoslav internal affairs led in June 1948 to Yugoslavia's expulsion from the Cominform. The break with the Cominform was in turn the catalyst for the extensive and systematic analysis of the limitations and defects of Soviet-type "administrative socialism."[21]

With the break, the deficiencies of the Soviet centralized planning system, the internal bureaucratization of the regime and its external imperialistic tendencies towards the "younger socialist brothers" became for the Yugoslavs natural and legitimate points of departure for the questioning of Stalin's type of Communism. The ideological uncertainty which resulted from the questioning, the feeling of isolation and vulnerability which emerged as a result of the break and the severe drought which struck Yugoslavia in 1950 (and again in 1952) led to a partial domestic political retrenchment, the most obvious example of which was the stepped-up collectivization drive of 1950-52, which in turn had further disastrous effects on the economy.

The impact of these diverse factors was that per capita consumption fell in 1952 to about 67% of what it had been before the war; the index of total productivity of industrial labor was 85% of that of 1939; the money income of the peasantry which still constituted 60% of the population was, before taxes, approximately 42% of their prewar average money income; and the 1952 national income fell in real terms to the level of 1939.[22] As a result, the First Five-Year Plan, inaugurated in 1947 and rendered effectively inoperative from the break with the Cominform in 1948, was formally abandoned in 1952 and replaced until 1956 by yearly plans deemed to be more suitable in this period of rapid systemic change.

19 Dragutin Marsenic, Interview, Economics Faculty, Belgrade, Serbia, January 17, 1983.

20 Shoup, 1968, p. 72.

21 Hoffman and Neal, 1962, pp. 113-151. For a fuller description of the events surrounding Yugoslavia's expulsion from the Cominform, see Adam Ulam, *Titoism and the Cominform*. (Westport: Greenwood Press, 1952).

22 Ljubo Sirc, *The Yugoslav Economy Under Self-Management* (New York: St. Martin's Press, 1979), pp. 4-6.

The cumulative effect of this ideological uncertainty, political vulnerability and economic chaos was that after an initial waiting and consolidation period of a year, at first tentatively, and from June 1950 and the Law on Worker Management more boldly, the CPY laid the foundation of Yugoslavia's "National Road to Socialism": social rather than state ownership of the means of production; worker management as the fundamental principle of social organization; decentralization of political and economic decisions from the federal government to republic communes and enterprises; and finally, as a result of the principle of self-management, a greater reliance on the market as a guide to the allocation of resources. The above were codified in 1953 in a new Constitutional Act and, along with non-alignment in foreign policy, remained the basic principles of Yugoslav socialism.[23]

For the development of the LDRs, this series of events following the break with the Soviet Union was decisive. The goal of equalization of economic development between regions through faster development of the LDRs, which even before the break had been based more on good intentions than on sound economic policies, was now all but eclipsed by the threatening international situation and resulting domestic siege mentality. As Branislav Mrkic, Assistant to the Director of the Development Fund, stated:

> I'll tell you the essence: Yugoslavia has six nationalities and seven borders to defend. . . . First we had to have a little accumulation. . . . Only when the situation between the 'east' and the 'west' was settled, could more thought be given to the aspect of regional development.[24]

The break with the Cominform, which both permitted and necessitated a search for a new road to socialism introducing an up-to-then unknown and unimaginable flexibility into a socialist system, in the words of Mihailo Radic of the Economics Faculty of Belgrade,[25] "imposed" a certain strategy of development. Unfortunately for the LDRs, that strategy pushed their development off the list of regime priorities for the rest of the decade of the 1950s.

For Yugoslavia, economically backward, feeling itself isolated between the "east" and the "west" and threatened by both, survival displaced all other goals. In developmental terms, maximization of

23 Hoffman and Neal, 1962, pp. 155-173.

24 Branislav Mrkic, interview, Federal Fund for the Development of the LDRs, Belgrade, Serbia, August 28, 1983.

25 Mihailo Radic, Interview, Economics Faculty, Belgrade, Serbia, March 4, 1983.

growth and the attainment of self-sufficiency became almost exclusive preoccupations. In policy terms, despite the break with the Cominform and the promulgation of the "Yugoslav Road to Socialism," the Yugoslav model continued to parallel the Soviet one. As a result, industrialization with emphasis on heavy industry and producer goods, underpricing of raw materials and agriculture and investment for priority sectors, including defense in regions where optimal development measured in terms of gross output could be most quickly achieved, displaced the goal of faster development of the LDRs.

This was corroborated in an interview with Svetozar Vukmanovic-Tempo, the fiery leader of the World War II Bosnia-Hercegovina uprising and one of Tito's chief lieutenants in the partisan resistance movement. According to Tempo, who from 1950 to 1952 was Kidric's replacement and, upon the latter's death in 1952, became chairman of the Federal Planning Commission with full responsibility for industrial development:

> the main issue was the accumulation of capital . . . and the primary plan was to transform the coal mines into modern production; to install electricity, and therefore to create power stations for an electrical system which would link the whole country. Here I clashed with the LDRs. I wasn't interested in how a specific republic would fare. I was interested in how the Yugoslav economy (as a whole) would fare.[26]

In terms of investment distribution, Vukmanovic-Tempo's statement explains why Slovenia, Bosnia-Hercegovina and Montenegro received disproportionately high per capita investments (Table 2.2). In the case of Slovenia, the most developed republic, the reason was economic, to maximize output. For the latter two, it was geopolitical, to ensure the military and defense capacity of the country.

The mind-set of this first period of postwar development which gave rise to these policies is well exemplified by the following quote of Tito's which found its way into his speeches time and again: "[political] independence can be safeguarded only if economic independence is safeguarded."[27] To the Bolshevik mentality of the lapsed Yugoslav Bolsheviks,[28] that meant above all electricity and steel. As

[26] Svetozar Vukmanovic-Tempo, Interview, Belgrade, January 23, 1990.

[27] Josip Broz Tito, *Borba za novi svet* [Struggle for a New World] collected and edited speeches of Josip Broz Tito, (Beograd: Preskliping, 1982). Reprinted from *Borba*, September 28, 1949, from a speech given in Stolicama, near Krupnja.

[28] Numerous respondents in both the DRs and LDRs used this term especially for this period, often for themselves, as well as for others.

Table 2.2
Distribution of Investments per Republic and Region
1952-1957

		SFRJ	BiH	Montenegro	Croatia	Macedonia	Slovenia	Serbia	Serbia Proper	Vojvodina	Kosovo
Participation in Investment in Fixed Assets	1952	100	24.7	3.6	20.2	6.7	14.8	29.9	–	–	–
	1957	100	13.9	3.6	23.1	5.7	13.6	39.2	–	–	–
Population	1953	100	16.8	2.5	23.1	7.7	8.7	41.2	26.3	10.1	4.8

Source: SZZS, 1973, pp. 227-228.

*Of the LDRs, Kosovo received by far the least investment per capita during this period. While figures are not available, both Kosovo's lag in development and corroboration in interviews point to this.

a result, in this first period of postwar development the geopolitical threat displaced all other concerns, and economic development, defined as growth of the primary industrial sector, displaced all other priorities, including that of regional development.

First Economic Decentralization: 1952-1957

By the end of the first period of postwar development, other factors besides the geopolitical were becoming increasingly important as determinants of Yugoslav regional development policies. In the first place, by 1952 the centralized apparatus of planning had been dismantled. The five-year plan, divided into yearly, quarterly, ten day and even daily plans (with a total physical weight of a ton and a half!), describing in detail the daily production quota for each firm throughout Yugoslavia, was replaced by yearly Key Investment Programs based on "planning by basic proportions."[29] Accordingly, the administrative allocation of investment funds through the central budget was replaced by a system of auctions for investment loans, most of which originated with the General Investment Fund with sectoral allocation specified by the center. This new and more decentralized method meant that while the federal plan specified the amount of money to be invested in the various sectors of the economy, it passed the allocative responsibility to the General Investment Fund; the latter then held public auctions at which enterprises interested in getting the investment funds for that particular industry competed on the basis of interest rates and repayment schedules.[30]

Because the loans were to be granted on the basis of economic criteria, that is profitability, special forms of financing were introduced to help the LDRs compete with the DRs for credit. These included free credits matching the amount of their own deposits, investment loans at preferential interest rates and special global subsidies to republic investment funds to enable the investors from these regions to pay the deposits required for free investment credits. Parallel to the General Investment Fund, there were investment funds in each republic, district, commune and enterprise, as well as specialized funds to finance

[29] Horvat, 1976, pp. 42-43.

[30] According to Bicanic (1973, p. 125), in 1958, 81% of investment funds still originated with the General Investment Fund. Egon Neuberger estimated that investments allocated through the auctions of the General Investment Fund between 1954 and 1956 were closer to 10% of total investment allocation, that is, that close to 90% of investment funds still originated with the General Investment Fund. Egon Neuberger, "The Yugoslav Investment Auctions," *Quarterly Journal of Economics*, Fall 1959, pp. 88-115.

investment for such purposes as road building, forestry, housing and agriculture.[31]

However, these measures proved to be inadequate to reverse the centuries-old trend of growing disparity between the developed and the less developed. In particular, this new, more decentralized method which was to increase the general rationality of investments and therefore the efficiency of the economy, was vulnerable to informal pressure by politicians who jockeyed for investments for "their" republic, region or town.[32] Furthermore, although the party leadership continued to articulate the importance of faster development of the LDRs, it also insisted on the necessity of continuing to channel investments to areas where they would give maximum returns, that is to the developed regions. For in 1952, the Yugoslavs still felt their position to be precarious. While the immediate threat of the Soviet Union had receded and a rapprochement with the West had begun, Yugoslavia as a whole was still an underdeveloped country; and as Tito himself was fond of repeating, "a backward country cannot be an independent country."[33]

Geopolitics

The Yugoslavs that I interviewed in the early 1980s overwhelmingly insisted that, throughout most of the 1950s, their continuing geopolitical vulnerability and economic poverty mandated the displacement of the development of the LDRs. This assertion is interesting for it indicates that the Yugoslavs had been so traumatized by the break with the Soviet Union that their perception of their geopolitical situation did not accord with the reality of the situation which, by the early 1950s, had changed in their favor. Furthermore, as this section will show, by the mid-1950s those who did perceive that the geopolitical threat had receded continued to use that defunct threat as an excuse to enhance their region's economic interests at the expense of the development of the LDRs.

First, in terms of the geopolitical situation, by the early 1950s, relations with the West were being normalized both politically and economically. With Truman's signing of the Yugoslav Emergency Act on November 29, 1950, which stated that "the continued independence of

[31] For more on the operation of the General Investment Fund see Bicanic; 1973; Cobeljic, 1974; Deborah D. Milenkovitch, *Plan and Market in Yugoslav Economic Thought*, (New Haven and London: Yale University Press, 1971), and Neuberger, 1959.

[32] Neuberger, 1959, p. 94.

[33] Josip Broz Tito, *Borba za novi svet* [Struggle for a New World], p. 41; reprinted from *Borba*, September 3, 1947, from a speech given to a work collective in Ljubljana.

Yugoslavia is of great importance to the security of the United States," Yugoslavia's political isolation had ended. Economically, starting with a twenty million dollar loan in September 1949, American assistance reached some 1.2 billion dollars by 1955.[34] Finally, in 1955 at a conference in Bandung, Indonesia, Tito, Nehru and Nasser established the non-aligned movement. Its purpose was the protection of national independence and sovereignty and the right of each country to choose its own socio-economic, political and cultural development without interference. Along with this insistence on national sovereignty, a position of "active neutrality" between the two Blocs became the basis of Yugoslav foreign policy and an affirmation of its position in the world.[35]

Furthermore, the break with the Soviet Union, which had precipitated Yugoslavia's fall into the abyss of isolation and vulnerability, was being reversed. Stalin's death in March 1953 began the slow but steady *rapprochement* between the Soviet Union and Yugoslavia which culminated in 1955 and 1956 with the much photographed exchange visits of Khrushchev and Tito. The signing of the Belgrade Declaration, confirming the "Yugoslav Road to Socialism" and pledging respect and noninterference in internal affairs, sealed this new relationship.

Thus by 1955, the geopolitical threat was no longer present. That the Yugoslavs had in fact recognized that a significant change in the geopolitical situation had occurred is indicated by this shift away from military investments in Bosnia-Hercegovina to nonmilitary investments in other republics and regions. Yet, no important shift in policy toward the development of the LDRs occurred.

Economics

An even more powerful version of this geopolitical explanation emerges if it is coupled with an account of Yugoslavia's economic situation. According to this explanation, given Yugoslavia's geopolitical vulnerability and overall backwardness, the scarce resources had to be channeled to areas and sectors where maximization of output could occur. That meant, first, strategic investments for security reasons; then, more generally, industrialization in the DRs for overall self-sufficiency and optimum growth. As a result, the Yugoslavs argued, the development of the LDRs had to be put on a temporary hold.

34 Rusinow, 1977, pp. 44-46.

35 For more on the non-aligned movement and Yugoslavia's role in it see Alvin Z. Rubinstein, *Yugoslavia and the Nonaligned World* (Princeton: Princeton University Press, 1970).

Upon closer scrutiny however, the economic argument for overall neglect of the LDRs is also found seriously wanting. The reason given for the consistently smaller per capita investment in the LDRs, most rational use of scarce resources for optimal national growth, is disproved by Montenegro's consistent lag in efficiency despite its high per capita investments, as well as by the fact that, as resources increased while the geopolitical threat decreased, no shift of priority to the development of the LDRs occurred. Thus, raw materials continued to be underpriced until the late 1960s, and the per capita investment of the LDRs continued to lag behind that of the DRs.

Once again, Vukmanovic-Tempo confirmed the available evidence:

> Because of the need for accumulation, we had a politics of prices; ... through prices we insured the fastest growth, and that was fundamental....Was it equally fair to all? That's a different matter....We had to create capital and enable it to circulate where it would be most profitable...as for individual republics, that's a different question ...a different matter. There were long discussions, arguments and clashes within the leadership, the Central Committee...we tried to have free prices....[36]

When we look at investment disbursement of the 1950s, two things are immediately apparent. The first is that the per capita investment in the LDRs was less than that in the DRs, despite the regime's proclaimed goal of faster development of the LDRs (Table 2.3). Secondly, a comparison of investments among the LDRs as well as between them and the DRs, shows that the distribution was highly unequal (Tables 2.3). As we can further see (Table 2.2), among the LDRs, Montenegro with 2.5% of the Yugoslav population received 3.6% of total investment for 1957; of the DRs, Slovenia with 8.7% of the Yugoslav population received 13.6% of investment, while Serbia proper, with a population of 26.3% received a preponderant share of the 39.2% of investment allocated.[37] Altogether then, Montenegro, Slovenia and Serbia proper with a total of 37.5% of Yugoslavia's population, received some 46% of the total investment.

There are a number of factors which show that, contrary to the Yugoslav claim, throughout the 1950s economic rationality was not the

[36] Svetozar Vukmanovic-Tempo, Interview, Beograd, January 23, 1990.

[37] In terms of investment in Serbia, it is known, accepted and born out indirectly by the pricing policies of agriculture and extractive industries that throughout this period Vojvodina and especially Kosovo received much less than their per capita share of investments; see Table 2.1. Furthermore, a quick comparison of Tables 2.1 and 2.3 yields the approximate investment figure of 46%.

Table 2.3
Per Capita Investment of Republics and Regions Relative to Yugoslav Average for 1952-1960 (in 1972 prices)

	SFRJ	BiH	Montenegro	Croatia	Macedonia	Slovenia	Serbia Proper	Vojvodina	Kosovo	LDRs	DRs
1952-1960	100	90.2	161.9	101.0	86.1	162.9	106.0	66.4	43.5	87.7	105.8

Source: Fond Federacije, *Razvoj privredno nedovoljno razvijenih podrucja u Jugoslaviji*, Belgrade: "Srbostampa,"1986, p. 108.

main criterion for regional distribution of investments and that, consequently, it does not account for the displacement of the goal of regional development. The first is that the three republics which received the most investment per capita were all at very different development levels; in addition, of the three, only in the case of Slovenia, the most developed republic, can the claim be substantiated that high investment might have led to the quickest output maximization.

This is further corroborated by the frequently poor investment decisions and the equally poor results of that investment. While subsequently there was disagreement in Yugoslavia over whether more irrationality in investment occurred during the centralized period of the 1950s or after the Reform of 1965, the concept and problem of "political factories" arose first in the 1950s. The building of the steel mill in Niksic, Montenegro, which was put into operation in 1953 while the rail connection to the Adriatic was not completed until 1961, a paved highway out of Niksic until 1963, or the standard gauge railway connecting it to the rest of the country until 1975, is only one example of suboptimal or irrational use of relatively scarce economic resources.

Furthermore, regarding the question of scarcity of resources as a reason for displacing the development of the LDRs until 1965, it is true that Yugoslavia's development needs, like those of all developing countries, far outpaced its resources. Yet, by 1955, the overall situation was stabilizing. The receding of the geopolitical threat meant that investments which had been channeled to military buildup could now be diverted to development. The high growth rate which began in 1953 and the continued low consumption meant that an economic base was being built up. And the almost 1.2 billion dollars of American aid, of which only 55 million dollars was loan, added substantially to this economic base. Yet, despite the changed geopolitical and economic situation, no substantial shift in policy regarding the faster development of the LDRs occurred.

Reality and Perception

Despite evidence of these changes in their geopolitical and economic situations, the Yugoslavs that I interviewed in the early 1980s insisted on explaining the displacement of the goal of regional equalization in the 1950s by reference to their isolation in the international arena and the consequent need to emphasize national security. In the words of Nenad Vujanic, non-party member who for sixteen years worked for PIK (at that time a large and very successful agricultural complex in Serbia), first as an agronomist and later as Director, and from 1971 worked in the Agrobanka in Belgrade: "We wanted Yugoslavia to be independent. Therefore we had to develop first the basic industries. . . . In that our development was similar to the development of other countries."[38]

From this shift in priority, from regional to overall development goals, two critical consequences for regional development emerged. The first concerned the nature of industrial investment; the second concerned the amount. In regard to the nature of industrial investment, it is important to note that from 1949 to 1956, and even to 1965, investments in the LDRs were neither channeled to more traditional labor intensive manufactures where the LDRs would have had a comparative advantage which could have created an economic base for their faster development; nor were they part of an overall plan for the economic development of Yugoslavia such as the one advocated by Kubovic at the time.[39] At this stage, the feeling predominated that whatever was built, wherever it was built, would be all right, since lacking "everything," "anything" would be useful.[40]

Ljubislav Markovic, professor of economics at the University of Belgrade, member of the 1982-1983 Krajger Commission for the Economic Stabilization and from 1957 to 1965 Head of Cabinet for Prime Minister Milentje Popovic, articulated this general view:

[38] Nenad Vujanic, Interview, Agrobanka, Belgrade, Serbia, August 27, 1983.

[39] For more on Kubovic's and other competing plans for the development of Yugoslavia in the 1950s, see Chapter 6.

[40] This position was reiterated consistently in the interviews. While some participants considered the position justified for the 1950s and others considered it deplorable, all agreed that it prevailed both in the planning and in resource distribution.

> Up to 1965 there were so few factories that mistakes in building could almost not be made; that is, almost everything was needed as a production unit, though not necessarily as an economic unit. The question 'How much does it cost?' was never asked as long as the item was produced.[41]

This mind-set, which was repeatedly articulated in interviews with policy-makers, bureaucrats and academics from all the republics and regions, owed as much to the traditional "peasant" mentality that in Yugoslavia, as in many developing countries, equated all things industrial with "progress," as it did to the still lingering influence of the Soviet model.

There are three significant points which emerge from these interviews in regard to the question of development in the 1950s. First, there was unanimity on the dominance of this mind-set in the 1950s. Second, although some of the respondents deplored this dominance, the majority justified it as the only possible thing to do in Yugoslavia's circumstances, which they continued to characterize in terms of geopolitical uncertainty and economic scarcity. In the words of Klime Corbe, Director of the Development Fund, " . . . because of the conflict with the Soviet Union, we first needed to solidify our material base."[42]

Third, the overwhelming majority of the respondents maintained the following contradictory claims: on the one hand, that faster development of the LDRs could not be a priority in the 1950s because of scarcity of resources and the consequent need for optimal investments and, on the other, that "mistakes" in investments could hardly be made since at Yugoslavia's low level of development everything was needed. Even the most reflective respondents were seemingly unaware of the contradiction between the two claims voiced above. Indeed, not one saw the necessity of justifying the simultaneous belief in these two contradictory propositions. Such tolerance for inconsistency alerts us to the fact that economic rationality in investment allocation may not have been the priority that the Yugoslavs claimed for it.

Effects

The repercussions for narrowing of economic inequality between the DRs and the LDRs, as we shall see, were serious. For by the early 1960s,

41 Ljubislav Markovic, Interview, Faculty of Political Science, University of Belgrade, Belgrade, January 28, 1983.

42 Klime Corbe, Interview, Federal Fund for Development of the LDRs, Belgrade, Serbia, May 9, 1983.

it was clear that major restructuring of Yugoslav industries needed to be undertaken in order to eliminate the waste of resources which resulted from both domestic production of unwanted goods, especially machinery, as well as from use of foreign exchange to purchase goods abroad which could have been produced at home, a practice which led to an accumulation of foreign debt. Yet, in an increasingly decentralized Yugoslavia, this became not only economically expensive, but also politically difficult and thus "dangerous." As a result, the restructuring was never done, and the duplication of inefficient factories, producing unsellable commodities, continued to plague the Yugoslav economy and to hinder the narrowing of regional disparity.

The second consequence of the shift in goal away from regional development concerns the amount of investment. Here it is important to remember that, beginning with the First Five-Year Plan and continuing through the 1950s, the LDRs received significantly less investment per capita than the DRs. According to the later findings of the Federal Fund for the Development of the LDRs, for the period 1952-1964, the index of growth for the LDRs measured at 132.8%, while that of the DRs was 131.6%.[43] Even this very slight increase for the LDRs gives a better picture than existed, since it is inflated by the military investments received by Bosnia-Hercegovina in the early 1950s following the break with the Cominform. (In 1953, for example, they received 38.5% of total investment.)[44] Because of their very limited spread effect, these investments had much less direct benefit for the development of the LDRs than the increased amount might indicate. Furthermore, not only did the LDRs receive less investment per capita and, on the whole, not much more investment than their GMP would qualify them for but, as we have seen, the distribution of that investment among the LDRs was heavily biased in favor of Montenegro. Although investments in the LDRs during the period 1952-1960, relative to their GMP, may appear to favor the LDRs (Table 2.4), it is necessary to remember that both the structure of investment and the pricing of products were decided by fiat at the center, and both worked against the LDRs by depreciating their contribution to the GMP by as much as 20%, while inflating that of the the DRs by up to 10%.

Secondly, an increase of investment of some 1.2 index points could hardly lead to a situation which could facilitate the LDRs' faster

43 Fond Federacije, *Razvoj privredno nedovoljno razvijenih prodrucja u Jugoslaviji* [Development of the Economically Insufficiently Developed Regions in Yugoslavia] (Belgrade: "Srbostampa," 1986), p. 106.

44 Data on investment amount channelled to defense installations has not been available up to now because of "security reasons."

Table 2.4
Investments in Fixed Assets Relative to GMP

	SFRJ	BiH	Montenegro	Croatia	Macedonia	Slovenia	Serbia Proper	Vojvodina	Kosovo	LDRs	DRs
1952-1960	100	114.5	230.4	84.8	126.8	93.5	112.0	65.2	106.5	125.7	92.8

Source: Fond Federacije, *Razvoj privredno nedovoljno razvijenih podrucja u Jugoslaviji*, Belgrade: "Srbostampa,"1986 p. 110.

Table 2.5
Grants-in-Aid:* Annual Average Expenditure per Capita, 1947-1965 (Thousands of Dinars)

Slovenia	7.94	BiH	4.59
Croatia	6.18	Macedonia	5.53
Serbia*	4.56	Montenegro	8.69

Source: Shoup, 1968, p. 231.
*The actual figure for Serbia proper would be higher since Kosovo received very little aid throughout this period.

development, especially since, except for Montenegro, all the LDRs received less investment per capita than the Yugoslav average (Table 2.3).[45]

The difference in the treatment, both between the DRs and LDRs and among them, is seen even more clearly in the regional allocation of the grants-in-aid. The idea behind the grants-in-aid was that regardless of its wealth, every republic and region should provide to its populace the same facilities in education, health, culture and other social services and benefits. Of special significance in a socialist society, the grants-in-aid were seen as a means of immediately equalizing the living conditions within the republics and regions while the LDRs were developing their economies. In view of that goal, it is particularly ironic to note that for the years 1947-56, when wage differentials between the DRs and the LDRs were still at their socialist minimum, the average annual expenditure per capita for the DRs, notably Croatia and Slovenia, was higher than for either Bosnia-Hercegovina or Macedonia (Table 2.5), whose increase in living conditions they were supposed to promote. The only exception was Montenegro which, as with investments, appropriated a preponderant share of the grants-in-aid.

Arguments over Regional Distribution of Investments

Before turning to an analysis of the Second Five-Year Plan, it is important to examine in some detail an argument often made, especially in the DRs, justifying the discrepancy in amounts of industrial investments between the developed and the less developed regions. Because the Yugoslav respondents that I interviewed repeatedly referred to 1957, 1960 or "around 1962" as the period when differences over the regional distribution of investments were first voiced and because 1957 was clearly, for most, their own initial referent, a more careful consideration of these disagreements over investment allocation is necessary before turning to the Second Five-Year Plan.

In essence, the argument states that the allocation of investment whereby the LDRs received less investment per capita than the DRs was both ideologically just and economically sound. It was ideologically "just" because, even though the amount of investment per capita was smaller, it was more than the LDRs were capable of

[45] Fond Federacije, *Razvoj privredno nedovoljno razvijenih prodrucja u Jugoslaviji* [Development of the Economically Insufficiently Developed Areas in Yugoslavia] (Belgrade: "Srbostampa," 1986), p. 106.

generating by themselves; that is, even this smaller investment included "aid" from the DRs. It was economically "sound" because economies have different absorptive capacities depending on their stage of development. The Slovenian economist, Pavel Sicherl, has noted:

> If the absorptive capacity of the LDRs had already been reached, then to put in more money at that time would mean an overall loss of development potential. Also, the DRs had to have their own growth rate. Therefore it is important to see what is happening in Yugoslavia as a whole since that influences much of what happens in the LDRs. Therefore again I emphasize the primary importance of development of Yugoslavia as a whole.[46]

Moreover, this argument continues, absorptive capacity for industrial investments in the LDRs was reached with the investments that they were getting, as shown by the fact that even these industries were operating at between 30% to 50% below their capacity level.[47]

Economic Efficiency and Investment Absorption

One of the major problems with such an explanation is that the question of amount and proportion of investment in the LDRs is far more complex than the "investment absorption" argument might imply. First, the problem of underutilization of industrial capacities or "efficiency of investment is a problem of all Yugoslavia, and not only of the LDRs."[48]

Secondly, as respondents in the LDRs repeatedly pointed out to me, there were industries in the LDRs which operated as efficiently as those in the DRs, and a few like the rifle factory in Kragujevac, Serbia, were more efficient. This suggests that the structure of industrial investment may greatly influence efficiency, a point often brought up in the LDRs. As Sulejman Kamenica of The Economic Institute of Sarajevo pointed out, "efficiency varies depending on whether you look at the capital coefficient which is high, or you take into account the structure of the economy, and then it is not so bad."[49]

46 Pavel Sicherl, Interview, Economic section of the Faculty of Law, Ljubljana, Slovenia, November 7, 1983.

47 Joseph T. Bombelles, *Economic Development of Communist Yugoslavia 1947-1964* (Stanford: Hoover Institution of War, Revolution and Peace, Stanford University Press, 1968), p. 34.

48 Klime Corbe, Interview, Federal Fund for the Development of the LDRs, Belgrade, Serbia, May 9, 1983.

49 Sulejman Kamenica, Interview, Economic Institute of Sarajevo, Sarajevo, Bosnia-Hercegovina, June 8, 1983.

The main point made here is that the structure of investment during this period was determined in Belgrade. In an economy where the central government largely decides who produces what, where, and under what conditions, as well as the relative value of the items produced, efficiency in terms of the ratio of cost per unit produced will depend more upon the government's allocative decision of investment and pricing than on any simple variable like productivity of a worker. Thus, had the decision regarding industrial investment in the LDRs considered the optimum development of the LDRs rather than that of the three more powerful republics or of Yugoslavia as a whole, a different structure of investment would have been pursued whose absorptive capacity and therefore efficiency for the LDRs would have been greater. Although there was less efficiency of investment in the LDRs, according to Ivan Turcic, specialist on regional development at the Economic Institute of Zagreb, "the efficacy of the LDRs, taking into account the structure of their economy, is lower by only 11% than that of the Yugoslav average, which is tolerable for me."[50]

A third problem with this argument is that even if greater investment in industry in the LDRs would have meant "wasting" money, that money "left over" once the "absorptive capacity" for investment had been reached could have been channeled into other sectors of the economy which desperately needed investments. In the absence of such policy, bottlenecks such as the one in the transportation system were created which then resulted in the lower "absorptive capacity" of investment in the LDRs. The building up of roads necessary for products to get to market, of apartments, schools, hospitals and other infrastructural investments, is critical for the long-range improvement of efficiency of an economy. Although the LDRs received grants-in-aid whose purpose was to equalize the social services and the infrastructure between them and the DRs, these grants were again less than those received by the DRs (Table 2.5). Not surprisingly, they were inadequate to cover the infrastructural needs.

Of course, improvements in infrastructure did occur in the LDRs, though much of it after the Fund for Development of the LDRs was put into operation in 1965-66, when the investment money was placed at the disposal of the LDRs themselves. However, because of the low infrastructural investments in the LDRs in the 1950s, in the later stages of development (post-1965), money from the Development Fund earmarked for productive investments was often used by the LDRs for building up their infrastructure. This, in turn, became a point of contention between the developed and the less developed, with the

[50] Ivan Turcic, Interview, Institute of Economics, Zagreb, Croatia, September 27, 1983.

former citing it as an example of the waste of productive resources by the less developed.

There are three "obvious" points which bear repeating because of their importance to an understanding of the issue of infrastructural investments, in general, and to the situation of the Yugoslav LDRs in the 1950s and thereafter, in particular. First, infrastructural investments are expensive; second, they do not themselves create income; third, they are necessary to develop a productive economy. Thus, the sooner the infrastructure is created, the sooner economic investments can be optimized.

Finally, the efficiency argument simply begs the question, in that a characteristic, indeed a definition, of underdevelopment is lesser efficiency. The only way to overcome it in the long run however, is to proceed with the developmental effort at some cost to efficiency, while ensuring that the gap in efficiency between the developed and the less developed areas is being narrowed. As Nadjenko Popovski, head of the Planning Ministry of Macedonia, had pointed out:

> Efficiency is an overall problem and not only of the LDRs . . . all . . . the developed and the less developed have the problem . . . sure the efficiency is less in the LDRs, but that can't be the basis for not developing them. Rather, we must look for solutions for increasing efficiency but not as some say with measures leading to the interest of the DRs.[51]

Economic Justice and Ideology

As to the question of "justice" or fairness regarding the disparity of investment, although it is correct that in the postwar period the LDRs were receiving more investment per capita than they were capable of generating from their own economies, that is only one side of the story. For not only was the structure of their investment decided at the center on the basis of what benefitted Yugoslavia as a whole, with the definition favoring the developed regions, but the price of their commodities, overwhelmingly raw materials and some agriculture, was kept artificially low, both in terms of domestic and world prices.[52] Sulejman Kamenica of the Economic Institute in Sarajevo articulates a commonly held view in the LDRs: "Low prices of raw materials, mostly

[51] Nadjenko Popovski, Interview, Planning Ministry of Macedonia, Skopje, Macedonia, May 11, 1983.

[52] For a more detailed analysis see Caslav Ocic, *Razvijenost Jugoslavenskih republika i pokrajina od 1950 do 1984* [Development of Yugoslav Republics and Regions from 1950-1984] (Belgrade: Institut Ekonomskih Nauka, 1986).

located in the LDRs, increased the disparity between the DRs and the LDRs, and further aided the development of the DRs."[53]

Respondents throughout Yugoslavia stated that the reason for this policy, which clearly disadvantaged the LDRs as well as agricultural Vojvodina, was to control inflation while stimulating the rest of industry, which, it is important for us to note, was located mostly in the DRs. In the words of Ivan Turcic of the Economic Institute in Zagreb, "We didn't want inflation to go up, because then everything else would go up too; so we kept the price of raw materials down. That was the federal policy."[54] The reason is given by Vukmanovic-Tempo: "Accumulation was primary."[55] As a result, not only was there a direct transfer of income from the LDRs to the DRs, which, to a diminishing extent, lasted until 1970, but because of the undervalorization of their products, the LDRs were contributing more to the GMP than they were being given credit for. Thus, contrary to the Yugoslavs' claims, the allocation of investment, supposedly based on "efficiency" and "absorptive capacity" which was used to justify the lower per capita investments in the LDRs, was neither ideologically just nor economically sound.

Another dimension of the question of "justice" frequently articulated by respondents in the LDRs focuses on the issue of "aid" as compensation. Briefly, the argument states that the aid received from the DRs was not aid but compensation for the initial twenty or twenty-five years of discriminatory policies towards the LDRs. A comprehensive study of the opportunity cost for the LDRs and how it balanced with the "aid" received has not been made or, at least, published. Questions that I asked in 1982-83, when the research was first undertaken, were met with a variety of answers, ranging from "that's all in the past . . . the present is what matters" to "everything came from the government budget, no specific accounting was made and therefore data does not exist for such a study." Nevertheless, several admissions were made confidentially, especially a notable one from an academic serving a term as a high-ranking government official in Bosnia-Hercegovina, that he had heard about a study made in his republic around 1975 whose publication had been blocked as too controversial. Finally, I was "advised" by several sources not to pursue that

53 Sulejman Kamenica, Interview, Economic Institute of Sarajevo, Bosnia-Hercegovina, June 8, 1983.

54 Ivan Turcic, Interview, Economic Institute, Zagreb, Croatia, September 27, 1983.

55 Svetozar Vukmanovic-Tempo, Interview, Beograd, January 23, 1990.

particular route of inquiry.[56] However, a rough comparison of prices indicates that unquestionably there was a considerable opportunity cost paid by the LDRs,[57] thus at least partially substantiating the argument of the LDRs that the Development Fund created in 1965 can be regarded as "reparation payment" rather than "aid."

There is one final argument which strengthens the case for the necessity of overall greater investments in the LDRs throughout the first postwar decade of Yugoslav development, that is, in the 1950s. This argument points to the essential continuation of a status quo situation which had advantaged the development of the DRs. For while most of the LDRs continued to develop haphazardly, on the basis of an investment amount, structure and pricing system which put them at a disadvantage, the DRs, notably Slovenia, Croatia and to a much lesser extent Serbia proper, began their postwar development with three major advantages. The first was that these were the industrial areas of Yugoslavia, and as such they had industrial plants which had survived the war. With the reconstruction completed, these plants could be expanded or converted to meet the requirements of the new regime. The second was that along with the industrial plants came the labor force, more educated and efficient, steeped in the industrial tradition and generally more amenable to the demands of a modernizing society (Table 2.6). Third, these areas possessed the infrastructure of roads, railroads, ports and so on, which were necessary for the maximum utilization of their resources. Thus, the investments that they obtained, first from the budget and after 1952 from the General Investment Fund, could be used directly to expand and enhance production. To borrow a term from Walt Rostow, whose model of stages of development was still often quoted in Yugoslavia in the early 1980s, the DRs were at the "take-off" point while much of the LDRs were barely entering the modern age. The cumulative effect of the above on the narrowing of economic disparity between the developed and the less developed regions at this crucial time in their development is, in retrospect, not surprising; the difference in GMP per capita between them was increasing.

[56] This refers to conversations held during the first part of this research, in 1982-1983. On this question all respondents requested anonymity, hence no reference is provided for these quotes. The respondents came from research institutes, government bureaucracies, as well as political positions in both LDRs and DRs.

[57] See study by Ocic, 1986.

Table 2.6
Comparison of Development Levels of Republics and Regions, 1953

		SFRJ	BiH	Montenegro	Croatia	Macedonia	Slovenia	Serbia	Serbia Proper	Vojvodina	Kosovo
Population	1953	100	16.8	2.5	23.1	7.7	8.7	41.2	26.3	10.1	4.8
	1961	100	17.7	2.5	22.4	7.6	8.6	41.2	26.0	10.0	5.2
Agricultural Level Total Pop.	1948	100	107	104	93	105	66	107	108	102	122
	1953	100	102	100	93	103	68	109	110	103	119
Level Working in Industry, 1952		100	91	39	121	48	233	79	82	88	45
Level Working of Entire Population		100	93	70	118	68	173	84	87	96	47
Participation by Illiterate in Pop.		25.4	40.2	30.1	16.3	35.7	2.7	27.9	29.5	12.9	54.8

(continues)

Table 2.6 *(continued)*
Comparison of Development Levels of Republics and Regions, 1953

	SFRJ	BiH	Montenegro	Croatia	Macedonia	Slovenia	Serbia	Serbia Proper	Vojvodina	Kosovo
Less than 3 grades of schooling	42.1	67.2	47.2	30.5	50.7	15.2	43.2	44.5	28.4	71.2
Grades 4-7	46.0	26.1	40.9	56.0	40.3	68.2	44.5	43.2	56.5	22.8
Completed primary school	4.2	2.4	5.7	4.8	3.5	4.5	4.4	4.0	6.5	1.9
Completed high school	6.6	4.1	5.3	7.3	3.8	11.2	6.6	7.0	7.5	2.3
Completed higher schooling	0.6	0.3	0.5	0.7	0.3	0.8	0.7	0.8	0.5	0.1
Industrial workers per 100, 1952	33	31	0.2	40	16	77	26	27	29	16

Source: SZZS, 1973.

Second Five-Year Plan: 1957-1962

As the Yugoslavs made preparations for their first non-Stalinist five-year plan, they had reason to be optimistic about the further development of the country as a whole, including the development of the LDRs. The break with the Cominform in 1948, and the resultant geopolitical threat which had caused the displacement of the goal of faster development of the LDRs in favor of maximizing the overall growth of the economy, had been successfully weathered. By 1955-56 Yugoslavia had created for itself an increasingly secure and respectable *niche* between the "east" and the "west", and was emerging as one of the leaders of a new movement whose members refused to align themselves with either of the two superpowers, the Soviet Union or the United States. Following the dismantling of collectivization, with its borders secured and its internal situation normalized, the leadership could turn its attention to the domestic scene. After ten years of sacrifice for the rapid construction of the socialist society, the general populace was to start reaping some benefits.

The aim of the Second Five-Year Plan, passed December 4, 1957, and made retroactive to January 1957, was to take account of the altered circumstances and to start the process of "inclusion"[58] in the socialist society. The objectives as articulated in the plan make clear the change;[59] notably, improvement of the standard of living became an articulated goal and was placed third in the ranking of priorities. As a result, not only was there a shift in investments from industry to agriculture (though only of the small socialist sector), transportation and trade, there were changes within the industrial sector as well.[60] In this case, there was a shift from almost exclusive investment in heavy industry (sector I) to the production of consumer goods and light industry (sector II).

For the LDRs, the Second Five-Year Plan mentioned for the first time as a separate objective "aid to development of underdeveloped areas"[61] and ranked its priority in fourth place. Moreover, because regional differences had continued to widen in the previous decade, a new instrument for developing the two most neglected regions, Kosovo-Metohija and Macedonia, was introduced. This was the so-called

[58] For more on the process of inclusion in Marxist-Leninist regimes, see Kenneth Jowitt, "Inclusion and Mobilization in European Leninist Regimes," *World Politics*, October 1975.
[59] Bicanic, 1973, p. 61.
[60] In 1957, the sector share of total investment shifted down from 58.7% to 43.8% in industry, in favor of agriculture (6.4% to 15.8%), transportation (23.7% to 27.4%) and trade (4.9% to 7.9%). Sirc, 1979, p. 34.
[61] Bicanic, 1973, p. 61.

"guaranteed investments," which provided the LDRs with a specific volume of investment for certain projects chosen by the center to ensure a relatively comprehensive development of Yugoslavia. Accordingly, Kosovo-Metohija (Kosmet) was to receive 10 billion dinars annually, ten times more than its previous annual amount and Macedonia was to receive 20 billion dinars annually, four times the amount received in the previous years.[62] However, the total amount of investments in the economies of the LDRs (in this period, this refers to Montenegro, Macedonia and for the first time Kosmet, though the latter was still administered by Serbia rather than being treated as a separate LDR) was not much larger than in the previous period, as Bosnia-Hercegovina was now no longer considered an LDR. Nevertheless, on a per capita basis, investment in the remaining LDRs increased, and because of their new permanent nature, a degree of planning could be applied. Finally, supplementary measures, such as priority on loans from the General Investment Fund, were carried over from the earlier period, and Macedonia, Montenegro and Kosmet were forgiven the principal on credits received to date.[63]

For the country as a whole, the Second Five-Year Plan was the most successful ever. With its goals achieved in four years (actually three, since the plan was passed December 4, 1957, retroactive to January 1, 1957), it stands as the only five-year plan to fulfill all its objectives. The achievements were indeed impressive: a 56.6% increase in social product, a 66.4% increase in industrial production and a 47.7% increase in agricultural production.[64] The average growth of GMP between 1953 and 1957 was 10.2%,[65] one of the highest in the world. Since most of the objectives of the Second Five-Year Plan were achieved in four years, and many were surpassed, it was decided to abandon it and begin the Third Five-Year Plan a year early.

Despite the overall success of the Second Five-Year Plan, its contribution to the development of the LDRs was an ambiguous one. On the one hand, the LDRs were "guaranteed" a certain sum of investments, and the actual investments came close to, or exceeded, the amounts foreseen. On the other hand, despite the LCY leadership's exhortation to help the LDRs develop, discussions between leaders of the developed republics regarding a formula for their development and, at

62 Shoup, 1968, p. 235, and Fond federacije, *Razvoj privredno nedovoljno razvijenih podrucja u Jugoslaviji* [Development of the Economically Insufficiently Developed Regions in Yugoslavia] (Belgrade: Instutut ekonomskih nauka, 1986), pp. 16-17.

63 Ibid.

64 Bombelles, 1968, p. 116.

65 Hoffman and Neal, 1962, p. 307.

least from 1954, increasingly frequent discussions in parliamentary committees concerning a program of aid for the LDRs,[66] criteria for defining the LDRs were still not agreed upon and, from the LDRs' perspective, a satisfactory policy geared to their development failed to emerge.

One result of the lack of agreement over regional development was the exclusion of Bosnia-Hercegovina from the LDR group during the Second Five-Year Plan period, a decision whose impact was a substantial economic setback for that republic.[67] Another important result was that "political" or personalistic criteria still could and did intervene in the distribution of resources for investment. This was facilitated by the low interest rates and soft budget constraints which meant that both at the republic and at the commune level it was economically rational from the individual unit's point of view to jockey for industrial investments because failure of an industry carried no penalty, while its mere presence provided some tax base and employment, and increased one's own and the region's prestige. Although this was a general problem of the Yugoslav economy, it tended to be especially severe when found in the LDRs.

Additionally, the continued absence of economic restructuring of the LDRs into areas where they would have comparative advantage--labor intensive processing industries--and the continuing lack of equitable valorization of their products, meant that their productive capacity for development remained constrained. Furthermore, the increase in agricultural investment benefitted them less than the DRs because it encompassed only the social sector agriculture, much more prevalent in the DRs (especially in Vojvodina and in Slovenia) than in the LDRs. Finally, the discrepancy in per capita investment between the DRs and the LDRs remained, and the economic disparity between them, as measured in GMP per capita, continued to grow.

Other problems which affected the general economy were also felt most acutely in the LDRs. For example, unemployment, whose main cause was the surplus labor force from agriculture, in turn partly a result of faulty government policies which stressed capital intensive mech-

[66] Shoup, 1968, p. 234.

[67] Because of strategic (military) investments in BiH in the early 1950s, its fixed assets per capita grew by some 10% by the latter half of that decade. As a result of this perceived "rapid development", it was excluded from the LDRs in the Second Five-Year Plan with the result that its per capita GMP fell by 35% during this period. Kasim Begic, *Jugoslovenski "sjever" i "jug"* [The Yugoslav "North" and "South"] (Sarajevo: Nisro "Oslobodenje", 1989), p. 95.

anization, rose nationwide from 3.6% in 1955 to 6.1% in 1959[68] and was the highest in the LDRs. Moreover, the continuous shortages in the consumer sector, especially that of housing, also became increasingly problematic at a time of rising expectations. The long delays in finishing investment projects, the "political" factories which continued to mushroom, the lack of attention to the location of raw materials, markets and other factors of profitability, though general problems throughout Yugoslavia, were always felt most strongly in the LDRs.

Regional Development in the 1950s

Thus by 1960, despite the successful completion of the Second Five-Year Plan a year ahead of schedule, important structural discrepancies in the economy continued to persist and were becoming increasingly felt. Furthermore, the problem of regional economic disparity was surfacing in a new light. For throughout this period, the LDRs had received considerably less investment per capita than the DRs, and less or barely as much investment as their unvalorized contribution to the GMP would warrant. Additionally, their investments had first been channeled to a defense build-up, much of which had neither a productive use nor a consumption benefit. Even the later industrial investments which were made were often reached on an ad hoc basis, often without sufficient concern for their future functioning, profitability or propulsive character in the regions where they were located. The grants-in-aid, whose sole purpose was to equalize living conditions between the developed and the less developed, were instead also instrumental in further increasing the gap between them as well as among the LDRs themselves. Finally, of the LDRs, only Montenegro received far more than the average in investments and in grants-in-aid and, along with Slovenia and Serbia, continued receiving preferential treatment throughout this period.

The evidence provided by the Second Five-Year Plan is consistent with that uncovered in examining the First Five-Year Plan, the period of economic decentralization and the arguments concerning per capita investments. This evidence shows that investments in the 1950s were not allocated solely or even primarily on the basis of economic rationality, that the grants-in-aid were not distributed on the basis of need and that, contrary to the Yugoslav claims, neither the geopolitical threat nor the scarcity of resources account for the con-

68 Savezni Zavod za Statistiku (SZZS) i Savezni Zavod za Drustveno Planiranje (SZDP), *Razvoj Jugoslavije 1947-1981* (Development of Yugoslavia, 1947-1981) (Belgrade, May, 1982), p. 63.

tinued displacement of the goal of regional equalization through faster development of the LDRs in the 1950s. If, however, contrary to the Yugoslav claim, neither the geopolitical situation nor the scarcity of resources can account for the displacement of the goal of faster development of the LDRs during the 1950s, why was regional equalization through faster development of the LDRs displaced in the first decade of postwar Yugoslav development?

The most complete explanation for the continuing and increasing disparity between the DRs and the LDRs throughout the 1950s; the most plausible explanation for why the prerequisites for narrowing that disparity, greater per capita investments and grants-in-aid, were not met; and why Montenegro, Slovenia and to a lesser extent Serbia proper, three republics which span the range of development levels in Yugoslavia, consistently received preferential treatment is the following: the disproportionately high representation in the top echelons of the government and party apparatus, partly a result of their wartime experience, enabled them to convert this presence into political power which they then used to enhance their or their republic's economic interests.[69]

That is, because of their role in the partisan resistance, Montenegro and to a lesser extent Serbia had a disproportionately large cadre presence in the political-bureaucratic apparat in Belgrade after the war. Croatia, one of the two most developed republics which, according to the economic rationality argument, should have received a large portion of investment, was presumably penalized for its wartime Nazi collaboration; Kosovo, by far the most backward and needy region, was similarly penalized for its attempted wartime rebellion against the partisans, as can be seen by its lack of national status, political representation and economic investments in the 1950s. Only in the case of Slovenia, the most developed republic in Yugoslavia, may economic rationality have played a role in its investment allocation. That in the process, as a result of the policies pursued (structure of the economy, pricing, investment distribution, grants-in-aid and others), development of the LDRs suffered a setback was an "undesirable consequence" rather than the result of some premeditated act. The intention or hope to narrow the economic disparity was always there; but the opportunity to enhance one's own interests, when it presented itself, proved irresistible.

The argument, that enhancement of a region's economic interests as a result of its political power best accounts for the otherwise seemingly

69 This disproportionately high representation already indicated greater political power.

haphazard choice of republics for investment in the 1950s, is strengthened by the strong correlation between a republic or region's party and state representation and its investment allocation. Thus, the composition of the Federal Executive Council, the top governing body in 1959, shows Montenegro and Slovenia proportionately highly overrepresented and Croatia highly underrepresented. While Serbia at first seems underrepresented, when we consider Serbia proper rather than Serbia as a whole, the underrepresentation is minimal.[70] Following Paul Shoup, if one further compares nationality rather than republic of origin, Montenegro, Slovenia and Serbia emerge clearly as politically overrepresented (Table 2.7).

Table 2.7
Composition of the Federal Executive Council, 1959

Republic	Nationality (Shoup)	Number	Percent	Percent of Total Pop.
Serbia	16	10	29	41.2
Croatia	5	2	6	23.1
Slovenia	6	6	18	8.7
BiH	–	4	12	16.8
Macedonia	3	3	9	7.7
Montenegro	4	9	26	2.5

Source: Shoup, 1968, p. 270; Rusinow, 1978, p. 72; SZZS, 1973, pp. 227-228.

Similarly, the 1957 national composition of the League of Communists of Yugoslavia shows a disproportionately large percentage of Serbs and Montenegrins and an underrepresentation of Croats (Table 2.8). It also shows the Slovenes to be a little underrepresented, a fact which is interpreted here as backing the earlier argument that, in their case, the high level of development and consequent economic rationality and their direct access to Tito through Sergej Krajger, one of the key personalities in shaping postwar Yugoslavia, were sufficient to ensure them disproportionately high investments.

70 Since no Albanians from Kosovo were in the government before 1965, considering Serbia proper is far more exact than Serbia as a whole.

Once again, corroboration is provided by Vukmanovic-Tempo. According to Tempo, between 1952 and 1957, decision-making regarding investment allocation was in his hands. When there was disagreement, the matter was taken by the aggrieved party to Tito for deliberation between the three (Tito, Tempo and the aggrieved party). Tempo's own priority up to 1957 was to invest in those units which were to maximize the development of Yugoslavia as a whole, without paying special attention to the LDRs. He also noted that Slovenia always "did very well" and that Bosnia-Hercegovina "did all right" because of the military investments.

We might note however that Montenegro, Vukmanovic-Tempo's home republic, did best of all and that BiH, which because of its strategic location received high investment in the early 1950s, was where the partisan uprising led by Tempo first began. Bosnia-Hercegovina ceased to "do well" in 1957, when it was dropped from the list of the LDRs.[71] In 1957 Vukmanovic-Tempo was also moved from leading the industrial sector to head the Trade Union. It was a move which he regards as a demotion, a way for the DRs to remove him from his influential position at a time when, in his words, he was "beginning to make trouble."

Table 2.8
National Composition of the League of Communists of Yugoslavia for 1957

	Percent	Percent in Population (1953)
Serbs	54.5	41.7
Croats	19.0	23.5
Slovenes	7.7	8.7
Macedonians	6.4	5.2
Montenegrins	6.7	2.1
Albanians	2.4	4.5

Source: Shoup, 1968, p. 270.

[71] As noted earlier between 1957 and 1963, BiH was excluded from the LDRs with the result that its GMP per capita fell by some 35%.

According to Tempo, by 1957 the prerequisites for the development of the country had been attained, and it was time to begin a much more active policy of development of the LDRs, a policy that would include a restructuring of their economies and a revalorization of their products, as well as direct aid for their development. The DRs were opposed to a shift in investments to the LDRs and the influence of their representatives, notably of Sergej Krajger and Edvard Kardelj, carried the day.[72] One result of their victory in development policy was the demotion of Vukmanovic-Tempo from head of the industrial sector to head of the Yugoslav Trade Union.

In terms of regional allocation of investments, the most frequent appeal to Tito, according to Tempo, came from Lazar Kolisevski, the representative from Macedonia. When we look at the investment disbursement of the 1950s, of the LDRs, Macedonia received the least. When we look at its representation on the Politburo, we note that in 1948 it had no representative, in 1953 it had one, and in 1958 it had one (Table 2.9). For the same time period, Montenegro, with a little over one-half of Macedonia's population, had in 1948 two representatives, in 1952 two and in 1958 three. In other words, proportionally, Macedonia had between 0 and 17% of Montenegro's representation. As for the Albanians, they had no representative at all on the Politburo until the fall of Rankovic in 1965. It is perhaps less surprising then that their investment continued to lag the most and that the economic disparity between them and the others continued to increase.

Table 2.9
Nationality of Persons Within the Party Politburo
(Executive Committee), 1948-1963

		Serbs	Croats	Slovenes	Montenegrins	Macedonians
Party Executive	1948	3	2	2	2	--
Committee	1953	3	4	3	2	1
	(spring) 1958	4	4	3	3	1
	1963	5	5	3	4	3

Source: Shoup, 1968, p. 275.

72 Svetozar Vukmanovic-Tempo, Interview, Belgrade, January 23, 1990.

Conclusion

To summarize, Yugoslavia's break with the Soviet Union and subsequent isolation between the two blocks may have been the *initial* event which displaced the goal of faster development of the LDRs and led to further channeling of scarce investment for strategic military purposes. However, the Yugoslavs' argument, that *throughout* the 1950s geopolitical necessity and economic scarcity compelled them to shift their goal of faster development of the LDRs to overall maximization of development, is not persuasive for two sets of reasons. The first is that, although both the geopolitical and economic conditions had changed by the mid-1950s, no equivalent shift in goal priority toward the LDRs occurred. The second is that, while additional investments were not channeled to the LDRs to help them develop faster, contrary to the Yugoslav claim, neither were they channeled to projects or regions which could maximize growth.

There is, moreover, significant empirical evidence which challenges the respondents' continued reliance on the argument of economic rationality to explain the shift in priority away from faster development of the LDRs. The growth of "political" investments like the steel mill in Niksic, Montenegro, are specific examples of economically irrational investments. The frequently repeated view that mistakes in investment could not really be made, since lacking everything all investments were useful, also shows that economic rationality was not the only, or even the main, criterion for investment.[73] Only in the case of Slovenia can high per capita investment be explained by pursuit of economic rationality. Low investment in Croatia cannot; nor can the high investment in Montenegro, a very underdeveloped republic, or the relatively higher investment in Serbia, the least developed republic among the DRs.

Finally, the official government stance that faster development of the LDRs was a priority goal from the beginning is directly contradicted by Svetozar Vukmanovic-Tempo, who was in charge of industrial development and claims to have made all investment decisions between 1952 and 1957. In a conversation I had with him in January 1990, Tempo stated categorically:

[73] While one can dispute the representativeness of the above view, it is important to note that irrespective of representativeness, it was voiced by a man who as Head of Cabinet from 1957 to 1961 had a direct input into and reflected the decision-making of the period.

> I wasn't interested in how a specific republic would fare. I was interested in how the Yugoslav economy (as a whole) would fare. Therefore with the accumulation, the government, I mean the banks, would give money to those firms that would give the fastest effects. In that process, Slovenia fared the best. [74]

When I pointed out that Montenegro did as well, or better, than Slovenia, Tempo explained at some length that due to Montenegro's isolation and backwardness, everything had to be built, from the infrastructure to industry, and that required a great deal of investment whose returns were not to be felt for a long time.

Although Vukmanovic-Tempo's claim for Montenegro is true, it bypasses the argument regarding the economic rationality criteria used by the Yugoslavs and is, therefore, irrelevant in this context. Additionally, if Montenegro had to receive such high investments through the 1950s (and beyond) because of its extreme isolation and backwardness, why did Kosovo not receive the same treatment? Its isolation and backwardness were even more acute.

The answer to this question as well as to the more general ones regarding investment allocation, goal priority and the place of the LDRs in the development scheme of the 1950s, as we have seen, lies in the realm of domestic politics rather than in that of geopolitics or economics.

To conclude, faster development of the LDRs was precluded throughout the first period of Yugoslav postwar development as a result of the political choice exercised by three politically stronger republics--Slovenia, Montenegro and Serbia proper--to optimize their individual economic interests at the expense of the development of the other republics and regions, including that of most of the LDRs.

[74] Svetozar Vukmanovic-Tempo, Interview, Belgrade, January 23, 1990.

3

1960s: Decentralization and Reform

Introduction

With the successful completion of the Second Five-Year Plan in 1960 and the feeling of exhilaration which accompanied its success, it was generally felt that Yugoslavia had crossed the threshold of development and was increasingly ready to compete in the international arena. Inaugurated in an atmosphere of optimism for the continuing high growth rates of the years preceding it, the Third Five-Year Plan sought to accelerate the pace of change by continuing the earlier liberalization and by bolstering it with a number of new, radical measures.

Unfortunately, along with the plethora of good news surrounding the achievements of the goals in the Second Five-Year Plan, the fundamental problems of poor economic planning and overinvestment in industries in which Yugoslavia had a comparative disadvantage persisted. Disproportions in the economy which had appeared alongside the high growth rate, notably the large stockpiles of unsellable goods like machinery, along with domestic underproduction of raw materials and food had created serious imbalances. More specifically, the high growth rate of industry (10.7% for the 1948-1960 period)[1] was a result of investments which were much higher than the output of the economy (as measured by yearly growth rate of GMP, Table 3.1), and were largely based on the forced extraction from the

[1] John H. Moore, "Industrial Production in Yugoslavia, 1952-72," U.S. Congress, Joint Economic Committee, *East European Economics, Post Helsinki* (Government Printing Office, August 25, 1977). Moore shows that the actual growth rate was about 1% per year less than the official Yugoslav index.

Table 3.1
Comparison of Gross Investment and Growth

1	Gross Investment in Fixed Assets (in billions dinars at 1972 prices)	1952-1960	214.1
2	Average Yearly Growth Rate of Investment	1953-1960	11.2
3	Share of Social Gross Investment in G.M.P.	1953-1956 1957-1960	31.7 35.0
4	Average Yearly Growth Rate of Industry	1948-1960	10.7
5	Average Yearly Growth Rate of G.M.P.	1951-1960	6.5

Sources: 1, 2, 4 and 5: SZZS, 1982, pp. 218-222.; 3 : Sirc, 1979, p. 33.

agricultural sector, the general impoverishment of the population, and on borrowed resources.

According to Nikola Cobeljic, fully one-third of Yugoslavia's investments in production came from foreign aid and loans,[2] while the growing balance-of-trade deficit was still covered by "soft," Western assistance. By the late 1950s and early 1960s, however, grants were increasingly replaced by credit, and old loans were coming to term, while the heavy industry and build-up of infrastructure for which they had been borrowed were not "yet" contributing to the growth of the economy. Additionally, the processing industries, the backbone of the economic boom, were operating largely on the basis of imported raw materials previously made cheap by the availability of foreign credits, low import duties and artificially low exchange rates. However, with the increased balance-of-payments difficulties and credit repayment due, outside sources of raw materials were becoming less available, while prices for raw materials produced in Yugoslavia continued to be so low that producers had little incentive to expand production. As a result, the processing industries were beginning to run out of raw materials.[3] Finally, in agriculture, two years of bad weather (1960 and 1961) led to a fall in output which necessitated food imports, while the government promotion of overall consumption, begun in the

[2] Nikola Cobeljic, *Politika i metode privrednog razvoja Jugoslavije 1947-1956* [Politics and Methods of Economic Development of Yugoslavia, 1947-1956] (Belgrade: 1959).

[3] For more on these problems see Ljubo Sirc, *The Yugoslav Economy Under Self-Management* (New York: St. Martin's Press, 1979).

late 1950s in the hope of thus spurring production, placed further strain on the economy.

Despite the overall problems in the economy, the Yugoslav regime reaffirmed its goal of narrowing regional economic disparities and for the first time incorporated into the constitution the guarantee that it was the duty of the DRs to help in the development of the LDRs. Moreover, in this period, development of the LDRs was finally to be ensured of a comprehensive treatment through a combination of measures, most importantly a Fund for Development which was to guarantee investment funds and grants-in-aid as well as an exchange of experts and expertise to help the LDRs in their developmental effort.

Nevertheless, despite both the Development Fund and other special measures designed to help the LDRs develop, and despite the decentralization which distributed power more equally enabling them presumably to enforce these special measures, by the end of the second decade of Yugoslav postwar development, economic disparities between the DRs and the LDRs, as measured in terms of GMP per capita, had once again increased. The explanation usually given by the Yugoslavs for the partial increase in economic inequality in the 1960s focused on two related phenomena both of which, according to the respondents, were surprise developments that mandated adjustments in regional development policy. Attempts to resolve these two negative phenomena, the increasingly public manifestations of ethnonationalism[4] and the appearance of economic cycles, had to take priority according to the Yugoslav explanation, though they usually added (contrary to existing evidence), that the goal of faster development of the LDRs was not short-changed in the process.

However, as we will see in this chapter, although the sharp downturn in the economy in the early 1960s and the accompanying rise of ethnonationalism were serious problems for the Yugoslav regime, they need not have displaced the goal of faster development of the LDRs for the entire decade. That they did so was largely due to the political decentralization and a turn to the market brought about by the 1965 Reform which both facilitated and justified the pursuit of regional economic interests. The Development Fund, created as a compensating institution, enabled Slovenia and Croatia to convince the LDRs to vote with them in favor of the Reform. The addition of the increased regional political power from the Reform would, the LDRs reasoned, enable them to enhance their economic interests.

Contrary to their expectations, however, neither the Development Fund nor the increased regional political power could compensate the

[4] For a definition of ethnonationalism please refer to discussion in the Preface.

LDRs for the absence of serious restructuring of the economies of both the DRs and the LDRs, the negative effects of the market and the continuing inadequate investment of resources.[5] The result was, economic disparities between the DRs and the LDRs which, once again, failed to narrow; those between Slovenia and Kosovo, moreover, further increased from 1:5 to 1:6.

The Yugoslav Economy and the Third Five-Year Plan: 1961-1965

Thus, by the early 1960s, investment and consumption had outdistanced production and fueled both domestic inflation and external balance-of-trade deficits, while pricing and fiscal policies had further discouraged the production of goods needed, especially in agriculture and raw materials, thus hampering any spontaneous recovery. These disproportions in the economy induced the government to adopt a more stringent fiscal policy in its Third Five-Year Plan. The goal was to instill a measure of discipline in the economic dealings between actors by insuring that the money supply did not rise faster than the social product. The policies which accompanied it had a dual character, reflecting both the brewing struggle between advocates and opponents of liberalization, as well as the general lack of certainty over the path to further development. This struggle and uncertainty indicated, in turn, the need for broader changes in the economic system.

The liberalizing character of the policies was clear enough. The role of self-management was to be enlarged in order both to bring it in line with the Yugoslav definition of socialism, as articulated in the new Program of the League of Communists in 1958, and to increase the efficiency of the labor force and improve the quality of the goods produced. A number of steps or economic reforms were taken to that end. First, decisions regarding the distribution of net income of enterprises, especially the decision to apportion this net income between reinvestment, reserve and personal income, were now to be made by the enterprises themselves. Second, the tax structure was rationalized to a flat rate as an incentive for enterprises to create profit (except for an "excess profits tax"), and an overhaul of the banking and credit system was designed to transform them into autonomous credit institutions rather than government disbursement agencies. To that end, the Yugoslav National Bank, the source of most short-term credit, was

[5] Despite the considerable flow of investment through the Fund, the LDRs continued to receive less or just about their "share" of investment per capita, a situation which could not promote their faster development.

turned into an autonomous credit institution in 1961, and investments were transferred to the three remaining federal banks: the Yugoslav Investment Bank, the Yugoslav Foreign Trade Bank and the Yugoslav Agricultural Bank. Finally, the dinar was devalued, multiple rates of exchange were replaced by a custom tariff, foreign trade was somewhat liberalized, and Yugoslavia became an associate member of the General Agreement on Tariffs and Trade (GATT).[6]

However, parallel to these liberalizing market-oriented policies, there were other, conservative ones. First, the share of industrial investment in overall economic investment increased slightly from 43.3% of GMP in 1957 to 47.2% in 1961, of which "basic" industries constituted 53%, a significant increase from the 31.4% of the Second Five-Year Plan.[7] This action was taken despite the fact that there were shortages of raw materials and stockpiling of machinery. This partial reversal to the earlier policies of emphasizing the so-called Sector I in industrial production showed that despite the 1948 break with the Soviet Union, the Soviet model of development remained attractive to many of the conservative politicians and bureaucrats. Moreover, this reversal was supported by a number of influential economists like Nikola Cobeljic, former head of the Federal Bureau for Social Planning, and Radmila Stojanovic, professor of economics at the Economics faculty of the University of Belgrade and frequent consultant to the Yugoslav government, for whom the appeal of central planning, especially for long-term decisions, prevailed. Furthermore, private agriculture remained without resources, and 70% of industrial commodity prices remained fixed by the state so that all potential benefit of the market as regulator of supply and demand was systematically undermined.[8] Thus, although the Third Five-Year Plan did generally increase the liberalization of the economy, it did so in an ambivalent and inconsistent manner.

Not surprisingly then, because the above policies failed to ensure the continuing economic boom, within the year, Yugoslavia experienced its first economic recession. When the recession deepened in 1962, the Third Five-Year Plan was abandoned. It was the shock of this first recession followed in quick succession by several others, resulting in the "discovery" of the existence of economic cycles in a socialist economy[9] (previously thought to be exclusive to capitalist economies), that was

[6] Horvat, 1976; Rusinow, 1977; and Milenkovitch, 1971.

[7] Sirc, 1979, p. 66.

[8] Milenkovitch, 1971 and Rusinow, 1977.

[9] First "discovered" by Branko Horvat, it was elaborated by him in his book *Business Cycles In Yugoslavia* (White Plains: International Arts and Sciences Press, 1971).

the impetus for the genuine public and broad-range debate which ensued[10].

Crisis and Debate

The economic debate began in December 1962 at a meeting of the Association of Yugoslav Economists in Belgrade, where it set two important precedents that henceforth were to define Yugoslav politics. First, the government had turned to a group of scholars for explanation of the malfunctioning of the economy and, just as important, had accepted their report. Second, the debate went far beyond the confines of research institutes to encompass the society as a whole. Thus, this debate marked the beginning of public acknowledgement and discussion of problems, the tolerance of sharper criticism, the tacit acceptance of conflicting views and, at times, the admission of differing interests.

These conflicting economic interests, which were difficult to reconcile because they were based on different levels and therefore different imperatives of development of the republics and regions, were often rationalized on the basis of ideology, that is, in relation to the "true" definition and implementation of self-management. Furthermore, the general correspondence of republics with ethnic-national boundaries meant that policies advocated on the basis of one's economic interests were so closely intertwined that it was often difficult to distinguish between them, or to discern the precise sequence of cause and effect.

For the developed regions, the search for a solution to the economic crisis led to the market system which, they argued, would increase the overall efficiency of the economy by linking wages to productivity. More specifically, an increased role of the market would mean both an increase in freedom of initiative as well as responsibility for an enterprise, over its investment as well as its production, and a general decrease of intervention in the economy. This, according to the DRs, implied an increase in power for workers and managers, at the expense of politicians and bureaucrats, over all aspects of "their" now to be truly "self-managed" factories. As the economically stronger, the DRs also stood to gain from competition in the market. Nevertheless, among the "liberals," those who stood for "decentralization" in the economy differed over where and how much decision-making power over investment, production and distribution should be allowed.

The economic decentralization favored by the DRs had political implications as well. These implications, specifically the devolution

10 For an excellent and comprehensive discussion of the liberalization debate of the 1960s, see Milenkovitch, 1971.

of power from the federal center to the republic or commune levels, as well as the broadening of self-management from the economic to the socio-political sphere to encompass nonproductive sectors like education, medical care and others, were generally agreed upon both within and among the DRs who favored the increased republic autonomy and lessening of interference from a distrusted Belgrade that decentralization would bring.

The "conservatives" or "centralizers," generally found in Serbia and the LDRs, were divided as well. On one side stood those who accepted the degree of self-management reached by Yugoslav society in the early 1960s. Some among them were willing to increase its scope; others were not and therefore were against the decentralization of investments. On the other side were those who believed that Yugoslavia's economic problems were due to the anarchic effect of market innovations and who called for an increase in central planning and greater control over enterprises. In both cases they claimed that an increase in the market would undermine socialism. As the economically weaker partner, they were keenly aware that it would also tend to undermine their economies.

Thus, the conflict between those who stood for an increase in self-management and those who opposed it was, above all, a conflict over perceived economic interests. It was potentially more explosive as the economic repercussions of decentralization and increased role of the market would be felt differently in the various republics and regions, according to their different levels of development. The historical polarization between the developed northwest (Slovenia, Croatia and Vojvodina), which stood to gain from the liberalization and a market-oriented economy, and the less developed southeast (Bosnia-Hercegovina, Macedonia, Kosovo and Montenegro), which stood to lose by it, with some in Serbia seeing their interests parallel to those of the less developed, threatened to make economic decentralization a political issue of exploitation of the "poor developing periphery" by a "greedy developed center."

Outside the economy there were problems as well. Fifteen years after the CPY had come to power, despite its impressive strides in modernization (including urbanization, industrial growth, education and so on), as well as its concerted attempt at creating and fostering a supranational Yugoslav consciousness and identity, in part through its policy of *Jugosloventstvo,* ethnonationalism was reappearing in new force. Certainly, the nationality question had arisen intermittently throughout the 1950s within the party circles and among government officials, occasionally warranting a rebuke by Tito. Nevertheless, it was still generally believed that the combination of socialist education and Marxist analysis, emphasizing the unifying elements in the history, culture and languages of the nations and nationalities, along with the "short-term" federal solution for assuaging national feelings, would attenuate and eventually extinguish these "retrograde" sentiments. Such, however, was not to be the case.

Thus, the background to the conflict of the 1960s was the sudden appearance of economic cycles after years of uninterrupted growth and the obvious failure of the policy of *Jugoslovenstvo* as seen by the rise in ethnic-nationalism. The territorial correspondence of republics and regions as homelands to the different nationalities meant, as always, that the existing cleavages, economic, political and national, could overnight turn explosive if they were to coincide. Although, in 1964-65 these cleavages were cross-cutting they, nevertheless, brought to the forefront the question of direction of the Yugoslav society.

Regional Development in the Third Five-Year Plan

The already muddled interplay between politics and economics in Yugoslavia of the early 1960s was further complicated by the disparities in regional economic development which, contrary to the Yugoslavs' early expectations, were not decreasing. Indeed, when measured in terms of GMP per capita, the differences in economic development between Kosovo and Slovenia had increased between 1950 and 1960 from 1:3 to 1:5.[11] Clearly, despite professed good intentions and promises of special concern for the development of the LDRs, the methods of the preceding period did not give the desired results.

The Third Five-Year Plan, inaugurated in 1962, proclaimed in a more forceful manner the goal of faster development of the LDRs. "Special concern in accord with the increased potential of the economy will be dedicated to the accelerated development of the LDRs; by accelerated development of these regions is understood a development which will be faster than in the previous period as well as faster in relation to the other regions in the country."[12] Two aspects of this statement deserve notice. The first is the admission that economic prerequisites for faster development of the LDRs had been created; the second is that the LDRs had to be enabled to develop faster than they had in the past, as well as faster than the developed republics and

11 SZZS i SZDP, *Razvoj Jugoslavije, 1947-1981* [Development of Yugoslavia, 1947-1981] (Belgrade: May 1982), p. 220.

12 *Drustveni plan privrednog razvoja Jugoslavije od 1961 do 1965 godine* [Social Plan for the Economic Development of Yugoslavia from 1961-1965] (Sluzbeni List FNRJ, no.53, 1961.), p. 975. (Author's translation.)

regions. Both the increase in regional economic disparities and the increase in nationalism mandated it.

Accordingly, the creation of a special fund for coordinating long-term plans for the development of the LDRs, which had been repeatedly brought up by the LDRs since the early 1950s, was supported in principle from spring 1961 when the prospective Third Five-Year Plan was first presented.[13] Its implementation, however, had to wait until the issue of manner and amount of aid, as well as the form that it would take, in turn closely tied to the brewing conflict over decentralization, was settled. This came about in two stages. The first was the promulgation of the new Constitution on April 7, 1963, which specified that it was the duty of the developed regions to help in the development of the less developed (Article 27). The second was a decree passed by the Federal Assembly in February 1965 which finally authorized the creation of a special fund for the development of the LDRs with permanent financial resources providing credits for economic investments and grants for upgrading their social services and infrastructure.

In terms of development of the LDRs, the years 1961-1965 brought no immediate change. Even though throughout this period a new system for financing investments, including those in the LDRs, was being formulated and slowly implemented, the financing of investments remained much like in the previous period, still largely occurring through the various government investment funds (Table 3.2). Thus, although the Fund for Accelerated Development of the LDRs and the Autonomous Province of Kosovo was created in 1963, it accounted for only 14.3% of total investments slated for the LDRs, and to even qualify for that, the LDRs had to invest a minimum of 30% from their own resources into projects financed by the Fund.[14]

Furthermore, with the exception of Montenegro and Vojvodina, per capita investments in the LDRs continued to be lower than those in the DRs,[15] and old problems of a structural nature persisted as well. That

[13] Ibid.

[14] Marija Ivanovic, *Finansiranje razvoja nerazvijenih podrucja Jugoslavije* [Financing the Development of the Undeveloped Regions of Yugoslavia] (Titograd: Institut za Drustveno-Ekonomska Istrazivanja, 1978), p. 89.

[15] Fond Federacije, *Razvoj privredno nedovoljno razvijenih podrucja u Jugoslaviji* [The Development of the Economically Insufficiently Developed Regions in Yugoslavia] (Belgrade: Institut ekonomskih nauka, 1986), p. 106. It is true that, as Yugoslav leaders were quick to point out, per capita investments in the LDRs lagged behind those of the DRs because of the high birth rate in the former. Nevertheless, given the regime's goal of faster development of the LDRs, one would expect that the LDRs would have received more, rather than less, investment per capita; an added incentive to give the LDRs more

Table 3.2
Source of Investments in Fixed Assets

Year	Total	Federation	Republics	Districts and Communes	Banks and Other	Firms
1960	100	37.1	7.0	17.5	7.4	31.0
1961	100	36.6	7.4	17.7	8.8	29.5
1962	100	30.5	9.0	20.2	10.6	29.7
1963	100	26.7	10.0	19.7	15.8	27.8
1964	100	6.8	8.3	21.4	37.6	25.9

Source: Vujicic, 1981, p. 53.

is, by the early 1960s, the demand for raw materials exceeded the supply, and the resultant pressure to import them to meet the needs of the processing industries further drained the foreign exchange. As the division between extractive primary goods and manufacturing of secondary goods bore some correspondence to the division between the developed and the less developed republics and regions, it followed that once again the less developed were left to shoulder a disproportionate amount of the burden of development. Finally, the definition of a less developed region was once again changed, this time to include the least developed areas of Serbia, Croatia and Bosnia-Hercegovina, as well as all of Macedonia and Montenegro.[16] The goal was to direct development to the least developed areas irrespective of republic or regional boundaries. It was also an attempt to increase the overall integration of the economy by treating regional development from the standpoint of the Yugoslav economy as a whole.

Yet, despite the awareness, present by the early 1960s, that development of the LDRs could and should be pursued more vigorously, major changes in development policy of the LDRs failed to occur.

money should have come from the knowledge that as development increases, the birth rate further decreases.

16 The LDRs were defined as all of the republics of Macedonia and Montenegro; the district of Kosovo-Metohija and the south and southwestern part of the republic of Serbia; the southern and western parts and a section of Posavina in the republic of Bosnia-Hercegovina; and parts of Dalmatia, Lika, Banija and Kordun in the republic of Croatia. Fond Federacije, *Razvoj privredno nedovoljno razvijenih podrucja u Jugoslaviji* [The Development of the Economically Insufficiently Developed Regions in Yugoslavia] (Belgrade: Institut ekonomskih nauka, 1986), p. 17.

Instead, domestic politics in the shape of the growing conflict over the direction of the Yugoslav economy and polity became the leaderships' focus of concern, displacing once again concern for regional development. More specifically, the debate-turned-conflict between the "liberals" and the "conservatives" within the top Yugoslav leadership centered on the optimal degree of decentralization for an efficient socialist economy and self-managed society. The resistance to liberalization crystallized around Aleksandar Rankovic, head of the secret police, Party Secretary in charge of cadres and heir-apparent to Tito. It was led by Serbia which, hoping to reestablish its position of leadership, appealed to the economic interests of the LDRs by arguing that, in any competition with the DRs, the LDRs stood to lose.

The DRs countered with a parallel appeal to the economic interests of the LDRs. By publishing a report showing that under the previous centralization, out of all the LDRs, only Montenegro received more than its per capita share of investment, Croatia and Slovenia were able to convince the LDRs that Serbia's support for centralization, supposedly out of concern for their welfare, was a mask for its own interest of political dominance. As a result, Bosnia-Hercegovina's and Macedonia's fear of Serbian hegemony was strong enough to make them cross over into tacit alliance with Croatia and Slovenia in support of decentralization, especially as the creation of the Development Fund, which would enable the LDRs to control their economic development, was part of the decentralization package. Furthermore, the split within the Serbian party between the centralizers led by Aleksandar Rankovic, head of the secret police, and Mijalko Todorovic, in charge of economic policy, weakened the former. The fact that the three formerly federal, now Serbian, banks were allowed to retain the assets that they had managed until 1964 when they were "defederalized" fueled the controversy over Serbian dominance and, in the process, further strengthened the position of the decentralizers.[17] Finally, Tito had been leaning on the side of the "liberals," so that, despite the ambivalent nature of the 1963 reforms, decentralization and liberalization had been continuing piecemeal through the early 1960s.

With the portrayal of the "centralizers" as Serbian-led and chauvinistically oriented, politicized ethnicity, that is ethnic-nationalism, specifically fear of Serbian domination, seemingly overrode immediate economic interests of the LDRs emanating from their fear of the market. Yet, even in this case, with their political sovereignty at stake, assurance of the preservation of their economic

[17] This was especially momentous in the case of the Yugoslav Foreign Trade Bank which had inherited the considerable assets of the GIF when the latter was abolished in 1963.

interests (by creating the Development Fund) was necessary before the LDRs would actually agree to switch their support in favor of decentralization and the market.

But switch they did. As a result, the impending division between a "progressive northwest" and a "conservative southeast" failed to materialize. By losing the bloc of support that they had counted on, the conservatives lost the initiative, a fact which contributed to their political decline in 1964-65 and enabled the subsequent passage of the Reform in 1965.

The Reform and the Fourth Five-Year Plan: 1966-1970

The main goal of the Reform was first, to increase economic efficiency by changing the economic system and second, to increase political stability through democratization and devolution of power to the republics and regions. The related problems of incompetent investment and disharmony between supply and demand had to be tackled first, because their palpable results, the rising inflation, unemployment and balance-of-trade deficits, were becoming intolerable. This was accomplished by removing the interventions which hampered the free operation of the market as allocator of investment and determinant of prices. In line with the above, enterprises were allowed to keep a far greater share of their net income to distribute as they chose, including for investment and personal income.[18] A price reform was also attempted to enable the market to start operating on the basis of supply and demand and to facilitate the restructuring of industries.

A major step taken to increase the rationality of investment was the abolition of investment funds and the reform of the banking system. With the abolition of the General Investment Fund (GIF) in 1963 and the handing over of the separate investment funds to the banks in 1964 (implemented in March 1965), the optimal use of investments was to be assured. This meant that decisions regarding the rate of capital formation, the distribution of investments and the size of the collective consumption expenditures were transferred from the previous essentially political sphere to the jurisdiction of the working organizations themselves via the banks.[19] The lowering of taxes on the enterprises and the abolition of social investment funds meant that enterprises were now left with more resources at their disposal. These,

[18] The net income that enterprises could keep after the Reform increased from 46% to 70%. Bicanic, 1973, p. 213.

[19] For an elaboration on the argument that decisions regarding investment were guided by political factors, see Rudolf Bicanic, "The Economics of Socialism in a Developed Country," *Foreign Affairs*, July, 1966, Milenkovitch 1971 and Waterston, 1962.

they were encouraged to deposit with the banks, thus increasing the availability of funds for investment capital. As a result, investment credits financed by the banks rose from 7.4% to 37.6% during the same period (Table 3.2).

However, the search for a price equilibrium, which began with a reduction in price subsidies, ended in a "temporary" price freeze (March 22, 1965), a general reduction of investments and a virtual credit freeze on consumer credits. Although prices were momentarily stabilized, inflation checked and the deficit lowered, unemployment increased and the annual rate of growth for the social product in 1965 fell to 1.4% from 12% in 1963 and 1964.[20] The price reform could not substitute for the necessary structural realignment of the economy, especially when inefficient enterprises, knowing that they would be "bailed out" of insolvency, continued to drain the economy. Yet the problems of increasing inflation, unemployment and the balance-of-trade deficit, clearly tied to problems of price disparities and low productivity of the economy, were in turn the manifestations of problems of a far deeper nature which had originated a decade earlier.

The first of these was the high investment in the 1950s,[21] based on the belief that all investment is "good," since everything is needed, which resulted in a lack of valorization of economic criteria. It was possible to hold this position while Yugoslavia was receiving large sums of money from the West, especially from the USA.[22] However, this money, which until 1956 was free, and for a number of years thereafter was virtually free, led to a disregard for the link between investment, employment and productivity. The reason for this disregard was the belief that investment, especially in industry (still seen as the only way to modernize), would automatically generate both employment and an increased demand for goods, thus acting as a boost to production and to the economy as a whole. As a result, investments were channelled to capital intensive, primary industries which had to be completed and sustained after the foreign largesse came to an end, despite locally high unemployment and scarcity of resources for completing the projects.

[20] Rusinow, 1977 p. 202.

[21] Throughout the 1950s the gross fixed investment represented between 28% and 33% of the Gross Social Product. SZZS, *Jugoslavija 1945-1964* [Yugoslavia, 1945-1964] (Belgrade: 1965).

[22] In all, between 1950 and mid-1959, Yugoslavia received $1,157.6 million of economic aid and $724 million of military aid from the United States, as well as the equivalent of $219 million in long-term credits and grants from other Western governments. Hoffman and Neal, 1962, Tables on p. 348 f.

Thus, pre-Reform investments had often been made without regard for local resources, economic or human, and were far above what the Yugoslav economy could finance on the basis of subsidies which had come to an end. Furthermore, they had been made with expectations of high returns in employment generation and productivity, both of which were precluded by, among other things, the type of industrialization taking place. By the mid-1960s, these misplaced investments were showing their undesirable effects on the economy as a whole, as well as on the regions where they were located, that is, disproportionately in the LDRs.

The second serious problem which needed to be dealt with was prices. Prices had been set by the government in accordance with its developmental priorities: namely, low agricultural prices to finance industrialization in the 1950s and low prices of raw materials to finance industrial production. Agricultural prices had been raised somewhat in 1957 and again in the mid-1960s as an incentive to increase production, since having to import foodstuff wasted scarce foreign exchange. However, the guaranteed minimum government purchase price, along with overinvestment in social sector agriculture in the absence of market incentives to increase the efficiency in production, meant that prices of agricultural produce were now distorted upward. At the same time, the continuing lag in the price of raw materials led to a fall in their extraction because it was correctly perceived by the individual republics and regions as economically unprofitable. As Slobodan Spasic of the Federal Fund for Development noted: "Secondary industry is protected while raw materials are not and prices are controlled...[so that] in a certain way the LDRs are punished."[23]

A third serious problem whose roots are traceable to the policies of the late 1950s is the conscious decision to promote consumption out of a belief that an increase in consumption would stimulate production and thus increase the vitality of the economy as a whole. By the late 1950s it was also politically attractive to encourage consumption in order to make the general populace feel the rewards for the years of sacrifice under socialism. It was, furthermore, economically possible to do so

[23] Slobodan Spasic, Interview, Federal Fund for Development of the LDRs, Belgrade, Serbia, August 20, 1983. Caslav Ocic has further shown that the pricing policies of primary and secondary products led to an undervaluation of the productivity of the LDRs and an overvaluation of that of the DRs; the policies remained in effect to a decreasing degree until the 1980s. Caslav Ocic, *Nacionalna ravnopravnost i regionalni razvoj* [National Equity and Regional Development] and *Razvijenost Jugoslavenskih republika i pokrajina of 1950 do 1984* [Development of Yugoslav Republics and Regions from 1950-1984] (Belgrade: Institut Ekonomskih Nauka, 1986).

because through the 1950s Yugoslavia had been receiving a large influx of money from the West.[24] The result, by the early 1960s, was that consumption outpaced production and spurred the beginning of a deficit. As Ljubomir Madzar pointed out, it had been much easier to encourage consumption than to discourage it when it later became necessary to do so.[25]

Thus, the government-sponsored drive for consumption led to a rise of expectations among the general populace for an ever better lifestyle on the basis of the existing work habits. These expectations were to grow from the mid- and late 1960s, as increasing numbers of Yugoslav *gastarbeitern* began sending part of their earnings home, thus fueling demand for new products and lifestyles.[26] Additionally, the opening of Yugoslavia to Western tourism, as well as the increase in the number of Yugoslavs travelling abroad, led to a demonstration effect which gave a boost to the consumer orientation, further increasing consumer demand.

Facilitated by the decentralization which had left decision-making regarding gross income in the hands of the workers, or at least in the hands of the governing boards of individual factories, and fueled by unrealistically high expectations, wages continued to increase at a rate which continued to outpace production. The individual psychological need to "keep up" the living standard and, after 1965, the possibility of doing so by controlling the apportionment of a factory's gross earnings meant that the increase in living standard derived from a reduction in capital investment. This, of course, created an additional inflationary tendency, further undermining future economic development.

The Development Fund: Strengths and Weaknesses for Regional Development

The Fourth Five-Year Plan (1966-1970), like the previous one, had as its goal the "accelerated development of the insufficiently developed regions and areas in order to lessen the differences in the degree of development."[27] That goal, which was defined in terms of

---

24 See footnote 18.

25 For more on this position as well as on the general debate regarding problems of the Yugoslav economy, see *Ekonomska Misao 3*, Belgrade, September, 1983.

26 By 1968, 350,000 Yugoslavs were working abroad, and by early 1971, according to government figures, 600,000. (According to Ivo Vinski it was closer to 700,000.) Their remittances accounted for more than 5% of the Yugoslav GMP. Sirc, 1979, pp. 201-203.

27 *Drustveni plan privrednog razvoja Jugoslavije od 1966 do 1970 godine* [Social Plan for the Economic Development of Yugoslavia from 1966 to 1970] (Sluzbeni List FNRJ, no. 28, 1966.) p. 975. The term "underdeveloped" was changed to "insufficiently developed"

GMP per capita and was set at 90% of the average Yugoslav level in 1965, was to be achieved by 1970.[28] It was further decided that priority should be given to finishing projects already started. Additionally, new kinds of industrial production were begun with the aim of creating a diversified economic structure approaching that of the DRs. Exploitation of natural resources and upgrading of transport and communications were also to be emphasized. In agriculture, both cooperation and labor-intensive crops were advocated to increase both efficiency and employment, as were handicrafts and cottage industries.

However, for the LDRs, the linchpin of the five-year plan and of the Reform lay in a new independent institution whose purpose was to create a "coherent politics of development so that in the LDRs they could count on the means necessary to provide a stable base for long-term development to get the effects of decreasing differences."[29] After years of developmental uncertainty because of changing criteria and amounts allocated for their development, a stable, long-term and guaranteed source of financial, human and technical resources for aiding the development of the LDRs was to be created. In that sense, 1965 was a watershed for regional development.

The Fund for the Accelerated Development of the Insufficiently Developed Republics and the Autonomous Province of Kosovo[30] was established by law in 1965 by an amendment of the 1963 constitution which specified that it was the obligation of the "social community in the interest of all" to help in the development of the less developed; these were defined as Bosnia-Hercegovina, Macedonia, Montenegro and Kosovo and accounted for 33% of the population and 40% of the area of Yugoslavia.[31] The source of finance for the Fund was a special tax on fixed assets of all firms in Yugoslavia (in the developed as well as less developed regions), which in the 1966-70 period stood at 1.85% of the GMP of the social product of enterprises in the social sector.[32] Low interest credits were extended by the Development Fund to the LDRs

(*nedovoljno razvijeni*), indicating a more inclusive attitude towards the LDRs, as well as a more specific goal for their development level.

28 This was a rather unrealistic expectation given that in 1965 the per capita GMP of the LDRs was only 54.5% of that of the DRs. Ivanovic, 1978, p. 59.

29 Marta Bazler-Madzar, Interview, Institute for Economic Studies, Belgrade, Serbia, June 3, 1983.

30 Henceforth referred to as the Fund or the Development Fund

31 *Ustav Socialisticke Federativne Republike Jugoslavije (SFRJ) 1963 godine "Osnovna Nacela"* [Constitution of SFRJ, 1963, "Basic Tenets"] (Belgrade: 1971).

32 Fond Federacije, *Razvoj privredno nedovoljno razvijenih podrucja u Jugoslaviji* [Development of the Economically Insufficiently Developed Regions in Yugoslavia] (Belgrade: Institut ekonomskih nauka, 1986), p. 20.

directly, thus removing the center from deciding on their use as had previously been the case.[33]

The allocation of resources between the LDRs was decided by the board of directors of the Development Fund (at that point made up of thirteen members, one from each of the republics, and seven appointed by the *Skupstina* or Federal Parliament) according to distribution criteria agreed upon by the members of the board in consultation with the Federal Planning Ministry. These were per capita income, volume and structure of savings in the area and efficiency of use of investments, that is proportion of production capacity employed in the area. The allocation of resources was also to follow the general developmental priorities of the country, the only requirement specifying 35% as the necessary minimum of local investment per project.[34] In the first five years, 8.973 billion dinars representing 1.85% of Yugoslavia's GMP was to be allocated to the Fund, with Bosnia-Hercegovina receiving 30.7%, Kosmet 30%, Macedonia 26.2% and Montenegro 13.1%.[35]

A separate category of supplementary resources to be similarly allocated to the LDRs was aimed at the narrowing of interregional differences in the quality of life (Table 3.3). These budgetary grants, which for the years 1965-70 constituted another .78% of the total GMP of Yugoslavia,[36] were to be provided to the LDRs to ensure the development of their social services, a necessary condition for faster development of these areas.

Whereas during the previous period special grants for the financing of social services in the LDRs were allocated through the central budget, as we have seen in Chapter 2, both the amount and distribution of these grants were biased against BiH, Macedonia, and Kosovo. In other words, with the exception of Montenegro, the LDRs had received fewer per capita grants-in-aid than the Yugoslav average, and much fewer than Slovenia and Croatia. Interestingly, interviewees throughout Yugoslavia repeatedly stated in response to questions concerning disbursement of grants-in- aid that "no one kept track of since it all came from one purse... and it went to whoever needed it the most."

33 For the period 1966-1970, these were given at an interest rate of only 2.1% and a repayment period of 19.5 years. Fond Federacije, *Razvoj privredno nedovoljno razvijenih podrucja u Jugoslaviji* [Development of the Economically Insufficiently Developed Regions in Yugoslavia] (Belgrade: Institut ekonomskih nauka, 1986), p. 20.

34 Ivanovic, 1978, p. 97.

35 Fond Federacije za kreditiranje brzeg razvoja privredno nedovoljno razvijenih republika i autonomnih pokrajina, *Priliv, plasman i utrosak stredstava fonda za period 1966-1970. Podaci iz zavrsnih racuna fonda za posmatrane godine* [Influx, Placement and Expenditure of the Fund for the Period 1966-1970. Data from the completed accounts of the fund for the years 1966-70] (Belgrade: 1971), p. 2.

36 Ivanovic, 1978, p. 128.

Table 3.3
Resources Allocated to the LDRs During 1966-1970

	Total for LDRs	BiH	Montenegro	Macedonia	Kosovo
Investment Resources from the Fund	100	30.7	13.1	26.2	30.0
Supplementary Resources (Budgetary grants)	100	41.0	11.0	21.0	27.0
*Population	100	52.3	7.4	23.0	17.3

Source: Ivanovic, 1978, p. 128. *Calculated by author.

This was the stock answer given by more than three-quarters of the respondents irrespective of the national, ethnic or functional background. It was curious response given that some of them were very critical of government policies. One hypothesis for this reluctance on the part of most respondens to critically address the question of allocation of grants in the 1950s was the realization that in the early 1980s, if specific knowledge of regional allocation of grants-in-aid had entered the public domain of discussion, the result would have been not only embarrassment for a socialist regime but also a threat to the political stability of the multi-ethnic-national Yugoslav federation. A number of individuals, who in their research had questioned the allocation of loans and grants, told me in confidence that they had been advised to move to other areas of research. Thus, well before the 1980s, it was clear to the Yugoslav leaders that regional economic disparities could precipitate a rise in divisiveness, as the various national groups argued that they were being discriminated against, offering as proof the economic "short-changing" of their republic or region.

In addition to providing cheap loans for the development of productive facilities and grants for upgrading their social sector, the Development Fund was to facilitate the exchange of human and technical assistance to the LDRs by becoming a liaison between the developed and the less developed, stimulating business cooperation between the two, as well as monitoring and analyzing the pace of development of the less developed regions. The failure of the Fund to fulfill this third function meant, in turn, that the money given for investments, both productive and infrastructural, was often not used in the most rational or productive way, with negative consequences for the narrowing of regional economic disparity.

Politics, Economics and the Fund

At this point, the question of why it is that the Fund's function of provider and coordinator of technical expertise never got off the ground must be raised. After all, this, presumably the least controversial aspect of the Fund, was to be divorced from special economic and political interests. The need for experts in the LDRs was clear; their educational and overall development lagged behind that of the developed regions, which is after all why they were less developed. Moreover, a cogent argument could be and was being made showing that it would have been in everyone's interest to have the LDRs develop faster. For them, it would have meant an increase in income and an improvement in the quality of life; for the DRs, the positive effects would have been felt in terms of expanded markets for their goods, assured sources of raw materials, as well as an end to the "drain" on their resources in order to help the LDRs develop.[37] Why then, when cooperation of experts would have been clearly beneficial to all, did it not occur?

Because of the Yugoslavs' general reluctance to address this issue, the answer has been pieced together from the interviews. The picture which emerges is the following. The LDRs were suspicious of the experts from the north and resentful of what they perceived to be their all-knowing attitude. To them, the northern experts' insistence on higher salaries as well as "hardship" bonuses was proof that their purpose in coming to the LDRs was to earn extra money rather than to help the LDRs develop. Furthermore, they felt that the northern experts sought to impose their views rather than work alongside local experts. Finally, respondents in the LDRs tended to express the views that the developed regions were much more concerned with establishing factories which would either produce goods that they needed or that would not compete with their goods, rather than in helping to establish whatever was best for the development of the

[37] A well known proponent of this argument is Kosta Mihailovic of the Economic Institute in Belgrade, considered an authority on regional development both within and outside of Yugoslavia.

local region. Illustrative of this attitude is the following typical statement: "If they wanted to help us, we would welcome them with open arms. But we don't need them to order us about, or to come here in order to make money off us."[38]

In the developed regions, on the other hand, the interviewees frequently expressed resentment over what was felt to be needless challenging of their expertise and advice by local political, bureaucratic and technocratic elite who despite, or because of, their backwardness felt that they "knew it all." It was to add insult to injury to expect, as was usually the case, that the northern experts would take a cut in pay in accordance with local salaries. This attitude can be illustrated in turn by the following representative quotation: "If they were interested in getting help we'd go; but why leave one's home, job, friends...to go where they don't want you?"[39]

These attitudes will not surprise us when we remember that although altruistic socialist motives were undoubtedly present for some, according to the respondents in the DRs as well as the LDRs, the majority of those in the developed regions who voted for the creation of the Development Fund did so for two reasons, both of which upheld their economic interests. First, the ensured support of the LDRs for liberalization and for a market-oriented economy, in return for their support of the creation of the Development Fund, was seen in the developed regions as a profitable exchange. Second, a fund which would define criteria and specify levels of development, as well as set the amount of aid to be given, also implied a limit and an end to that aid, as measurable and defined levels of development would be achieved over time. Since in the DRs the prevailing view of aid to the LDRs was of a bottomless pit into which their profits were being drained, the Fund, with its clearly defined limits, offered the hope of an end to what the DRs increasingly saw as a waste of their resources. Finally, some like Nikola Cobeljic and Kosta Mihailovic, two of the foremost Yugoslav experts on regional development, argued that, on economic grounds, faster development of the LDRs would benefit all the republics and regions by increasing the size of the market as well as the scale of production, leading to an economically rational, regional (geographical) division of labor based on maximum rates of return.[40]

[38] Quotations taken from interviews conducted in Yugoslavia during 1983-84 (anonymity was requested).

[39] Ibid.

[40] Kosta Mihailovic, Interview, Economics Institute, Belgrade, Serbia, February 14 and March 3, 1983.

In the LDRs, even for those who saw that the market would put them at a relative disadvantage and thus could potentially hurt their developmental effort, the guarantee of a fixed sum of money and the freedom to allocate it as they deemed necessary seems to have tipped the balance in favor of the compromise. Here, economic considerations were joined to the nationalist political ones. According to Branko Horvat, a bargain was struck; "The DRs got the money to be a loan rather than a grant, while the LDRs got sovereignty over the use of the money."[41] For most in the less developed regions then, the creation of the Fund for Development signaled the abandonment of a much resented tutelage. As Budislav Soskic noted, "Well, you know how it is: everyone wants to be master in his own house...that he himself should be able to decide."[42] Additionally, since under the previous centralized system Bosnia-Hercegovina and Macedonia received less per capita investment than was due to them, they had no economic interests to protect, whereas support of the developed regions, and therefore of the market, was seen as safer than support of Serbia and its presumed goal of political dominance.

Given that this mutual suspicion kept the DRs and the LDRs from cooperation, why didn't the Development Fund(ers) step in? The answer lies in the very limited powers of the Development Fund. First, it is important to note that the Development Fund did not have the right to monitor the use of money once it had been distributed. Thus, how the money was spent was left to the discretion of the individual LDRs. In the decentralized federation where the center's ability to direct investment had been undermined while the constituent republics firmly believed that they had, and ought to have had, sovereignty over all decisions affecting them,[43] coordinating attempts by individuals or by groups outside the republic or region were seen as political interference in one's sovereignty.

That view was generally and sometimes avidly disputed in the DRs: "development has nothing to do with sovereignty. When Yugoslavia gets a loan from the International Monetary Fund (IMF) or the World Bank for development, 'sovereignty' doesn't enter into it; it has to abide by certain conditions set by the donor, or it gets no loan. So it should be with the LDRs."[44] Nevertheless, in decentralized

41 Branko Horvat, Interview, Faculty of Economics, University of Zagreb, Croatia, October 6, 1983.

42 Budislav Soskic, Interview, Academy of Sciences, Titograd, Montenegro, June 12, 1983.

43 See statement by Budislav Soskic in the previous footnote.

44 Branko Horvat, Interview, Faculty of Economics, University of Zagreb, Croatia, October 3, 1983.

Yugoslavia where decision-making proceeded by consensus, divergent short- and medium-term economic interests, further enforced by a climate of suspicion, meant that cooperation, coordination and exchange of expertise, all of which rely on good will as well as good planning, were most difficult to achieve.

Furthermore, coordination and exchange of expertise would have disturbed the operation of local patronage networks which continued to flourish as new crops of "political factories" could testify. Thus, given the problems and dangers of attempting cooperation, the natural inertia against undertaking difficult tasks and the overall hesitancy of all concerned, it is more understandable that the Fund never fulfilled its tasks as a source of expertise and liaison between the DRs and the LDRs

Of course, it is plausible that in the first years following the Reform, the general lack of efficiency and slowness in setting up programs may have been as responsible for the lack of cooperation as the problems examined above. However, within a few years the above became more salient, as decentralization led to the closing off of republic boundaries, a symptom and in turn a cause for greater suspicion between republics and regions. For while on the one hand, the differing and divergent economic interests gave the republics and regions a reason to be wary of cooperation, a reason which at least from the point of view of their immediate economic interests as well as the interests of the local elite, was rational, on the other, the political and economic decentralization following the Reform enabled them to avoid cooperation if they so wished.

Problems Continuing After the Reform

The Reform had for many led to unrealistic expectations for a better life, that is, a higher living standard, greater openness in the society and an increase in self-management. In a study conducted by The Center for Public Opinion Research in Belgrade in 1966, when asked to identify "the most important problem before which Yugoslavia finds itself today," respondents in every republic and region cited most frequently "the carrying out of economic reform." Whereas the next most frequent problem cited was "the preservation of peace in the world," the next two were, like the first, economic in nature: "improvement in the standard of living" and "economic development."[45] Since a year earlier, the same Center had concluded a study which indicated that

[45] Steven Burg, *Conflict and Cohesion in Socialist Yugoslavia* (Princeton: Princeton University Press, 1983), pp. 46-7.

the main causes for the rise in the divisive national chauvinism were economic and developmental differences, it was clearly imperative that for reasons of national stability as well as economic rationality the Reform be successful.

Yet the Reform was faltering, and the repercussions, as was so often the case in Yugoslavia, were political. Dissatisfied with the Development Fund's allocation of resources for the Fourth Five-Year Plan, and having failed to change it, Bosnia-Hercegovina appealed to the Chamber of Nationalities for redress. While BiH's allocated amount of 30.7% was not increased, it did receive some special credits as compensatory measures.

Other open manifestations of popular dissatisfaction followed. In June 1968 university students, first in Belgrade and within days throughout Yugoslavia, staged a strike to protest against the conditions at the university; they soon broadened their grievances to include unemployment, the increase in economic inequality, the bureaucratization of the polity and the embourgeoisement of the political elite. A combination of persuasion and manipulation by the authorities split the student movement, summer recess intervened, and the Soviet threat posed to Yugoslavia as a result of the Czechoslovak invasion in August 1968, all acted to dissipate the student protests.[46]

Within six months of the student strike, widespread, sometimes violent demonstrations of Albanians broke out in Kosovo and in neighboring northwest Macedonia. The demands, "a product of perceived economic deprivation,"[47] took on a ethnonationalist expression. These ranged from the extreme, namely separation from Yugoslavia and unification with Albania, to more moderate and plausible demands such as the elevation of Kosovo's status from autonomous region to that of a socialist republic within the Yugoslav Federation. Although the latter was refused, both Kosovo and Vojvodina were granted separate constitutions, though both remained integral parts of the Serbian republic. The economic position of Kosovo relative to other republics and regions had been deteriorating throughout the postwar period, and the riots of 1968 were a sharp reminder that ethnonationalism remained an unsolved question in Yugoslavia, especially prone to surface whenever the region's economy faltered.

[46] For more on the student strike see Rusinow, "Anatomy of a Student Revolt," I, II in *American Universities Fieldstaff Report*, Southeast Europe Series, 5, 4 and 5, (Hanover: American Universities Fieldstaff, 1968).

[47] For a comprehensive treatment of the Albanian question see Ramet, 1984.

The Slovenian Road Crisis, which broke out soon after, was another reminder of the importance of regional economic interests and the politically volatile character of the latter.[48] The "road crisis," like the BiH and the Kosovo crises before it, further expanded the realm of legitimate political action by republics and regions. It also strained the liberal coalition, specifically relations between the two main partners, Slovenia and Croatia, who were involved in the conflict over the allocation of investments. In the process, it demonstrated once again that regional pursuit of scarce economic resources was, in the final analysis, the key element in coalition-building and the most important determinant of political action.

Regional Development in a Changing Society: 1961-1970

Despite their "liberal" approach to the "national question,"[49] as Marxists, the Yugoslav Communists believed that nationalism, a product of false consciousness of the bourgeois-capitalist stage of development, would, with modernization and the establishment of the communist society, be superseded almost automatically by a supranational "Yugoslav," and eventually inter-national, proletarian consciousness. In the words of Slobodan Milic, Director of the Institute of Agricultural Economics in Belgrade, "After the war, the idea especially in Serbia and Montenegro was that Yugoslavia could be one country...that republics would be just a temporary thing." [50]

By the early 1960s, however, the "National Question" had not been resolved. Neither the policy of *Jugoslovenstvo*, the attempt at cultural, historical and linguistic unitarism, nor the abandonment of this widely resented policy were able to attenuate ethnonationalism either among the party or among the general populace. In the prevailing atmosphere of open discussion over the direction of the economy and its implications on the polity, ethnonationalism was exacerbated when individual regions' economic interests were seen as being harmed by federal policies.

48 The Slovenian Road Crisis was precipitated by a decision of the Federal Executive Council to exclude Slovenia from a World Bank loan for construction of highways in Yugoslavia, despite Slovenia's need to upgrade its deteriorating highways, which as the Slovenians pointed out, were the main commercial link between Europe, the Balkans and the Middle East. For more on the Slovenian Road Crisis see Rusinow, 1977, and Burg, 1983.

49 "Liberal" in terms of forming a federation in which the six largest nations were granted republic status and, along with it, both recognition and, on paper at least, quasi-political sovereignty.

50 Slobodan Milic, Interview, Institute of Agricultural Economics, Belgrade, Serbia, September 8, 1983.

For the argument that ethnonationalism was responsible for the continuing regional economic inequality to be valid, the same ethnic-national group, or coalition of groups (at republic level), would have had to hold over a number of issues, when according to particular interests, one would have expected them to diverge. Diverge they did. The informal "coalition" of Slovenia, Montenegro and Serbia, which throughout the 1950s had been able to channel a disproportionately large percentage of investments for their own development, was not able to survive the divergence of interests brought to the fore by the issue of decentralization in the early 1960s. In fact, Slovenia and Serbia each took the lead in the opposing positions, with Montenegro siding with Serbia. That decentralization would most benefit Slovenia, economically the strongest republic, was clear; it was equally clear that Montenegro, as an LDR, stood to lose by it. In the case of Serbia, since decentralization was more likely to hurt its economic interests than to enhance them, and would certainly undermine its political dominance, continued centralization was in its overall interest.

By showing that despite the redistributive power of the centralized state of the 1950s, redistribution had not sufficiently benefitted the LDRs, the DRs were able to persuade the LDRs that the Serbian argument of faster development of the LDRs within the centralized system was not convincing. In addition, the DRs' argument that Serbian hegemonic tendencies were on the rise, as illustrated by their ability to keep the assets of the "defederalized banks," helped to convince both Bosnia-Hercegovina and Macedonia to cross over to the DRs on this issue and to vote for decentralization and the market. The price that the LDRs exacted was the creation of a Development Fund to guarantee a consistent predetermined amount of investment resources to aid in the narrowing of regional economic disparity. Thus, the shift in regional development policy in the mid-1960s was to some extent due to the convergence of ethnonationalism with regional economic interests, resulting in a realignment of actors who were then strong enough to pass the economic Reform.

Furthermore, although the continuing Serb-Montenegrin alliance may indicate some support for the ethnic-national argument, it is argued here that while ethnic-national/cultural affinity may have predisposed these two republics to act in unison, it was economic interest that created and maintained the alliance. This is corroborated by the divergence in the alliance among the LDRs in 1968 when BiH petitioned for a more equitable redistribution of investments among the LDRs; it can also be seen in the conflict among the DRs, notably between Slovenia and Croatia, over the distribution of World Bank funds in what became known as the Slovenian Road Crisis of 1968-69.

Conclusion

To summarize, the purpose of the Reform passed in 1965 was twofold: first to maximize economic rationality through reliance on the "invisible hand" of the market; second, to increase political stability by satisfying ethnic-national aspirations through a devolution of power from the federation to the republics and regions. By taking power away from the federal center and giving it to the republics and regions, it was also thought by the LDRs that the equality among the republics and regions which would ensue would enable the LDRs to ensure the passage of measures necessary for preserving or enhancing their economic interests. The result, however, was the opposite of what the LDRs had anticipated. That is, the effect of the market undermined the development of the LDRs since its "spontaneous operation" led to a gravitation of investments to the DRs.

In terms of regional development, the result of the Reform and the creation of the Development Fund as the compromise between the DRs and the LDRs meant that the Development Fund's potential as coordinator in the development of the LDRs, and thus its role as agent for "coherent" development, was undermined by the Fund's de facto role as disbursor of money. Although the Fund also acted to some extent as the arena for articulation of regional economic interests, its lack of power over allocation or use of money meant that this articulation led more often to bickering and jockeying for patronage than to solving disagreements by rational behavior.

As a result, rather than increasing political stability, the devolution of power to the republics and regions further destabilized the federation because regional economic interests and ethnonationalism became even more intertwined. Since, on the one hand, ethnic-national groups coincided with regional political boundaries and economic interests of regions differed according to their varying levels of socio-economic development, while on the other, the increase in power of republics and regions at the expense of the federation enabled the former to pursue these often irreconcilable interests, a situation which could easily become explosive was created. Moreover, given the correspondence of regional economic interests with ethnic-national groups, the pursuit of regional economic interests tended to manifest itself in the rise of ethnonationalism as exemplified by, among others, the 1968 riots of Kosovo and the Slovenian Road Crisis.

Although the connections between economic interests and ethnonationalism were so intertwined in Communist Yugoslavia that it was frequently difficult to separate them or to determine which was more important in explaining Yugoslav development, there is considerable evidence that economic interests were most often the cause, whose manifestation was ethnonationalism and effect was the displacement of the goal of faster development of the LDRs and consequent increase in regional disparity.

The argument that the rise of ethnonationalism was not solely, or even mainly, responsible for the increase in regional disparity is underscored by the fact that no coalition based on ethnonationalism held across issues when economic interests were at stake. Thus, as we have seen, the resolution of the question of centralization vs. decentralization of the economy and polity split the alliance of Serbia, Slovenia and Montenegro; the issue of apportionment of the GMP to the Development Fund split the DRs and the LDRs; and the issue of apportionment of the Development Fund among the LDRs split the LDRs among themselves.

Nor were the DRs overwhelmingly concerned with the faster development of the LDRs when development of the latter risked hurting the economic interests of the DRs. Thus, despite evidence that the market led to increased autarchy, "spontaneously" allocating a preponderant share of investment to the DRs, very little effort was undertaken to restructure the economy and thus rechannel investments to the LDRs. As a result, throughout the 1960s, with the exception of Montenegro, the LDRs continued to receive less or barely as much investment per capita as was due to them (Table 3.4). Furthermore, of the special credits from the International Bank for Renewal and Development, 33.2% was allocated to the LDRs, no more than was their fair share if considered on a per capita basis.[51] The distribution of

Table 3.4
Credits from the International Bank for Renewal and Development 1947-1970

Republic/Region	Credits
BiH	57.1
Montenegro	22.7
Macedonia	15.4
Kosovo	4.8

Source: SZDP, *Analiza* (Belgrade: November 3, 1988), p.14

51 SZDP, *Analiza* [Analysis] (Belgrade, November 3, 1988), p. 14.

these was once again highly skewed in favor of Montenegro (Table 3.5). Not surprisingly, this was not conducive to the narrowing of the economic inequalities between the developed and the less developed regions.

To conclude, although the sharp downturn in the economy and the rise of nationalism were serious domestic problems which thrust themselves into the Yugoslav limelight in the early 1960s, of themselves, they would not have impeded the faster development of the

Table 3.5
Per Capita Investment in Fixed Assets (in 1966 prices)

	BiH	Montenegro	Croatia	Macedonia	Slovenia	Serbia	Serbia Proper	Vojvodina	Kosovo
1952-1961	5.1	4.1	22.7	6.6	13.8	37.5	-	-	-
1962-1971	13.3	3.0	24.9	8.0	13.5	37.4	-	-	-
Population 1971	18.3	2.6	21.6	8.0	8.4	41.2	25.6	9.5	6.1

Source: SZZS, 1973, p. 228.

LDRs for the entire decade. That they were able to do so was the result of the ability of the most developed, Slovenia, Croatia and Vojvodina, to ensure through the reform the passing of measures which would benefit their more developed economies.

The relative increase in the political power which accrued to the LDRs as a result of the decentralization did not lead to a decrease in regional disparity, as this political power of the LDRs (with the exception of Montenegro) was not strong enough to compensate for the negative effects of either the market or the local "subjective" factors. The subsequent withdrawal of the DRs from active participation in the development of the LDRs, leaving the latter to fend for themselves in a situation in which they could not compete effectively, undermined the possibility of accelerated development of the LDRs, with the result that, on the whole, throughout this period as in the previous one, the disparity between the DRs and the LDRs continued to increase. In the case of Slovenia and Kosovo, by 1970 it had increased to 1:6.[52]

52 Fond Federacije, *Razvoj privredno nedovoljno razvijenih podrucja u Jugoslaviji* [Development of the Economically Insufficiently Developed Regions in Yugoslavia] (Belgrade: Institut ekonomskih nauka, 1986), p. 87.

4

1970s: Institutional Change and the Price of Reform

Introduction

There was both good and bad news as Yugoslavia entered the 1970s. The good was very visible. The economy had begun to pick up in late 1968 with the growth in social product averaging 8% per year for 1968-71, the industrial output more than doubling its recession growth to 43% and employment rising at approximately 4% per year.[1] The bad, while less visible at the time, was no less present as the unsolved imbalance in the economy from the previous period was once again increasing. Thus, the foreign trade deficit for 1971 was a record U.S. $1,437 million out of a total turnover of U.S. $5,000 million; the percentage of imports covered by exports fell to 55.8%, and the balance of payments deficit continued to grow reaching U.S. $434 million in 1971, despite tourism and remittances from workers abroad which offset much of the trade deficit. Domestically, the official cost of living index increased in 1970 by 11% and in 1976 by 16%; problems of liquidity forced workers in a number of firms to go without pay, sometimes for several months; and the number of migrant workers in Western Europe approached 700,000 by 1971, almost 20% of total domestic employment.[2] Effective intervention in the economy was badly needed just when it was hardest to achieve, for decentralization had proceeded to a point where the influence of republics and regions had become strong enough to block

[1] Rusinow, 1977, p. 251.

[2] Sirc, 1979, pp. 199-203. This was of particular embarrassment to a socialist regime which prided itself on providing all its members with the right to a job.

policies that went against individual regional interests while the federal government was increasingly unable to arbitrate between them.

In terms of the polity, federal level decision-making, which since the Reform could proceed only by consensus, was difficult to achieve when interests differed. That is, members of the central party organs were now directly responsible to the constituents and peers in their republics and regions, to whom they owed their positions and by whom they could be recalled. This added incentive to represent their region's interests made it virtually impossible to compromise, even on issues they otherwise might have been willing to compromise on. The result was a shift in primary allegiance for members of central party organs away from the center toward their home republic or region. As a result, there followed a period of virtual immobilization in political decision-making as indicated by the figures on the legislation passed.[3] Furthermore, the devolution of power from the federal center facilitated competition for resources and power among the local elites, so that within republics and regions development was also increasingly subject to the pursuit of individual interests.[4] Thus, at both the republic/regional level and within republics and regions, one could portray oneself as the defender of one's nation's (or sub-region's) interests against the exploitation of the "others." One could also point to the mass support at home, support which could be used in a subtle manner as leverage, especially in federal-level negotiations over competing demands. The general correspondence of ethnic-national groups with political boundaries and the linking of ethnonationalism to economic issues made it even more difficult to arrive at future compromises among the republics and regions. It also meant that the goal of faster development of the LDRs was displaced once again, this time more openly than in the past, by the pursuit of individual republic and regional interests.

[3] Dennison Rusinow has noted that 134 controversial issues were resolved in six months following the resolution of the Croatian crisis in December 1971, most between December 1971 and March 1972--approximately 130 more than had been resolved in the previous two years. Rusinow, 1977, p. 286.

[4] The purpose of this study did not mandate, and time constraint did not permit, a parallel study of development of the less developed districts within republics and regions. However, a dozen-and-a-half interviews conducted mostly in 1988, 1989 and 1990 in the republic development fund, bureau for social planning and economic institutes and universities, of Slovenia, Serbia and Croatia, suggest a very strong parallel between the less developed and developed republics and regions on the one hand, and less developed and developed districts within republics and regions on the other. Generally, problems, approaches and explanations for the perpetuation and, in places, increase in economic inequality are reminiscent of those encountered at the federal/republic level; so is the role of the personal nexus and the goal of fulfilling one's own economic interests narrowly defined as district, county or town.

Nevertheless, throughout the third decade of Communist rule "faster development of the economically underdeveloped republics"[5] continued to be one of the articulated goals of the five-year plans. Furthermore, in the course of the 1970s, the Yugoslav regime seemed to have understood that in addition to the ideological and humane motivations for equalizing development levels, there were more immediate pragmatic ones as well. Thus, the Sixth Five-Year Plan (1976-1980) specified that promoting faster development of the LDRs was necessary for "inter-nationality relations," as well as for the "common economic interest." In view of this realization, one might have expected the regime to seriously pursue development of the LDRs.

Yet, once again, by the end of the decade, the disparities between the DRs and the LDRs had failed to decrease, and those between Slovenia and Kosovo had further increased to 1:7. The Yugoslav officials in Belgrade and in the DRs explained this failure to narrow regional disparities in the 1970s by focusing on two problems which emerged in the 1970s. The first was the rise of ethnonationalism in the early 1970s, the second, problems of the overall Yugoslav economy which became manifest in the latter part of the decade. Those, according to the official Yugoslav view, mandated the regime's primary attention and energy although they insisted that they continued, simultaneously, to pursue the goal of regional equalization through faster development of the LDRs. As evidence they offered the continuing role of the Development Fund as well as a new mechanism instituted to increase the economic linkages between the DRs and the LDRs, the joint ventures.

However, as we will see in this chapter, pursuit of individual regions' economic interest remained the main impetus behind economic policy in this, as in the previous two decades. First, throughout the 1970s as in the earlier periods, the LDRs continued to receive less investment per capita than the DRs and even less than agreed on in the five-year plans. Montenegro was again the exception despite the continuing low efficiency of its investments. Additionally, the much touted joint ventures between the DRs and the LDRs were negligible (only 2.3% of the allowed 20% of the investments through the Fund, or less than 0.5% of all investment in the LDRs, were in the form of joint ventures[6]) and the lack of mechanisms to enforce or even encourage these

[5] Through this period the LDRs received both less investment than had been planned, 28.8% as comapred to 33.1%, as well as less investment per capita than the DRs (Table 4.2). For more on this, see Marija Ivanovic, *Finansiranje razvoja nerazvijenih podrucija Jugoslavije* [Financing the Development of Underdeveloped Areas of Yugoslavia] (Titograd: Institut za Drustveno-Ekonomska Istrazivanja, 1978), pp.105-6

[6] See footnote 43 for full reference.

shows the (lack of) importance granted to them. Furthermore, the attempt and failure of the republics and regions to agree on the criteria and measures of development highlights the fact that the major conflicts between republics and regions centered on economic interests and that in this conflict between the republics and regions, each primarily look out for itself.

The Croatian Crisis: 1970-1971

As the decade of the 1970s opened, rapid modernization and the changes that it entailed were creating in many ambivalence towards the present and uncertainty regarding the future. This ambivalence was understandable. For the idealists, the system was becoming too pragmatic and materialist; for the pragmatists, lack of coherent planning, continuing state meddling and ever-changing laws were equally frustrating. At the enterprise level, while self-management was generally lauded for bringing freedom through democracy in the work-place, it also required endless discussions and meetings which resulted in very little effective action thus generating more cynicism. At the federal level, the overall stalemate in policy promulgation increased general frustration. Thus, while the ambivalence, uncertainty and social tension that they generated were understandable, they were potentially also dangerous if mobilized and channeled against the regime.

In terms of living standard, although people were living better than at any previous time, the expectations engendered by the increase in consumerism in the 1960s, the promises of the Reform and the increasing contact with the West often surpassed what the current reality could offer. Furthermore, as mentioned above, a crisis of identity faced the uprooted individual as rapid social change due to rapid urbanization, opening up of the West and the overall process of modernization forced a redefinition of the self relative to the family, the work-place and society in general. The frustration was aggravated whenever the economic situation worsened, whether because of unemployment, liquidity of some firms or wages which had not kept up with expectations; it was felt even more acutely when political stalemate resulted in the lack of direction in the society. In this climate of uncertainty and anxiety, general fears, specific grievances and acute conflicts of interests, always easy to project unto other identifiable groups, could take on an ethnonational coloration. With the Croatian crisis they did just that.

Much as the 1948 break with the Cominform had resulted in a turning inward and questioning of Soviet-style socialism out of which emerged the "Yugoslav road to socialism" with its cornerstone of self-management, so the Croatian crisis of 1970-71 precipitated a soul-searching and questioning, this time, however, of the system of self-management itself as it had evolved up to the time of the crisis. Although the Yugoslav regime had in the late 1960s faced and weathered a number of domestic crises that had had ethnonationalist manifestations,[7] the Croatian crisis of 1970-71 was different from these others in two ways. First, it represented the most serious threat since 1948 to the viability of the Yugoslav nation-state; second, the resolution of the crisis entailed major changes in the Yugoslav socio-political system, with important repercussions on various aspects of the polity and the economy, including on regional development.

The Croatian crisis, which developed over a period of almost two years culminating in the December 1971 purge of the "left" faction of the Croatian leadership, sprang from economic grievances over what the Croatians saw as their continuing exploitation by Belgrade. Despite the reform of the banking system and the general Economic Reform of 1965, resources continued to be centralized, with the Belgrade banks still controlling more than half of all the credits and more than three-quarters of foreign credits. Furthermore, despite the fact that Croatia brought in about half of all foreign capital, as of 1969, according to a Croatian economist, it was allocated only about 15% of the total credits,[8] an amount insufficient for its level of development, as well as unjust in terms of its contribution.

Although there were other more specific grievances as well,[9] for many in Croatia, by late 1970 or early 1971, the issue of foreign exchange was paramount. In part, this was because it was seen as part of a larger pattern of economic exploitation which centered on the unfair distribution of money and advantages among the republics and regions, especially pertinent to Croatia, which produced most in foreign currency earnings and enterprise profits and received much less than its share through the redistribution process. The articulated grievances which arose from this situation were threefold: first, Croatia was losing out economically by its membership in the federation; second, it

[7] Demands for increased allocation of resources by BiH in 1966-67, Croatia in 1967, and Kosovo and Slovenia in 1968 were resolved in what appeared to be a satisfactory manner. For more on these, please see Chapter 3.

[8] Ramet, 1984, p. 104.

[9] Serb penetration of the Dalmatian coastline, mainly through manipulation of investments into the hotel industry obtaining highly advantageous agreements through bribery or political pressure, their exploitation of Croatia through the sale of ships built for the Croatian merchant fleet, their ability to set up two airlines before Croatia was granted permission for even one--all were additional indications to the Croats that they were once again being exploited by Belgrade.

meant that the political decentralization which had occurred with the Reform granting power to republics and regions to articulate and pursue their interests was largely inconsequential since, with the financial decision-making in Belgrade, the republics and regions were unable to exercise that power; third, this situation was especially galling to Croatia as it meant that Belgrade, the federal capital as well as the capital of Serbia, had become not only the political center of the country but had, as a result of this political power, replaced Zagreb as the financial center as well. The result was that while Croatia produced 27% of the Yugoslav Social Product, 30% of its industrial production and 36% of its foreign currency earnings,[10] Serbian banks controlled 63% of total bank assets of Yugoslavia. Furthermore, four of the ten largest foreign trade enterprises which accounted for 70% of total Yugoslav foreign trade were also located in Belgrade, while only one was to be found in Zagreb.[11] To the Croatians, Serbia was clearly prospering at their expense.

Although the grievances which arose from this situation were economic, the demands which resulted were both political and economic in nature. They were vocalized by Croatia which, supported by Slovenia and Macedonia and tacitly supported by other republics and regions (developed and less developed), argued for a greater devolution of power over investment policies to the self-managed economic enterprises that generated capital. More specifically, Croatia wanted a reform of the banking and foreign currency system, curbs on wealthy Belgrade export-import firms and redistribution of former federal assets which had been appropriated by Serbia when, following the 1965 Reform, the Yugoslav banks had been defederalized.[12]

The correspondence of ethnic-national groups with republic boundaries, especially as in this case the issue was between Zagreb and Belgrade with its inter-war legacy of suspicion and animosity, facilitated an interpretation of ethnic-nationalist exploitation which gave it a more volatile political character. This was reinforced as the Croatian leadership, seeking to increase its positive power[13] in relation to Belgrade, first allowed and then encouraged the economic issues to take on both a public and increasingly a ethnonationalist expression. The escalating ethnonationalist demands voiced in the

[10] Rusinow, 1978, p. 323.

[11] Ibid.

[12] Burg, 1983, p. 104.

[13] Positive power to act, as compared to negative power stemming from its ability to merely veto decisions of the federal government; for more on this see Gregor Tomc, "Social Stratification and National Formation in Post-War Yugoslavia" (Paper presented at the Wilson Center, Smithsonian Institution, Washington, DC, September 4-6, 1986).

press, and the split within the Croatian leadership which evolved in the course of 1971, further radicalized the situation and polarized the positions within both the Party and society. The liberal faction's subsequent attempt to solidify their position by using ethnonationalist appeals to mobilize broad popular support as an implicit threat to Belgrade should it fail to meet their demands, in turn, backfired.

As the Croatian leadership's demands escalated, Croatia found itself increasingly isolated and without support within the federation; meanwhile, the escalation of ethnonationalist demands within the republic and the disagreement over its handling split the Croatian leadership. Finally, as the ethnonationalists gained increasing popularity through influential journals like the *Matica Hrvatska* and the student movement, the liberals within the Croatian leadership, despite a number of warnings by and meetings with Tito, found that they could no longer control the situation. The student strike in late November 1971 was the proverbial last straw. Troops were called in and amid arrests of leaders of both the ethnonationalist and the student movement, and resignation and purges of party elite, order was restored. With the subsequent forced resignation of the liberals in Serbia, as well as to a lesser extent of the leaderships in Vojvodina, Kosovo, Macedonia and Montenegro, central authority of the party was restored as well.[14]

The Croatian crisis convinced Tito that party discipline and authority had been eroded to the point where there was no longer a unified League of Communists. "Democratization" had gone too far; it was time to reassert elements of "centralism." However, although leaders of republics and regions were willing to support the purge of the Croatian leadership, because of the nationalist and chauvinist character of that variation of "democracy," they were much less willing to give up the power they had accrued as a result of the 1965 Reform and of the 1967, 1969 and 1971 Constitutional Amendments. The republics were now "sovereign", and judging by the difficulty Tito had in recentralizing the Party, they wished to remain that way. According to

[14] On December 12-13 the leadership of the "liberal" faction, Dabcevic-Kucar, Pirker, Kopita and Tripalo, was forced to resign; their resignation was followed by mass nationalist demonstrations in Zagreb which resulted in the arrest of some 550 demonstrators, mostly students. In the months that followed there was a massive purge of the Croatian Party mostly at the elite level, ranging from forced resignations of high ranking party and government officials, to disciplinary actions, removal from positions and expulsions. Justifiable economic grievances had been transformed into the most volatile political issue possible in Yugoslavia, that of ethnic-national domination. In the process, the regime had suffered the most serious internal postwar challenge to its legitimacy and its rule. For a comprehensive treatment of the Croatian crisis see Burg, 1983, Chapter 3, and Ramet, 1984, Chapter 7.

a number of respondents including Branko Horvat, a compromise was made between Tito and the regional leaders: "They let Broz have a lifetime term in the Presidency in exchange for leaving the republics alone to decide on everything...which they still do. They went so far in this process as to destroy scholarly circles; for example, the Yugoslav Statistical Society was disbanded and everything was regionalized. Politically, regional oligarchies were created."[15]

The most vocal and serious opposition to Tito's attempt at reasserting central authority in the party came from Serbia. Not only did the Serbian leadership continue to ignore Tito's emphasis on re-centralization, but it refused his call to action regarding the concentration of banks and foreign trade companies in Belgrade. When to Tito's public reprimand and thinly veiled parallel to the Croatian excesses no response was forthcoming, the Executive Bureau of the LCY drafted in mid-September 1972 a sharply critical letter. Subsequently known as "The Letter," it called for increased central authority in the party, the reaffirmation of democratic-centralism in the relationship of the center to the republics and regions and for "moral-political suitability" (*moralno-politicka podobnost*), as a necessary qualification for occupancy of social and state positions, especially in the economy, education, information, administration, judiciary and security.[16]

By spring 1973 the ensuing purge of the Serbian party restored party unity and reaffirmed the importance of "democratic-centralism" with the usual emphasis on centralism. In the course of the following year, similar though less extreme purges were undertaken in other republics and regions. Finally, with the closing of the Croatian intellectual journal *Praxis*, and the suspension of eight liberal professors of the Faculty of Philosophy in Belgrade in early 1975, a decade of unprecedented experimentation with the "democratic" aspect of "democratic-centralism" had come to a close. The tail would no longer wag the dog. The LCY's leading role was firmly reestablished.

The Croatian crisis which led to the Yugoslav crisis was until the 1980s the most extreme example of economic grievances taking on ethnic-nationalist manifestation with serious repercussions on the political stability of the regime. It is important to note, however, that although it is often difficult to separate economics from politics in Yugoslavia, ethnic-nationalist disturbances which caused the reassertion of party control in 1972 were caused by *perceived economic* exploitation which, because of the multinational nature of the

[15] Branko Horvat, Interview, Economic Institute, Zagreb, Croatia, September 26, 1983.
[16] Sirc, 1979, p. 226.

Yugoslav federation and the general correspondence of ethnic-national boundaries with political ones, transcended the purely economic demands, taking on the more volatile ethnonationalist aspirations.

Fifth Five-Year Plan: 1971-1975

The reestablishment of the LCY in the leading role did not, however, mean a complete turning back to the pre-Reform days. Despite the recentralization of authority within the party which occurred between 1972 and 1974, the decentralization of the federation which had occurred through the Constitutional Amendments of 1967, 1969 and 1971, proceeded on course. This was true even as "democratic-centralism," "dictatorship of the proletariat," "party unity," "purges of rotten liberals and technocrats" and other clearly centralizing slogans and measures in the social and political realms, were reaffirmed.

Thus, self-management, the ideological justification of the regime, interpreted as decision-making at the most basic social, political and economic levels (republic, commune and, from the mid-1970s, OOUR or BOAL, and SIZ or "interest communities"),[17] ensured that the devolution of power which had occurred remained untouched. As a result, the June 1971 Amendments to the Constitution specified that the federal government retained power only over the six areas specifically allocated to it;[18] all residual power was vested with the republics and regions, virtually ensuring their sovereignty.

Furthermore, not only did the federation continue to have jurisdiction only over those matters specifically allocated to it, but in many important instances like social plans, monetary policy, foreign exchange, trade and aid to the LDRs, agreement by republics and regions was needed before the federation could act.[19] Additionally, the creation of the Collective Presidency in 1969 and its eventual

[17] OOUR (*Osnovne Organizacije Udruzenog Rada*) or BOALs, (Basic Organizations of Associated Labor) legally and financially independent units forming part of the enterprise were constituted in the mid-1970s; SIZ, (*Savezne Interesne Zajednice*) for social services in which "consumers" of social services (delegates from enterprises) bargained with the "producers" (the social-service agencies) over all aspects of social services like price and quality--thus breaking the latter's monopoly. The result was to be a system of checks and balances between economic units, government bodies and mass organizations, enabling "true" self-management. For more on the above see Ellen T. Comisso, "Yugoslavia in the 1970s: Self-Management and Bargaining," and Steven Sacks, "Divisionalization in Large Yugoslav Enterprises," *Journal of Comparative Economics*, 4: 192-208, 209-225.

[18] These federal powers were defined as defense, foreign affairs, ethnic equality and individual liberty, a single Yugoslav market, common monetary and trade policies and upholding the "principles of the political system."

[19] Sirc, 1979, p. 226.

composition of nine members, one from each republic and region and a representative from the party, the creation of two federal chambers and increased grass roots participation through the system of delegates, as well as the de facto obligatory parity through the "ethnic key" (*kljuc*),[20] all show the degree of decentralization which had occurred by the early 1970s. The upgrading of the two chambers in the assembly, the Federal Chamber and the Chamber of the Republics and Provinces, to equal status while ensuring that their membership be based on regional parity and the delegate system with the delegates responsible to their regional assemblies also shows the increased power of the republics. This was especially true as control over regional cadres appointments, either within republics and regions or at the federal level, remained under the jurisdiction of republics and regions. Finally, the principle of consensual decision-making based on inter-regional consultation and harmonization of interests was reaffirmed, as was the role of President Tito as the ultimate arbiter in political conflict.

A parallel decentralization took place in the economy. The milestone in this process was the Constitutional Amendment XXI passed in June 1971 which created self-managed, semi-autonomous economic units, *Osnovne Organizacije Udruzenog Rada* (OOURs) or, Basic Organizations of Associated Labor (BOALs).[21] The purpose of the BOALs was to bring self-management closer to the worker by disaggregating the firm into units of workers who produce a marketable item, so as to tie more closely the result of their labor to the amount and quality of labor. It was a way of compensating for the huge growth of enterprises since their creation in the 1950s, (the average size of a BOAL in the 1980s was the size of the enterprise of which it was a part when the latter was first formed), as well as dealing with the resultant worker alienation from an increasingly impersonal environment.

Relations between BOALs were to be governed by *samoupravni sporazumi*, or self-managed agreements (SMAs). These SMAs were binding agreements whose main purpose was to coordinate development strategies between actors at the micro-level. They were supplemented

20 This was an attempt at appeasing fears of national exploitation or repression by ensuring an equitable representation of interests of all republics and regions, and thus all major ethnic-national groups, in most important federal organs and institutions including the Federal Executive Council (FEC), the Council of Nationalities, the Constitutional Court and among the personnel of ministries.

21 For more on BOALs see Laura D'Andrea Tyson, *The Yugoslav Economic System and Its Performance in the 1970s* (Berkeley: Institute of International Studies, University of California, 1980), Chapter 2.

by *drustveni dogovori*, or social compacts (SCs), non-binding agreements which regulated matters of "general social concern," like planning and investment policies, prices and employment. The purpose of SCs was to coordinate economic affairs at the macro level, thus displacing governmental agencies in economic planning. Thus, from the mid-1970s, bargaining and voluntary consensual decision-making based on shared interests were to replace the imposition of central authority in both polity and economy,[22] to become the operating principles of the Yugoslav federation.

A consequence of this decision-making by consensus was a high degree of "negative power" of all republics and regions because of their de facto right to veto legislation that they deemed harmful to their particular interests. This "negative power," which was to guard against the domination of any single republic, region or coalition within the federation, an important concession in multinational Yugoslavia with a history of national exploitation and oppression and one of the legitimizing factors of the regime, also paradoxically raised two dilemmas for the regime. The first, the question of fairness in representation arose from the equal vote of republics irrespective of their size: it was most often brought up in relation to Montenegro and Serbia (proper) where population ratios were 1:10. The second, as has been pointed out repeatedly in the Western literature (Burg, Comisso, Milenkovitch, Ramet, Rusinow, Tyson and others), as well as by various "Yugoslavs" (Bajt, Horvat, Korosic, Mihailovic, Tomc and others), was the problem of decision-making by consensus, when for objective reasons (different levels of development and therefore different interests) consensus was so difficult to arrive at. In this case, the results ranged from decisions arrived at by compromise, which so diluted the original proposal that its purpose or potential effectiveness was lost, to decisions arrived at with so much delay that their efficacy was largely surpassed by a changing situation, to a complete stalemate in decision-making. All three occurred in Yugoslavia with increasing frequency from the late 1970s as the economy began its downward spiral into stagnation and regional oligarchs competed for the distribution of the increasingly scarce resources. The negative consequences for

22 Together Amendment XXI of 1971, the new Constitution of 1974 and the Law of Associated Labour of 1976 decentralized economic decision-making, creating a complex set of checks and balances. This decentralization was carried out at two levels, from the federal to the republic and provincial governments, and within enterprises from central management to the semi-autonomous BOALs. As a result, since the mid-1970s, economic planning in Yugoslavia has (at least in theory) proceeded from the bottom up, through a process of harmonization and coordination of interested parties from BOALs to enterprises within a sector, as well as within the republican Economic Chambers, and among various levels of government.

planning and development were especially obvious in the more vulnerable LDRs.

Regional Development in the Fifth Five-Year Plan: 1971-1975

The Fifth Five-Year Plan 1971-75, like all medium term plans before it, listed as one of its priorities the faster development of the LDRs specifying that "the growth rate of the GMP of the insufficiently developed republics and the region of Kosovo together should surpass by about 25% the growth rate of the GMP of the country as a whole, along with the faster development of each insufficiently developed republic, and especially of the region of Kosovo."[23] As in the previous plan, the Federal Fund for Development, in operation since 1965, was to be the main measure of intervention. However, unlike in the previous period, only the LDRs were to receive Federal Fund assistance; the less developed areas of developed regions, which from 1966 to 1970 were included as recipients of the Federal Fund, were now to be solely at the charge of their respective developed republics and regions.

In addition, at Kosovo's request, all credits granted up to 1970 were cancelled so that in effect all money transfers which had occurred in the previous two decades (to both the developed and less developed republics and regions) became grants. Third, the Fund's board of directors was increased from thirteen to fifteen with both Kosovo and Vojvodina acquiring their own representatives. Fourth, from 1971 all organizations of associated labor in the socialized sector had to subscribe to an obligatory loan to the Federal Fund. This amount to the Fund was increased from 1.85% of the GMP of the socialized sector in the 1965-70 period to 1.94% in the 1971-75 period. While all LDRs received favorable terms, loans at an interest rate of 4% with a repayment period of fifteen years, because of its low level of development, Kosovo was given preferential treatment with an interest rate of 3% and a repayment period of nineteen years; additionally all areas had a grace period of three years.[24] The allocation of supplementary resources for the faster development of social services in the LDRs accounted for another .83% of Yugoslavia's GMP in this period.[25] Together, these two transfers formed about 10% of the GMP of

23 *Drustveni plan razvoja Jugoslavije za period od 1971 do 1975 godine* [Social Plan of Development of Yugoslavia for the Period 1971-1975] (*Sluzbeni List* FNRJ, no. 35, 1971), p. 692. (Author's translation.)

24 *Sluzbeni list* SFRJ, no. 33, pp. 642-645.

25 *Sluzbeni list* SFRJ, no. 35, pp. 711-712.

the LDRs, though in the case of Kosovo, they represented more than 60% of that region's GMP. And though 60% of the transfers were credits which would later have to be repaid, the low interest rate at a time of rising inflation and the favorable repayment schedules meant, in effect, that the grant element was very high. Finally, the allocation of loans given by the International Bank for Renewal and Development increased to 45.2%, for the first time to a little above their per capita share, and the distribution among the LDRs was improved (Table 4.6).

Table 4.1
Economic Growth Rates in Yugoslavia in Percent, 1966-1975

	1966-70		1971-75	
	A	B	A	B
Yugoslavia	18.1	14.6	25.5	15.9
LDRs	14.9	14.1	26.9	27.3
DRs	19.4	14.7	25.0	25.5

A = Annual growth rate of investment in fixed assets.
B = Annual growth rate of gross material product.

Source: Vujicic, "Investment, 1966-1975," *Yugoslav Survey* 18 (2) (May 1977): 61-62 as reported in Ramet, 1984, p. 179.

Despite a positive impact of the above on the economic growth of the LDRs, that is, the growth of the LDRs was not only substantially higher than it had been during the 1966-70 period but was slightly higher than that of the DRs for the period 1971-75, (Table 4.1), their share of investment per capita relative to that of the DRs continued to lag. In 1972, for example, the LDRs, with a population of 36% of Yugoslavia's total, received only 30% of investments in fixed assets[26] and for the entire 1971-75 period the LDRs received 82.1% of the Yugoslav average, compared to the DRs 109.7% (Table 4.2).

Furthermore, the distribution of investments among the LDRs, especially of those originating with the Development Fund, did not

[26] SZZS, *Materialni i drustveni razvoj SFRJ 1947-72* [Economic and Social Development of SFRY 1947-72] (Belgrade 1973), pp. 227-229.

Table 4.2
Per capita Investment of Republics and Regions Relative to Yugoslav Average for 1971-1975 (in 1972 prices)

	SFRJ	BiH	Montenegro	Croatia	Macedonia	Slovenia	Serbia Proper	Vojvodina	Kosovo	LDRs	DRs
1971-1975	100	89.8	114.1	112.5	77.2	190.1	86.3	95.1	46.9	82.1	109.7

Source: Fond Federacije, *Razvoj privredno nedovoljno razvijenih podrucja u Jugoslaviji,* Belgrade: "Srbostampa," 1986 p. 108.

Table 4.3
Disbursement of Credits from the Development Fund, 1966-1980

	1966-1970[1]	1971-1975[2]	1976-1980[3]	Total Population[4]
Disbursement Total	100.0	100.0	100.0	100.0
BiH	30.7	32.4	30.6	52.3
Montenegro	13.1	11.4	10.8	7.4
Macedonia	26.2	22.9	21.6	23.0
Kosovo	30.0	33.3	37.0	17.3

Source: 1. and 2. SZZS, 1982, p. 206: 3. Fond Federacije, 1981, p. 24:
4. Calculated by author.

Table 4.4
Disbursement of Funds and Effects on
Growth in the LDRs in Percent: 1971-1975

	BiH	Macedonia	Montenegro	Kosovo
Credits from the Development Fund	32.4	22.9	11.4	33.3
Supplementary Resources	40.15	18.3	10.3	31.25
Growth Rate Above the Country Average	3.7	14.9	-11.2	14.2

Source: Mladenovic, 1976, p. 224.

enable the best possible development of each. Thus, although Kosovo, by far the least developed, finally began receiving in the post-Reform period credits from the Development Fund well above its per capita share which, moreover, increased in each five-year plan period resulting in a growth rate of 14.2% above the national average for 1971-75, investments in Bosnia-Hercegovina once again remained well below its per capita share (Table 4.3). As a result, BiH suffered a loss of development as shown by its growth rate which was only 3.7% above the national average. Additionally, Macedonia's share of investment decreased throughout the 1965-80 period even though next to Kosovo it was the least developed and its utilization of investments was the most efficient as can be seen by its growth rate of 14.9% above the national average for the 1971-75 period. Finally, Montenegro continued to receive well above its per capita investment share despite evidence of underutilization of capital as shown by its growth rate, which for the 1971-75 period measured 11.2% *below* the national average[27] (Table 4.4).

Thus, despite the devolution of power to the republics and regions and the new equalization of power that it entailed, some regions clearly did much better than others. It may be understandable that Kosovo as the most underdeveloped region received more than its share of investment per capita. It is more difficult to explain why Montenegro, which by the early 1970s already had one of the highest per capita investments and fixed assets in the country, continued to

27 Mihailo Mladenovic, "*Neki rezultati razvoja privredno nedovoljno razvijenih republika i pokrajine Kosovo 1971-74*" ["Some Results of the Development of the Economically Insufficiently Developed Republics and the Region of Kosovo, 1971-74"] *Jugoslovenski pregled godina* XIX, 1975-6, p. 224.

receive the highest per capita disbursement of the Development Fund loans (Table 4.3), the budgetary grants (Table 4.5) and of World Bank credits (Table 4.6),[28] especially since the efficacy of its investments remained by far the lowest in the country (Table 4.4).

Table 4.5
Disbursement of Supplementary Resources to LDRs, 1966-1980

	1966-1970	1971-1975	1976-1980	Population
BiH	40.6	40.3	35.8	52.3
Montenegro	11.4	10.4	12.4	7.4
Macedonia	20.5	18.5	16.3	23.0
Kosovo	27.5	30.8	35.4	17.3

Source: SZZS, 1982, p. 208.

The most plausible explanation for Montenegro's continuing success in garnering development resources, despite both the opposition from the other LDRs as well as the economic irrationality that it entailed in view of the low efficiency of these investments, is that its party membership, the highest per capita in the country, facilitated both the continuation of old networks of influence (*veze*) predating the Reform, as well as the forging of new ones, enabling it to remain an effective actor in behind-the-scenes bargaining despite the institutionalization of parity in political and administrative positions[29] (Table 4.7).

28 Only in the last few years has Kosovo surpassed Montenegro in per capita disbursement; in view of Kosovo's extreme backwardness, the point made about Montenegro still stands. Furthermore, although the old "Yugoslav" argument which stated that--given the small size and extreme backwardness of Montenegro, a great deal of capital was needed to bring it to a level of self-sufficiency--clearly had some validity, it failed to account for the large discrepancy in the investment between Kosovo (which is small and even more underdeveloped) and Montenegro, which lasted until the 1980s.

29 This was well understood in Yugoslavia as the following saying, repeated in a number of interviews, shows: "Montenegrins are found in only two places in Yugoslavia: Montenegro and Dedinje." Dedinje is the wealthy area of Belgrade where foreign and domestic dignitaries (including Tito) resided.

Table 4.6
Credits from the World Bank for Renewal and Development of the LDRs

	1949-1970	1971-1975	1976-1980	Population
Total	100.0	100.0	100.0	100.0
BiH	57.1	40.6	27.1	52.3
Montenegro	22.7	17.4	18.7	7.4
Macedonia	15.4	20.5	22.4	23.0
Kosovo	4.8	21.5	31.8	17.3

Source: SZZS, 1982, p. 207.

Table 4.7
Party Membership as Percent of Population over Sixteen Years of Age

Republic/ Region	Party Membership	Republic/ Region	Party Membership
Kosovo	5.6	BiH	8.9
Slovenia	6.5	Serbia	9.5
Macedonia	7.2	Vojvodina	10.7
Croatia	7.4	Montenegro	12.4

Source: *Statistical Herald of Yugoslavia*, 1985, cited in Tomc, 1983, p. 17.

As a result, in the decentralized Yugoslavia of the Fifth Five-Year Plan period, though individual republics and regions could block or at least delay legislation, they could not necessarily ensure the passing of legislation which would benefit them. At most they were able to achieve a compromise through which they would receive something more than they would have had otherwise. That "more" usually took the form of supplementary measures and included reduced import duties, preferential credits by the national bank system, special access to foreign exchange, preferential participation in institutional borrowing abroad and tax preference to foreign partners in joint ventures.[30] Although the LDRs were on the whole not fully satisfied with either the amount of investment disbursed by the Development Fund for the 1971-75 period or by its allocation, they were placated by supplementary measures passed to promote their faster development as well as by promises of more investment in the next five-year plan.

However, the effect of these measures on narrowing regional disparity was marginal. Lacking adequate financial means and a concerted effort at developing the LDRs, perennial problems like the shortage of experts, the low level of education, inadequately developed and defined ideas and plans on regional development and embezzlement of funds continued to retard the development of the LDRs. The gradual return of Yugoslav workers from Western Europe following the 1974-75 recession and the subsequent increase in domestic unemployment and decrease in foreign exchange remittances, further aggravated the overall economic situation with negative effects felt even more acutely in the LDRs. Additionally, the 1973-75 increase in the price of oil caused a first sharp deterioration of Yugoslavia's terms of trade and, along with the 1974 European Economic Community (EEC) ban on imports of meat from non-member countries, resulted in a doubling of the balance-of-trade deficit between 1973 and 1974 from U.S. $1,658 to U.S. $3,737 million.[31]

The combination of these general economic problems (whose results were always felt most intensively in the more vulnerable LDRs) with the lower investment in the LDRs, in conjunction with the skewed distribution of the inadequate investment among the LDRs,[32] was that

30 SZDP, SIV, *Analiza funkcionisanja sistema podsticanja brzeg razvoja privredno nedovoljno razvijenih SR i SAP sa predlogom ocena i zakljucka saveznog izvrsnog veca* [Analysis of the Functioning of the System of Faster Development of the Economically Insufficiently Developed Socialist Rupublics and Socialist Autonomous Regions] SIV, 20 no. 30-23/88, (Belgrade, November 3, 1988).

31 Schrenk Ardalan and El Tatawy, 1979, p. 84.

32 Through this period the DRs received both less investment than had been planned, 28.8% as comapred to 33.1%, as well as less investment per capita than the DRs (Table

instead of the projected growth rate of 25% above the national average for the period 1971-75, the LDRs grew at 9% above the national average. Although this growth rate was impressive in light of their adverse economic conditions, it proved insufficient to decrease the economic disparity between them and the developed regions.

Regional Development in the Sixth Five-Year Plan: 1976-1980

"Faster development of the economically underdeveloped republics with the socialist province of Kosovo exceeding most of the country's average development,"[33] was once again an articulated goal, the fourth out of five in the new five-year plan. It is interesting to note the two reasons highlighted by the Sixth Five-Year Plan for promoting that goal. The first is "for inter-nationality relations"; the second, for the "common economic interest" of all. By the mid-1970s, then, it was deemed politic to supplement the ideological appeal of regional development with concrete appeals to self-interest in the form of political stability and pecuniary gain in order to secure the support necessary for faster development of the LDRs. A second point of special significance in the Sixth Five-Year Plan was the stipulation that objectivized criteria for determining the level of development of republics and regions be formulated by no later than the end of 1978, in order to decide which republics and regions would be considered underdeveloped after 1980.

The above again indicate that disagreement and tension over "aid" versus " compensation" to the LDRs (through easy credits by the Fund and the free supplementary resources) was steadily increasing. As we have seen, disagreement and some tension between the republics and regions over the role of the Development Fund as a source of aid (as articulated by the DRs) or compensation (by the LDRs) had been present from the beginning. Thus, Kosovo had requested cancellation of all debts acquired through the Fund for the period 1966-70 (granted) and had asked for interest-free credits for the future (refused); Macedonia had requested a much greater expansion of credit from the Fund, 2.3% to 2.5% of the national GMP instead of 1.94% for the 1970-75 period (refused); and BiH wanted a greater share of the Fund's resources (partially granted).

4.2). For more on this, see Marija Ivanovic, *Finansiranje razvoja nerazvijenih podrucja Jugoslavije* [Financing the Development of Underdeveloped Regions of Yugoslavia] (Titograd: Institut za Drustveno-Ekonomska Istrazivanja, 1978), pp.105-6

33 *Drustveni plan razvoja Jugoslavije za razdoblje od 1976 do 1980* [Social Plan of Development of Yugoslavia for the Period 1976 to 1980] Part 1, Section 5.1.

Although these specific conflicts were resolved, other more fundamental ones persisted. This is shown by the increased use of both appeasement and threat by all parties in the conflicts of the 1970s, invoking both the proverbial carrot, economic interests, and the proverbial stick, the threat to social cohesion and political stability. It is also shown by the more specific promise to the DRs that they would not be required to give to the Development Fund indefinitely because criteria to determine which republics and regions would be in the "club" of the less developed, and thus receive the loans and grants, was to be agreed on by December 1978. Before we look at these, however, let us turn to the Sixth Five-Year Plan and its effect on regional development.

In the second part of the 1970s, the Development Fund continued to be the main means of intervention in the LDRs. Along these lines, first, the allocation of resources was raised to 1.9% of the GMP of the social sector, .17% of which was set aside for Kosovo's development and another .03% for its share of the Ibar-Lepenac Hydrosystem. The rest was to be distributed among the LDRs according to criteria agreed on by all (Table 4.4). These credits were extended at an interest rate of 4.166% with a repayment period of fourteen years and to Kosovo at an even more favorable rate of 3% with repayment of seventeen-and-a-half years. Additionally, budgetary grants were increased from .83% to .93% of Yugoslavia's GMP, of which .07% was set aside for Kosovo and .03% for Montenegro,[34] while the rest was divided among the LDRs in the same proportions as during the 1971-75 period. However, because of the overall economic difficulties in the latter part of the plan, budgetary grants for 1976-80 were decreased to .80% of GMP and the distribution among the LDRs was also revised, once again in favor of Montenegro and Kosovo (Table 4.5).

A potentially significant innovation for the development of the LDRs was the possibility of fulfilling up to 20% of one's financial obligation to the Development Fund through the pooling of labor and resources of work organizations in the developed and less developed.[35] The only criteria was that these investments be in line with the social plans of the LDRs and the autonomous region of Kosovo. The purpose of this innovation was to enhance self-management integration in the

[34] *Drustveni plan razvoja Jugoslavije za razdoblje od 1976 do 1980* [Social Plan of Development of Yugoslavia for the Period 1976-1980] Part II, Sections 10.1.1, 10.1.2 and 10.1.3.

[35] The Law on the Permanent Resources of the Federal Fund for Crediting the Faster Development in Economically Underdeveloped Republics and the Autonomous Province in the Period 1976-80, Article 7. Additional provisions were made for those who wanted to fulfill more than 20% of their obligations through cooperation.

economy--in banking, transportation and other branches--between the developed and less developed regions. In the next chapter we will examine in greater detail the advantages and disadvantages of this innovation for regional development. In this first period of its operation, however, this cooperation between work organizations which totalled only thirteen ventures was negligible,[36] so that the goal of a more integrated and better functioning economy through the joint ventures was not met. To the question of why so few used this seemingly advantageous innovation, respondents in the DRs admitted that there was considerable political pressure locally against investing "their" money outside of "their" republic or region. To my suggestion that joint ventures could surely benefit the DRs as well as the LDRs by ensuring the former access to needed raw materials or goods produced in the LDRs, the response in the DRs generally held that, given the variety of problems associated with joint ownership in the LDRs, it was more trouble for them than it was worth. Thus, once again, claimed socialist solidarity regarding regional development was displaced by what the respondents saw as "their" regional economic interests.

Other measures for stimulating the faster development of the LDRs in the Sixth Five-Year Plan were the use of two-thirds of the credits granted by the International Bank for Reconstruction and Development of Yugoslavia,[37] priority in the use of foreign credits and loans, access to needed foreign exchange for the import of equipment and others. In addition, Kosovo, the most underdeveloped region in Yugoslavia, was to receive supplementary capital of U.S. $80 million for imports of equipment outside Kosovo's foreign currency quota, up to 1,500 million dinars for construction of priority projects and another 1,500 million dinars of foreign financial loans with no obligatory deposits for the construction of above projects. Kosovo was also exempt from part of the contribution due to the federal budget for 1978-80, and steps were being taken to examine the possibilities for opening a special credit line with the International Bank for Reconstruction and Development for the construction of plant manufacturing industries.[38]

However, once again, regional development met with setbacks as Yugoslavia's overall economic problems grew more acute. First of all, the worldwide recession of 1974-75 reduced the demand for Yugoslav exports while the sharp increases in the price of oil in 1973-75 and again in 1978-79 increased their import bill by an equivalent of 7% of

36 Mladenovic, 1981, p. 64.

37 For the 1976-80 period, 64% of credits were given to the LDRs, SZDP, *Analiza* [Analysis] (Belgrade: November 3, 1988), p. 14.

38 Ibid.

Yugoslavia's GNP for 1974-76, and 8% for 1978-81.[39] The consequences included a foreign debt which in early 1980 stood at some U.S. $18 billion,[40] soaring inflation of some 35% in 1979-80 and a resultant "temporary" price freeze in August 1979 further interfering with the market, as well as over-investment resulting in exhaustion of Yugoslav bank liquidity and inability to meet credit commitments without further borrowing. Secondly, the return of some 40,000 *gastarbeitern* per year had, by the end of 1980, swelled the number of unemployed in Yugoslavia to 785,000.[41] Finally, a GNP increase of only 2.4% in 1980 compared to 7% during the preceding years led to a real fall in personal income which by 1980 had receded by 7.1% to the 1975 level, the first decline in more than two-and-a-half decades.[42]

The overall slackening of the growth of the economy was once again felt most strongly in the LDRs. First, in terms of overall investment, the LDRs continued to receive less investment than was planned and considerably less per capita than the DRs (Table 4.8).[43] Nor was the distribution among them optimal; in BiH, Macedonia and even Kosovo,

Table 4.8
Per Capita Investment of Republics and Regions Relative to Yugoslav Average for 1976-1980 (in 1972 prices)

	SFRJ	BiH	Montenegro	Croatia	Macedonia	Slovenia	Serbia Proper	Vojvodina	Kosovo	LDRs	DRs
1976-1980	100	78.1	114.8	118.5	75.5	180.2	85.2	116.3	55.7	76.9	113.0

Source: Fond Federacije, *Razvoj privredno nedovoljno razvijenih podrucja u Jugoslaviji*, Belgrade: "Srbostampa," 1986, p. 108.

39 Balassa and Tyson, 1981, quoted in Christopher Martin and Laura D'Andrea Tyson "Can Titoism Survive Tito: Economic Problems and Policy Choices Confronting Tito's Successors," in *Yugoslavia in the 1980s*, edited by Pedro Ramet, (Boulder: Westview Press, 1985), p. 3.

40 Ibid. Martin and Tyson, p. 27.

41 Kosta Mihailovic, *Ekonomska stvarnost Jugoslavije* [The Economic Reality of Yugoslavia] (Belgrade: Prosveta, 1982), p. 46.

42 Mihailovic, 1982, p. 25.

43 Fond federacije, *Razvoj privredno nedovoljno razvijenih prodrucja u Jugoslaviji*, [Development of the Economically Insufficiently Developed Regions in Yugoslavia] ("Srbostampa," Belgrade, 1986), p. 108.

Table 4.9
Investment in the LDRs: 1976-1980

	Planned	Received
BiH	16.5	12.6
Montenegro	3.4	3.5
Macedonia	8.9	6.6
Kosovo	5.2	3.9

Source: Fond Federacije, 1981, p. 9.

investment was cut by a third, while in Montenegro it was slightly increased (Table 4.9). Furthermore, their share of supplementary resources was also reduced from .93% of the country's GMP to .80%. Thus, adequate material resources, a minimal criterion for bridging regional disparity, were once again not present.

Nor were other measures for stimulating the faster development of the LDRs successful. The inter-regional cooperation, on which much hope had been placed, achieved a negligible 2.3% of the possible financial cooperation between enterprises of the DRs and those of the LDRs.[44] This lack of inter-regional cooperation in joint ventures is not surprising when we remember that all forms of cooperation between the DRs and LDRs had been minimal. One evidence of this lack of inter-regional cooperation was the Development Fund's failure to become a facilitator and coordinator in the exchange of experts and expertise across regional boundaries. Additional evidence was provided by the chronic disunity or malintegration of the Yugoslav markets as illustrated by the inter-regional price dispersion, economic specialization, personal income dispersion, location of the BOALs[45] and, importantly, by inter-regional trade which, as Caslav Ocic has shown, fell from 27.7% in 1970 to 21.7% in 1980.[46]

[44] Fond Federacije, *O Priticanju i usmerivanju sredstava fonda u periodu od 1976 do 1980 godine* [On the Flow and Direction of Means of the Fund in the Period from 1976 to 1980] (Belgrade: May 1981) p. 41.

[45] Burkett and Skero, "Inter-Regional Economic Integration in Yugoslavia, 1963-84" (Unpublished paper presented at the European Program of the Wilson Center, Smithsonian Institute, Washington, DC, September 4, 1986).

[46] *NIN*, June 5, 1983, pp. 10-11.

Regional Development: Criteria and Measures

A final area which highlights and crystallizes the nature and importance of the problem of regional development is that of criteria for defining and measuring levels of development. A growing issue from the early 1970s and a stumbling block in the negotiations over the 1976-80 Five-Year Plan and of every five-year plan since, the question of criteria and measures of development had been set aside to enable all regional economic institutes to produce studies by 1978, in time for negotiations over the 1981-85 Five-Year Plan. Three studies were produced by 1978-79: Slovenia and Croatia collaborated on one; Serbia (proper) produced its own; the LDRs together produced a third; Vojvodina chose not to participate.[47] Not surprisingly, each study presented the problem of regional development from its perspective and arrived at a definition of criteria and measure of development which would accord best with its interests, while claiming to be the one "objective study." Thus, while all agreed that Kosovo, as the least developed, was to receive preferential treatment "for a long time," agreement on specific criteria and measures of development was not reached.

Faced with an impasse and the prospect of another delayed five-year plan, the Federal Executive Council (FEC) submitted in July 1980 a draft proposing the following as the criteria and measures of development: first, GMP per capita with 70-75% or alternatively 72-77% of the country's average; second, employment per 1,000 with 80-95% of the country's average, and third, value of fixed assets per capita with 72-82% or 80-85% of the national average. Two additional stipulations were made in the proposal. The first was that those regions below the national average in two of the three indicators, including GMP per capita, would be considered underdeveloped and would continue to receive money from the Development Fund until they reached the lower boundaries of two of the indicators; at that point they would

[47] Ekonomski institut, Zagreb; Institut za ekonomska raziskovanja, Ljubljana; Institut za financije, Zagreb; *Politika i sistem posticanja brzeg razvoja privredno nedovoljno razvijenih republika i autonomnih pokrajina* (Zagreb: lipanj 1979). Institut ekonomskih nauka, Belgrade; Ekonomski institut, Belgrade; *Jedinstveni objektivizirani kriterijumi za odredjivanje stepena razvijenosti republika i autonomnih pokrajina* (Belgrade, 1978). Ekonomski institut univerziteta "Kiril i Metodij," Skopje; Ekonomski institut ekonomskog fakulteta, Sarajevo; Institut za drustveno ekonomska istrazivanja, Titograd; Ekonomski institut, Pristina; *Utvrdjivanje jedinstvenih objektiviziranih kriterijuma za odredjivanje stepena razvijenosti republika i autonomnih pokrajina i politiku i sistem podsticanja brzeg razvoja privredno nedovoljno razvijenih republika i autonomnih pokrajina* (September, 1978). [The institutes which authored the above documents are also responsible for publishing them, therefore, they are regarded as one and the same].

begin a transitional period with reduced funding until the upper boundary was reached. The second stipulation was that a region with two of the three indicators below 55% of the national average, including per capita social product, would be considered least developed and would receive additional stimulative measures.[48] However, as an agreement on the proposal could not be reached in time for the 1981-85 Five-Year Plan, the proposal was withdrawn and the previous criteria and measures defining the four LDRs were continued into the Seventh Five-Year Plan.

This lack of agreement over criteria and their measure for determining development levels in turn highlights two key aspects of Yugoslav development which characterized the 1980s. First, in terms of decision-making, it shows that not even the Federal Executive Council (FEC), the strongest decision-making body in post-Tito Yugoslavia, could get its measure passed even when so shortly after Tito's death republics and regions were particularly sensitive to the importance of presenting a united, "business-as-usual" image. It also indicates that the influence of the central party apparatus which had been reestablished in the 1970s was either not strong enough to override inter-regional disagreements, or itself reflected this regional conflict and was thus unable to obtain agreement on the measure.[49]

The second aspect which is highlighted by the failure to pass the draft agreement is that once again conflict between the republics and regions converged on the issue of regional development, specifically over concrete economic interests of the republics and regions. As this study argues throughout, the conflict between republics and regions in Yugoslavia has most often centered around their divergent economic interests. These regional economic interests were, however, not admitted to because in socialist, self-managed Yugoslavia the pursuit of individual economic interests was not considered ideologically legitimate until, that is, the mid-1970s when the existence and pursuit of particular, even contradictory, interests were for the first time, however briefly, legitimized.

In Pursuit of Interests, Pluralist and Particular

First presented at a meeting of the Presidium in June 1977, Kardelj's "pluralism of self-managed interests" described Yugoslav society as one in which a "multitude" of interests that arise out of class, economic, political, social and other conditions of life, work and the activity of

[48] *Politika*, June 21, June 24, July 2, July 10, 1980.
[49] For more on this see Burg, 1983.

people,"[50] characterize and will continue to characterize Yugoslav politics. He went on to state that these interests which "concern issues such as the further development of socialist society; the resolution of current economic, social, cultural and other problems; the direction and tempo of the further development of socio-economic, political and other relations; ideological and political differences that appear in connection with the treatment of concrete questions, etc."[51] give rise to "differences and conflicts" and that it is the "free emergence" of these conflicts that forms the basis of a self-managing democracy.[52]

What exactly Kardelj meant by "pluralism of self-managed interests" has been debated since Kardelj's pronouncement, and even more since his death. However, for our purpose it is important to first note his definition of the Yugoslav self-managed democracy:

> Self-managed democracy is not a system based on an ideal harmony, rather, on the contrary, on the struggle of thought and on criticism of practice, and often even on the direct confrontation of partial interests where the decision must be arrived at by a majority rather than by social compacts or self-managed agreements.[53]

This ideological justification of individual, that is partial, interests rests on the fact that there is "neither democracy nor freedom for man if he cannot freely express his interests and his thought, his yearning and creative view."[54] With these words, Kardelj admitted the presence of multiple conflicting interests and further set up the free expression of these as a prerequisite for democracy in a socialist society. For those who yearned for a politically more open society, one in which individual interests were legitimized and freely pursued, where conflicts were logical manifestations of differing interests and where decisions "must be arrived at by a majority rather than by social compacts or self-managing agreements,"[55] this pronouncement by Yugoslavia's ideological beacon had cleared the way.

However, the goal for Kardelj was not to create a truly open society predicated on the maximization of individual interests; rather, it was to undermine the decision-making monopoly in both economy and polity, thus increasing economic efficiency and political legitimacy of the regime. Kardelj sought to ensure political stability by first

[50] Kardelj, 1978, p. 86.
[51] Ibid.
[52] Ibid. pp. 92-93.
[53] Ibid. p.106. (Author's translation).
[54] Ibid. p. 116.
[55] Ibid. p. 106.

admitting to the existence of conflicting interests and then channeling these conflicts into the party-controlled institutions, where they could ultimately be diffused. However, for those who wished to emphasize only the first part of Kardelj's "pluralism of self-managed interests," the pronouncement provided an ideological justification for the pursuit of individual interests. At the same time, veto power inherent in consensus decision-making ensured that no legislation harmful to one's interests was passed. Thus, the possibility for increased particularization of interests was granted quasi-legitimacy, while the institutional changes of the early 1970s which strengthened the power of the regional leaderships enabled them to promote, or minimally safeguard, those interests.

Consequently, Kardelj went on to elaborate, because the expression of conflicting and partial interests occurs within groups that are changing and impermanent, the conflicts among them are also "non-antagonistic" enabling them through the democratic process of debate and compromise, to arrive at an agreement and aggregation to common social interests. This aggregation is to occur under the guidance of the League of Communists with other socio-political organizations. Thus, although the decision-making in Kardelj's ideal self-managed democracy would still be arrived at by majority, a majority whose composition would change with the change in issues so that the cleavages would remain cross-cutting and therefore "non-antagonistic," ultimately it would be the LCY along with other socio-political organizations that would determine "the common social interest by means of the confrontation and selection of partial interests."[56]

These particularistic interests, which since the mid-1970s could so much more easily be pursued, occurred mainly on two fronts. The first was at the federal level where republics and regions viewed legislation mainly in terms of its impact on their own region. This parochial regional tendency was, as mentioned, reinforced by the institutional innovations of the 1970s. The direct dependence of federal representatives on the regional organization which elected them resulted in their acting almost exclusively on behalf and in the interests of their region, rather than as representatives of the federation as a whole. With decision-making at the federal level dependent on consensus, and the consequent de facto veto power of republics and regions over legislation that they saw as impairing their individual interests, particularistic interests were further emphasized. This led to parcelization of the federation with negative effects for overall development, and especially for the development of the LDRs.

[56] Ibid. p. 86.

In the words of Misa Mitrovic, the result was that "we decentralized so much our interest that each person is an individual at each level...many difficulties have come from that," among them, that "neither we (the DRs) nor the Development Fund can influence how the money is used, and so money is not used as efficiently."[57]

While the "pluralism" aspect of self-managed interests was de-emphasized within a year after Kardelj's address in 1977, and subsequently attempts were consistently made to emphasize the consensual over the conflictual aspect of Yugoslav politics, the ideologically sanctioned "pluralism of self-managed interests," was never rescinded. The openness of debate in the post-Tito era was a tacit recognition of its existence and perhaps even of its legitimacy or at least of its inevitability; while the frequency with which it was mentioned in conversations, especially in the DRs, shows that it had taken firm root in the collective consciousness. For some, "pluralism of self-managed interests" was seen only in a positive light: thus Bozo Marendic considered Kardelj's "*Pravci razvoja...*" (*Directions of Development...*) his best work, because in it Kardelj encourages us to "state our interests openly first, so we can see how to agree on things. . . . It's a great advance; now we can at least tell what our interests are. . .maybe in the future we'll learn to agree as well."[58] Others, like Alexander Bajt cautioned that "pluralism of self-managed interests" has been distorted creating new and greater problems:

> I thought it would lead to a kind of multi-party; instead it has become a major problem for the federation because it has enabled the direct and personalistic relations of rulers of communes and republics, with the economy...and it has enabled each republic to act only in its own interests.[59]

Thus, the post-1965 decentralization and the de facto veto power of republics and regions over federal policy, as well as the appointment of federal personnel according to the nationality "key," greatly facilitated this pursuit of "partial" interests. While these interests were multiple and cross-cutting, operating within regions as well as among them, they were most contentious when the issue was money and its allocation between republics and regions. It is here that interests

57 Misa Mitrovic, Interview, Regional Institute for Social Planning for Vojvodina, Novi Sad, Vojvodina November 15, 1983.

58 Bozo Marendic, Interview, Economic Institute of Zagreb, Zagreb, Croatia, September 27, 1983.

59 Alexander Bajt, Interview, Institute for Economics, Ljubljana, Slovenia, November 9, 1983.

collided most directly and that consequently compromise was most difficult to achieve.

The second area where pursuit of interests occurred is at the republic/regional level, where communes and smaller socio-political and economic units such as "self-managed interest communities" and BOALs also vied for scarce economic resources to enhance their individual interests or the interests of their sub-unit. This further parcelization to sub-unit level meant that regional coordination and rational decision-making in broader economic planning of the region also became more difficult to achieve.

The result for the LDRs was to further relegate them to a permanently disadvantaged position. On the one hand, decentralization and the market had created a situation of competition in which the LDRs, economically weaker and therefore also less competitive, were unable to draw the capital necessary for investment or to find markets for their products. At the same time, the ideological justification of the pursuit of interests condoned this situation in which they were less competitive.

The main compensating factor, the Development Fund, proved unable to overcome these institutionalized disadvantages. Its original function as source of expertise, of research and development and as a coordinating institution facilitating the interaction and cooperation between the DRs and LDRs, failed to develop. In addition, the cooperation in investment between the DRs and LDRs which was begun in the 1976-1980 Five-Year Plan, depending on one's point of view, either as an addition (LDRs) or an alternative (DRs) to the Fund, had by the end of the Sixth Five-Year Plan met with dismal failure; that is, barely over 2% of all possible cooperative ventures had been carried out.

Conclusion

In the 1970s, then, as a result of the internal threat posed by the Croatian crisis of 1970-71 and the Yugoslav leadership's perception that the survival of an integral Yugoslavia was at stake, the focus of concern shifted to domestic politics and to a search for instruments and institutions to reestablish political stability. As a result, while development of the LDRs continued to be proclaimed as a primary goal, it was in fact once again relegated to a function of the broader goals, this time of the goals of internal political stability and overall economic development. As in the earlier periods, when the crisis passed, regional development was not reinstated as a priority; rather, it was once again displaced by economic regionalism, the pursuit of the individual regions' economic interests, now facilitated by the decentralization and the constitutional amendments of the late 1960s and 1970s.

Not surprisingly, the combination of overall economic difficulties and increase in regional disparity with the possibility of airing publicly one's grievances led to political repercussions. Tensions in Kosovo over the extent of aid encouraged the late Marshal Tito to visit the region in October 1979 where he declared that "Kosovo should become the concern of Yugoslavia as a whole" and promised that other republics, notably Croatia and Slovenia would invest more in Kosovo's economy to change the economic structure of the province. The promise, along with Yugoslavia's awareness of the extent of dissatisfaction in Kosovo, was coming too late. Albanian discontent in Kosovo (as well as in Macedonia, Montenegro and other areas where there were sizeable Albanian communities) had been growing throughout the 1970s as evidenced by consistent, if sporadic, student demonstrations, distribution of subversive material, propaganda actions, chauvinist outbursts and separatist activities.[60]

By 1980, Kosovo's situation relative to that of the other republics and regions had further deteriorated, while the overall development of the LDRs had once again faltered. Instead of the economic growth rate of the LDRs exceeding that of Yugoslavia as a whole by 20% to 25% as stipulated by the Sixth Five-Year Plan, it exceeded it by only 7%.[61] Overall, the disparity between the DRs and the LDRs had failed to narrow, while that between Slovenia and Kosovo had further increased to 1:7.[62]

This increase in disparity is not surprising when we consider that, despite the proclaimed goal of regional equalization through faster development of the LDRs, steps necessary to bring it about, starting with more investment per capita to build up both the productive capacities and the necessary infrastructure in the LDRs, as well as broad systemic measures geared to regional development of the LDRs, were not pursued. The most important reason for the failure to pursue the goal of regional equalization, it is argued here, was economic regionalism: that is, the pursuit and preservation of one's own regional

60 For more on the Albanian nationalism and the Muslim question see Ramet, 1984, Chapter 8.

61 Fond Federacije, *U funkciji ostvarivanja dogovorene politike razvoja privredno nedovoljno razvijenih republika i SAP Kosovo u razdoblju 1976 do 1980 godine* [In the Function for Implementing the Agreed upon Policies of Development of the Insufficiently Developed Republics and the Region of Kosovo for the Period 1976 to 1980] (Belgrade: October, 1981), p. 11.

62 SZZS i SZDP, *Razvoj Jugoslavije 1947-1981* [Development of Yugoslavia, 1947-1981] (Belgrade, 1982), p. 220.

economic interests. In that pursuit, the developed regions were automatically favored in the increasingly market-oriented Yugoslav economy, while the shift in ideology to a legitimation of "self-managed interests" helped to rationalize and sanction the continuing economic inequalities between the LDRs and the DRs.

The result for regional development was that 35 years after the CPY had come to power, its goal of bridging economic inequalities between the developed and the less developed republics and regions had not been achieved. The effect on the political stability of the country was becoming palpable. Ten years after the Croatian crisis shook the Yugoslav regime, economic grievances once again took on a violent ethnic-nationalist manifestation. In the decentralized, post-Tito Yugoslavia of the early 1980s, where pursuit of economic interests had acquired de facto legitimacy, these proved much more difficult to contain and, ultimately, impossible to subdue.

5

1980s: From Decline to Disintegration

Introduction

Speculated on for more than a decade before it occurred and feared for its impact on Yugoslavia's stability, the death of the man who had led the CPY to power and had become the symbol of the postwar, socialist, self-managed, non-aligned Yugoslavia had remarkably few consequences. The decentralization measures of the early 1970s and those following the 11th Party Congress of 1976, including the "Tito initiative" which had created the rotating collective leadership and, with it, the "old man's" virtual withdrawal from the daily operations of the state culminating in his total absence from political life in the last four months before his death, had provided a little time to his successors to acquire some experience and operational know-how, as well as institutional legitimacy.

No *fuehrerist putsch*, no regional supremacy, no army coup occurred; rather, within hours of Tito's death on May 4, 1980, the new President and Vice-President were duly elected from among the eight representatives of the republics and regions. Ten days later, the first rotation in the Presidency occurred smoothly and on schedule (yearly on May 14), and later that month the order of rotation among the republics and regions was formally established. Similarly, the Presidium of the LCY, the arbiter in domestic policy deadlocks, and the Federal Executive Council (FEC), the executive body of the Federal Assembly whose combination of knowledge of issues and power over the agenda placed it at the center of political power in Yugoslavia, functioned smoothly in terms of rotation of power. Thus, the transition to a stable, institutionalized rotation of political power, the prerequisite for both overall and regional development, was successfully carried out.

In terms of regional development, while faster development of the insufficiently developed republics and the region of Kosovo continued to be proclaimed in the Seventh and Eighth Five-Year Plans of the 1980s, the struggle over a diminishing economic pie was becoming increasingly evident. As the decade progressed, loud accusations of selfishness (from the LDRs) or of squandering of resources (from the DRs) displaced the old appeals to "brotherhood." The situation was further complicated by the 1981 student riots in Kosovo whose brutal suppression convinced the Albanians that nothing less than full republic status (and thus, autonomy from Serbia) could guarantee their economic development or their civil (and human) rights. A renaissance of Serbian nationalism among a key group of Serbian intellectuals linking Serbia's economic problems to national exploitation coincided with the rise of Slobodan Milosevic. Milosevic's ability to broaden his power base by overtly linking Serbia's decline to Yugoslavia's poor leadership, specifically concerning the Albanian "irredenta," unleashed an expansive nationalism among the Serbian masses who henceforth claimed Milosevic as their undisputed and unchallenged leader. As the decade came to a close, the "Yugoslav road to socialism" was abandoned in favor of a nationalist road to disintegration. Soon thereafter, all remnants of unity and all concern for development of the LDRs gave way to a desperate scramble of "*sauve qui peut.*"

Seventh Five-Year Plan: 1981-1985

While the system set up by Tito in the 1970s in preparation for his absence from the political arena continued to function relatively smoothly after his death, no small matter considering the turbulent history of the area, the magnitude of the social, political and economic problems which began to emerge in the 1980s proved ultimately unsurmountable.

Following the death of Tito, the most pressing task for the new leadership was to stabilize the negative phenomena of increasing unemployment, inflation and balance-of-trade deficits, which had suddenly appeared after a decade of much heralded prosperity. This prosperity of the 1970s, which had been largely based and fueled by the foreign loans, was now giving way to a deceleration of growth. The second increase in oil prices (1978-1979) had led to a deterioration of the terms of trade, while the world recession which began in 1980 (1980-1983) was reducing demands for Yugoslav exports. The sharp increase in interest rates on the once cheap and abundant Western loans, which were beginning to come to term, further drained Yugoslavia's foreign exchange reserves.

The response of the new leadership was to negotiate the first of a series of packages of stand-by-agreements with the International Monetary Fund (IMF, 1980-1984) to devalue the dinar by 20% (June 1980) and to appeal repeatedly to the population to "tighten the belt." The goal of these measures was to reduce the domestic demand in order to reduce the demand for imports and to rechannel domestic output from consumption to exports.

Although the trade deficit improved, it did so at great cost. The general slowdown in the economy which resulted led to a 3% fall in consumption between 1980 and 1983; this in turn led to a further slowdown in overall growth of the economy. Thus, the growth of the GMP, which in 1978-1979 had measured 7.5%, fell to 2.2% in 1980, 1.4% in 1981, .9% in 1982, and in 1983, for the first time in the postwar era, it measured negatively at -.5%.[1]

It was in this situation of overall economic decline that the awaited Report of the Krajger Commission for the Economic Stabilization of Yugoslavia was completed in the summer of 1983. The thirteen "leading people" from the party, government and "learned" circles of Yugoslavia[2] with an additional thirty-five to forty "experts" drawn from the various republics and regions, concluded their year-and-a-half long study with an endorsement of full marketization of the economy. In order to reactivate the economy and to stabilize the "negative phenomena," the commission found that the market had to assume a central role, with production based on criteria of profitability, linking responsibility for economic outcomes with the decision-makers involved. It was also to operate in foreign trade where the goal was to set Yugoslav prices in line with world prices, with a view to reaching the ever elusive convertibility of the dinar.[3]

However, a major problem regarding the recommendations for the economic reform remained: how to ensure its implementation. It was clear to all that without a political reform, involving displacement or

[1] Christopher Martin and Laura D'Andrea Tyson, "Can Titoism Survive Tito: Economic Problems and Policy Choices Confronting Tito's Successors," in *Yugoslavia in the 1980s*, edited by Pedro Ramet (Boulder: Westview Press, 1985), p. 192.

[2] Description given by Ljubislav Markovic, one of the nine members of the Krajger Commission interviewed.

[3] For an evaluation of the Krajger Commission Report, see John P. Burkett, "Stabilization Measures in Yugoslavia: An Assessment of the Proposal of Yugoslavia's Commission for Problems of Economic Stabilization," U.S. Congress, Joint Economic Committee, *East European Economies, Slow Growth in the 1980s*, Vol. 3 (Washington, D.C., 1986), pp. 561-74.

"shake-up" of those in whose interests it was to keep the economic status quo, implementation of the reform would be short-circuited. Yet a political reform was not forthcoming. For despite the general consensus that political reform was necessary, when it came time to consider it, individual interests from the republic/regional level down prevailed. In addition, consensus-based decision-making enabled the established interest groups to block or dilute whatever legislation was being considered.

The inability to go beyond the economic recommendations in implementing the reform meant that a mostly covert and unorganized opposition was able to block it.[4] The result was the overall worsening of the economy with negative effects in unemployment, salaries and shortages of goods, once again felt most sharply in the LDRs. The parcelization of the Yugoslav market into eight closed regional economies, and the further parcelization of these to sub-regions (that is, to the commune level) strengthened the ever present "subjective factors" and, further, negatively affected the overall development of Yugoslavia, particularly that of the poorer and less competitive LDRs.

Regional Development in the Seventh Five-Year Plan: 1981-1985

In this climate of overall economic crisis, struggle over scarce resources intensified. In the LDRs, where even during the prosperous 1970s the economic growth rate exceeded that of Yugoslavia by only 7% instead of the 20% to 25% stipulated in the Sixth Five-Year Plan, development had faltered.[5] The disparity between them and the DRs had not narrowed, while that between Kosovo and Slovenia had further increased to a little over 1:7.[6]

For the DRs, whose economies were suddenly contracting after a decade of unprecedented growth, socialist concern and solidarity were giving way to a sharper examination of costs and benefits. After fifteen years of giving what amounted to almost 10% of their investment potential for the development of the LDRs, the progress in bridging the development gap remained at best mixed. Increasingly, the feeling prevailed in the DRs that their hard-earned money was appropriated

[4] The modest recovery under Prime Minister Milka Planinc in the first half of 1985 was undermined by the conservatives in the government led by Branko Mikulic, who succeeded Planinc as Prime Minister. For more on the economy under Planinc see *OECD Economic Surveys: Yugoslavia* (Paris OECD, 1987).

[5] Fond Federacije [Federal Fund], op. cit. October 1981, p. 11.

[6] SZZS i SZDP, *Razvoj Jugoslavije 1947-1981* [Development of Yugoslavia 1947-1981] (Belgrade, May 1982), p. 220.

and used irresponsibly by nameless individuals who were benefitting themselves more than their republic or region. The answer, they argued, was to increase accountability, devise criteria for defining an LDR and, at the latest by the Eighth Five-Year Plan, phase out all but Kosovo from the Development Fund.

Despite continuing rhetoric emphasizing their identity of goals (development) and minimizing the differences in means (membership in the "Club" of the LDRs), the struggle over criteria for defining development levels and consequently membership in the Development Fund was intensifying. This can be seen, among other things, by the fact that the Seventh Five-Year Plan was passed a year-and-a-half late because of the inability of the republics and regions to agree on the criteria and measures and, thus, on membership in the "Club."

A compromise was finally reached in the fall of 1982 which enabled the five-year plan to be passed. Accordingly, 1.86% of the GMP of the social sector of all republics and regions was set aside for the development of the LDRs, down from 1.97% in the previous five-year plan. Once again these loans were given at a highly favorable interest rate of 5.5% with a twelve-year repayment period, and for Kosovo at 4.4% with a repayment period of fifteen years.[7] In an effort to break through the autarchic tendencies of the republic economies and to increase trade among them, it was stipulated that of the 1.86% set aside for the development of the LDRs only 50% be given as a mandatory loan to the Fund with the other 50% of the resources given through joint ventures. These joint ventures were to be mutually agreed upon by individual firms in the DRs with those in the LDRs for the benefit of both. For Kosovo, this was amended to 60% in cash and 40% in joint ventures in recognition of its extreme poverty. In addition, .79% of the GMP was to be allocated as supplementary resources to aid in the building up of social services in the LDRs, down from .93% in the previous period.[8]

This decrease in Development Fund loans and supplementary resources from the previous five-year plan meant that for the 1980-1988 period, total investment in the LDRs was falling by an average of 10.7% per year.[9] As such, it was part of a broader and continuing trend of deceleration of growth, which by the early 1980s had become

[7] Fond Federacije, *Razvoj privredno nedovoljno razvijenih prodrucja u Jugoslaviji* [Development of the Economically Insufficiently Developed Areas in Yugoslavia] (Belgrade: "Srbostampa," 1986), p. 20.

[8] SZDP i SZZS, *Kriza i reforme, Drustveno-ekonomski razvoj Jugoslavije u periodu 1970-1989 godine* (Belgrade: Izdavacki centar Komunist, 1989), p. XXVI.

[9] Ibid.

painfully apparent.

Although, in the 1980s, the distribution of credits among the LDRs from both the Development Fund (Table 5.1) and from the International Bank for Renewal and Development (Table 5.2) for the first time heavily favored Kosovo,[10] it could not make up for three decades of insufficient investment, faulty development policies and mismanaged implementation--as the increasing disparities between the DRs and the LDRs were making clear (Table 5.3).[11]

One effect of the diminishing resources was the further exacerbation of conflict between the DRs and the LDRs over the definition of an LDR, specifically over the threshold level at which an LDR would be considered sufficiently developed to further pursue its development on the basis of its own resources. This was seen in the delay of the promulgation of the Seventh Five-Year Plan; it was encountered again by the Krajger Commission's sub-group on regional development.[12] Of the seventeen sub-groups commissioned to study specific problems of the

Table 5.1
Disbursement of Credits from the Development Fund

	1981-1985	1986-1990	Population (1989 estimate)
BiH	28.3	26.3	48.8
Montenegro	9.4	7.7	7.0
Macedonia	21.1	16.6	23.0
Kosovo	41.2	49.4	21.2

Source: Fond Federacije, Evropski Centar za mir i razvoj (ECMR) [Federal Fund, European Center for Peace and Development] *Dvadesetpetogodisnje iskustvo* Belgrade, 1991, pp. 68 and 93.

Table 5.2

[10] The one thing that all the republics and regions could agree on was that a concerted long-term effort had to be made towards Kosovo which, according to all indicators of development, was falling further and further behind.

[11] Fond Federacije, *Razvoj privredno nedovoljno razvijenih prodrucja u Jugoslaviji* [Development of the Economically Insufficiently Developed Regions in Yugoslavia] (Belgrade: "Srbostampa," 1986), p. 90.

[12] The Krajger Commission of thirteen "notable" people delegated the task of in-depth study of seventeen major problems facing the Yugoslav economy to seventeen sub-groups.

Distribution of Credits from the
International Bank for Renewal and
Development

	1949-1970	1971-1975	1976-1980	1981-1985
BiH	57.1	40.6	27.1	30.6
Montenegro	22.7	17.4	18.7	10.9
Macedonia	15.4	20.5	22.4	19.1
Kosovo	4.8	21.5	21.8	43.4

Source: SZDP, *Analiza,* [Analysis], Belgrade: November 3, 1988, p. 14.

economy, the group dealing with the faster development of the LDRs was the only group whose head resigned three-quarters of the way through the study in "disgust at the political-bureaucratic interference" into its work;[13] it was, furthermore, the last group to finish its report and present its conclusions to the Krajger Commission; and finally, one of its core tasks, determining the threshold level of development of the LDRs, remained undone as once again consensus could not be reached.

The Program for the Economic Stabilization of Yugoslavia made the following point concerning the importance of regional development:

> The significance of the politics of regional development of Yugoslavia lies in the fact that its presence within the framework of overall development politics, in all the republics and regions, in the interest of each individual nation and nationality as well as the entire entity, contributes to the equality of our nations and nationalities and to the solidarity of the working people on the unified territory of Yugoslavia, on the basis of the socialist self-managed socio-economic and political systems.[14]

[13] Bosko Gluscevic, leader of the sub-group on Regional Development; Interview held at the Economic Institute, Titograd, Montenegro, June 13, 1983.

[14] Komisija saveznih drustvenih saveta za probleme ekonomske stabilizacije, *dokumenti komisije knjiga 4: Regionalni aspect razvoja Jugoslavije,* [Commission for Federal Social Councils for Problems of Economic Stabilization, Documents of the Commission, book 4: Regional Aspect of Development of Yugoslavia], (Belgrade: Centar za radnicko samoupravljanje, 1983), p. 143. (Author's translation.)

Table 5.3
Comparative Overview of Relationship of Main Criteria for Development

	1952		1953	1965			1989	1988	1989*
	Employ-ment	Fixed Assets	GMP per capita	Employ-ment	Fixed Assets	GMP per capita	Employ-ment	Fixed Assets	GMP per capita
Croatia	113.0	113.4	111.6	114.7	117.7	120.7	117.6	130.6	128.4
Slovenia	166.7	223.7	182.8	165.2	191.7	177.3	149.0	206.2	222.9
Serbia Proper	82.7	86.1	90.3	87.0	79.7	94.9	100.9	81.8	93.9
Vojvodina	90.5	82.0	95.1	113.4	97.5	122.4	105.9	109.8	126.7
DRs	104.9	112.1	110.2	110.0	109.0	118.2	113.3	117.9	126.7
BiH	102.6	86.3	80.2	80.3	86.5	69.1	81.5	78.7	66.3
Montenegro	80.2	36.3	57.7	84.2	125.7	71.2	91.8	121.7	72.8
Macedonia	75.9	58.2	68.1	90.3	71.8	69.8	88.6	66.8	72.8
Kosovo	55.6	43.1	52.1	52.5	47.8	38.6	51.3	41.0	26.1
LDRs	87.7	69.6	71.3	78.9	80.4	64.4	78.3	72.0	57.7
Yugoslavia	100.0	100.0	100.0	100.0	100.0	100.0	100.0	100.0	100.0

Source: Evropski Centar za mir i razvoj, Belgrade, 1991, pp. 90, 105 and 113
* in current prices

Lacking the will to reach a consensus which none of the participants saw in their interest, and in the absence of a center with the ability to enforce a compromise, the measures recommended by the Krajger Commission for the stabilization of the Yugoslav economy went unheeded. As a result, the Report of the Krajger Commission was de facto abandoned within a year of its publication, the much needed reform failed to take place, and the overall economy continued to deteriorate. Not surprisingly, except for Montenegro, the disparity between the DRs and the LDRs increased in both fixed assets and employment per thousand, as well as in their effect, GMP per capita (Table 5.3). In addition, the disparity between Kosovo and Slovenia had, by 1984, further increased to 1:7.5.[15]

Considering the Yugoslav leadership's awareness of the importance of regional development, both for the stability of the nation-state and for the creation of the socialist society, as well as given the urgency of the Yugoslav economic problems of the 1980s, its inability to reach a consensus on a core issue was quite remarkable. This lack of agreement highlighted once again the extent to which economic regionalism--the pursuit of one's own region's economic interests--was the main priority for the republics and regions. It remained the priority even when, as a result of this pursuit, both the interests of the republics and regions as a group, and those of the individual members, would suffer negative consequences. The price for the lack of agreement was the increased parcelization of the economy, as well as the increased political deadlock. The combination of the two, as was clear to all, could lead to serious political instability.

Regional Development in the Eighth Five-Year Plan: 1986-1990

By 1985 the economic crisis was characterized by stagflation, that is, stagnation of economic growth along with a sharp increase of inflation. Almost all the economic indicators were negative. For the 1980-85 period, GMP growth measured a yearly average of -.2%, prices of consumer goods increased an average of 45% yearly, and the average personal income in 1985 had fallen by 27% in relation to 1979. In addition, investments in fixed assets had decreased in 1985 by 40% in relation to their 1979 measure, work productivity had fallen by 9%, and the value of the dollar in relation to the dinar had increased

15 SZZS, *Jugoslavija 1945-1985, Statisticki prikaz* [Yugoslavia 1945-1985, Statistical Overview] (Belgrade, 1986), p. 187.

sixteen times during the preceding period.[16] Finally, the external debt had increased to some $19 billion, while a recently discovered internal debt was estimated to be twice as large.[17]

Even though industrial production had increased in 1984 and 1985, which meant a relative stability in internal consumption and a decrease in the foreign trade deficit,[18] this was but a breathing spell. The accumulated problems were structural; radical changes would be needed for an economic turnaround. However, the political leadership remained unwilling to take the difficult steps. Instead, price controls were lifted and inflation shot up to 115% in 1986 and 130% in 1987. It was in this climate of economic uncertainty that the Eighth--and what proved to be Yugoslavia's last--Five-Year Plan (1986-1990) was passed.

Throughout this period, the complex question of Yugoslavia's overall development continued to politicize the question of regional development. The latter, in turn, took the form of an increasingly open struggle for the status of underdeveloped. Not surprisingly, an agreement on measures for development failed to be reached. Instead, once again, the obligatory loan given to the LDRs through the Development Fund was reduced, now to 1.56% of the GMP of the social sector, which after inflation amounted to barely .86%.[19] A stipulated minimum of 60% was to be provided through joint ventures (for Kosovo, 50%), while all of Serbia's and Vojvodina's contributions intended for Kosovo were to be given through joint ventures.[20]

The generous terms of the loans meant once again that, given the high inflation rate and low interest payment, the loans were in reality grants. The interest rate for the LDRs was 11% with a repayment period of twelve years, and for Kosovo 9% with fifteen years while Yugoslavia's inflation rate during this five-year plan period increased from an annual 115% in 1986 to 2,500% in December of 1989.[21] Supplementary resources for social services were to be allocated as a variable percentage of the falling GMP; for 1986 it amounted to .53% of

[16] Ibid, pp. 10-11.

[17] For an explanation of Yugoslavia's vast internal debt and its origin, see Ljubomir Madzar, "The Economy of Yugoslavia: Structure, Growth Record and Institutional Framework," in *Yugoslavia in Transition: Choices and Constraints*, edited by John B. Allcock, John J. Horton and Marko Milivojevic (New York and Oxford: Berg Publishers Limited, 1991).

[18] In 1984, industrial production increased by 5.6% in relation to the previous year, and in 1985 it was 19% larger than in 1979, while the inflation rate dropped to 15% and in 1985 to 10%. Ibid.

[19] Slobodan Spasic, Interview, Fund for the Development of the Insufficiently Developed Republics and the Region of Kosovo, Belgrade, November 16, 1989.

[20] SZDP, *Analiza* [Analysis] (Belgrade: November 3, 1988), p. 4.

[21] SZDP, *Analiza* [Analysis] (Belgrade: November 3, 1988), pp. 4, 6.

the GMP and for 1987, .50%. Thereafter, it was increasingly difficult to tell.[22]

Most startling in the second half of the 1980s was the frequency with which at the federal level and in the DRs (and sometimes in the LDRs as well) it was held that this would be the last five-year plan to keep the Development Fund as the institution for development of the LDRs. By 1988, there was an active search for a way to aid the LDRs while increasing their accountability for the money transferred. By 1989, this search had led the Yugoslavs to the Italian model which, the LDRs feared, would recreate something like the General Investment Fund of the 1950s. This, the LDRs felt, would be more conducive to corruption by *veze* (connections) as well as generally being more amenable to pressure from well placed special interests in the DRs. In addition, by giving loans to the economically most "viable" projects based on a national competition, the LDRs argued that this new institution would once again, like in the 1950s, favor the development of the DRs.

By June 1989, as the development of the LDRs hobbled along amidst a plunging economy and a commitment by Prime Minister Ante Markovic's government to streamline the bureaucracy, including the Development Fund, new measures were being promulgated. In an attempt to revitalize the Fund and, most of all, to encourage genuine development with spread effects in the LDRs, measures aimed at increasing economic incentives to professional cadres from the DRs were passed. Doubling of salaries and newly built company apartments were meant to lure the skilled to less developed areas, especially to Kosovo, to set up joint ventures. In addition, there was an attempt to awaken the individual's entrepreneurial spirit by allowing, for the first time, loans from the Development Fund to be given to the small private entrepreneur (*mala privreda*).[23]

However, while some were preoccupied with the nature of the future development institution, and their place in it, and others were more focused on ways to stimulate the economy in the LDRs, another problem was emerging which soon all but eclipsed the question of regional development.

22 SZDP, *Analiza* [Analysis] (Belgrade: November 3, 1988), p. 13.

23 Hasan Zolic, Director for the section on regional development, Federal Bureau for Social Planning, November 16, 1989, Belgrade.

Social, Political and Economic Crises in the 1980s

Kosovo

In addition to the sudden and rapidly deteriorating economy at the beginning of the 1980s, a second and equally dangerous problem re-emerged, that of ethnonationalism. It began in Kosovo where the economically motivated student strikes of March 1981, within days, had broadened into grievances over Kosovo's general underdevelopment and high unemployment rate of 27.5%, mainly among the young.[24] The brutal attempt at suppression which followed the student strikes had an incendiary effect. In the coming weeks, the student strikes spread beyond the University of Pristina to high schools and even grade schools, taking on a more nationalistic form, with demands ranging from republic status for Kosovo to the first voicing of outright secession. By late April and early May, the student strikes had spread to coal miners and other workers in towns and cities throughout Kosovo; by July, they had spread to Montenegro and Macedonia and to areas outside Kosovo that had a sizeable Albanian community.[25]

Within Kosovo, the situation continued to deteriorate. Incidents of arson, sabotage and terrorism became commonplace; the school year ended a month early so that the students could be dispersed, a state of emergency was declared, the army was brought in "to restore order," and Kosovo was sealed off for two months in the summer of 1981. A purge of the Kosovo party followed with some one-hundred League of Communists of Kosovo (LCK) members expelled by late July 1982; additionally, Mahmut Bakali, head of the LCK, resigned and was subsequently expelled from the party. Nevertheless, the unrest, pamphleteering, arson, bombings and intimidation of Serbs living in Kosovo continued. Between 1981 and 1987, some 1,500 Albanians were convicted of political crimes, 6,650 of misdemeanors and 1,430 of military offenses. During the same period, more than 40,000 Serbs and

24 For more on the Kosovo crisis, see Mark Baskin, "Crisis in Kosovo," *Problems of Communism*, March-April, 1983; Pedro Ramet, 1984, Chapter 8; and Jozef Darski "Reformism and Nationalism: Two Responses to the Crisis of Communist Power in Yugoslavia," *Uncaptive Minds*, Vol. 11, No. 2, March-April, 1989.

25 The 1981 riots began the most serious clashes between Serbs and Albanians in post-World War II Yugoslavia. Rooted in both Serb and Albanian historical claims to the territory of Kosovo as the cradle of their respective civilizations, the conflict was exacerbated by the Albanians' lack of enthusiasm at joining the Yugoslav federation as shown, among other things, by the 1944 Albanian uprising against the Partisans and, more recently, by the Serb subjugation and domination of Kosovo until the ouster of Rankovic in 1966. In addition to their political underrepresentation in the LCY and their severe economic underdevelopment, Kosovo had been consistently falling further behind the Yugoslav average.

more than 9,000 Albanians emigrated, many on both sides for economic as well as political reasons.[26]

Although the Kosovo crisis may have seemed at first less directly threatening to the integrity of the Yugoslav nation-state than the Croatian crisis of 1971-72,[27] the disturbances in Kosovo created serious problems for the regime. By directly linking regional economic inequalities to ethnic-nationalist exploitation within the Yugoslav federation, the Kosovo riots spurred other republics and regions to increased vocalization against their economic "exploitation." Because of the general correspondence of the major ethnic-national groups with (regional) political boundaries, the perceived regional economic inequities took on a nationalist manifestation. As a result, there was a steady increase in national disturbances in all republics and regions of Yugoslavia throughout the 1980s.

The sharp downswing in the economy experienced in the 1980s made it far more difficult to arrive at solutions to regional problems of both economic equalization and of the rise of ethnonationalism. With the steady worsening of the overall economic situation and fear of losing economic ground, the attempts at preserving one's own regional economic interests once again displaced the concern for the faster development of the LDRs.

By the summer of 1988, throughout Yugoslavia, one could hear echoes of the sentiment expressed by a Belgrade sociologist in the following statement: "The situation in Yugoslavia today is catastrophic. One can expect a real explosion."[28]

For many, the sharply escalating turmoil of the previous nine months had been expected. Indeed, the surprise was not at the "sudden" rash of demonstrations, strikes and riots that had been breaking out since the beginning of the year. Rather, it was that it had taken so long for the anger at the economic failure and the socio-political breakdown to manifest itself. For the more acute Yugoslav observers, both within and outside of the country, the relevant questions, since at least 1983 and the publication of the Krajger Commission Report, had been directed at the continuing passivity of the masses, at their seemingly unlimited and endless acceptance of the deteriorating conditions of life.

[26] Ramet, 1984, and Darski, 1989.

[27] The Kosovo crisis involved a far smaller population; Kosovo could not possibly survive as an independent nation-state while Croatia could; incorporation into Albania, attractive to some Kosovars for nationalist reasons, (and unattractive to others for economic reasons) would pose difficulties for the Albanian as well as Kosovo leaders.

[28] Radmila Nekarada, Interview, Economic Institute of Belgrade, July 14, 1988.

Economy

By 1988, the recession of the 1980s, which since 1986 had led to negative growth of Yugoslavia as a whole, had encompassed Slovenia, the most developed and prosperous republic. The yearly GMP per capita had declined from $3,000 to some $2,400 in 1988,[29] the foreign debt had increased to an estimated $23 billion,[30] and approximately 30% of large industrial complexes were working under capacity, some by as much as 40% to 50%.[31] As ominously, the official unemployment rate stood at 17%, with another 20% of the population underemployed. In Kosovo, the most underdeveloped and politically volatile region, unemployment measured some 56%, with the unemployed drawn mostly from the young and often the educated.

The result, a sharply critical stance towards the leadership and demands which went beyond the purely economic, showed that the workers had some understanding of the proportion of the crisis. However, mixed in with these demands of a "classic workers' movement" was the continuing brewing national conflict over the question of Kosovo, where eight years of turmoil for an increase in autonomy precipitated a Serbian backlash.[32]

"*Mora da pukne*" - "It must snap," those in the know kept repeating to each other. When that would happen, what would set off the masses, what form the protests would take and what the consequences of these would be, remained the unknown. That it must happen, and sooner rather than later, had been the prevailing wisdom for some time.

Leaderism, Mass Mobilization and Federal Destabilization

It began in Serbia, where a draft memorandum from the Serbian Academy of Sciences was leaked to the press in September 1986. Calling for a reversal of the 1974 Constitution, which had granted de facto republic status to Kosovo and Vojvodina, and more generally calling for a restoration of Serbia's "rightful place" in the federation, the memorandum caused a furor in the non-Serb areas of Yugoslavia where it was seen as a renewed attempt at "Great Serbian

29 *Radio Free Europe*, SR, No. 10, November 11, 1988.

30 Ibid., pp. 3-7.

31 *Vjesnik*, September 11, 1989.

32 The discussion of the 1988 workers' strikes and the role of Milosevic, the importance of these for development in Serbia and, more broadly, in Yugoslavia, owes a great deal to Milovan Djilas. Interview, at his home, August 17 and 18, 1988, Belgrade.

hegemonism." Among the Serbs, however, there was both a general acceptance of the memorandum's main thesis that Serbia had been systematically discriminated against in Tito's Yugoslavia and anger at the perceived attempt at sabotage and discrediting by "unnamed enemies" of what they insisted was only a draft for discussion, not a final product. Thus, a dozen years after Tito's 1974 purge of liberals and half-a-dozen years after "the old man's" death, liberalism and nationalism were reappearing in Serbia.

A few months earlier, a relatively unknown banker-newly-turned-politician, who was the brother-in-law and *protégé* of Serbia's president-elect, Petar Stambolic, assumed (Stambolic's) vacated position of chairman of the Central Committee of the LC of Serbia. Slobodan Milosevic's appearance on the political scene thus coincided with a renaissance of Serbian nationalism among a key group of Belgrade intellectuals. It was a coincidence which he was to use to his advantage.

Following his soon-to-become legendary "defense" of the Serbian common man in Kosovo Polje in April 1987, Milosevic's star was on the ascendance. Presenting himself as the guardian and defender of the downtrodden peasants and workers, Milosevic promised that, while he was there, no one would ever beat them again. Placing himself squarely on the side of "the people," Milosevic was the first to tell them that they had a right to demand of the politicians to give account for bringing Yugoslavia to ruin, promising that he would always be on their side. In turn, in growing numbers, "the people" responded. A few months earlier, in September 1987, Milosevic had engineered a bloodless, "nightmarish palace coup"[33] in Serbia which had ousted the liberal Stambolic, subsequently cleaning out all vestiges of liberalism in the press and in the media in general. With all opposition silenced, Milosevic could concentrate on mobilizing support among the masses.

From spring 1988 and on, no public meeting in Belgrade or elsewhere in Serbia, or in other republics and regions with a substantial Serb or Montenegrin population, took place without incantations of Milosevic's name, linking it with freedom, *Slobo-Sloboda*, or with Serbian patriotism and unity, *Slobo, Srbine, Srbija je uz tebe!* (Slobo, o Serb, Serbia stands with you!). Along with the many variations of the above, posters and pictures of Milosevic began appearing not only at rallies but in public places like buses, above the driver's mirror, a place traditionally reserved for pictures of Tito.

[33] Description of a delegate who was present through the day and night-long meeting and who requested anonymity.

In addition to his heroic and nurturing[34] attributes, Milosevic was above all depicted as a man of the people. A feature article in the premier issue of *ON* (Winter/Spring, 1989) portrayed Milosevic as a quiet, humble, family man who lives in an apartment, which he himself repainted the previous summer, in an ordinary section of Belgrade. It further described how Milosevic drives his own car, a Yugoslav-made Fiat rather than an expensive imported car, and pays his own bills. Additional evidence of his personal integrity was presented with the examples of his refusal to accept a suit length of cloth offered in a clothing factory, or the gift of a car offered in Kragujevac. Thus, unlike the corrupt "armchair" politicians, Milosevic was portrayed as a man who shies away from the usual perks of office. Preferring to live like the "common man," he was clearly to be seen as the person whom the "common man" could trust.

This direct appeal of Milosevic, portrayed simultaneously as *of the people* and having the heroic stature to lead them, along with his ideological "flexibility,"[35] enabled him to vary his platform to suit the audience and the occasion. It also freed him to explain the various political, economic and social problems confronting Yugoslavia as a result of an oppressed and shackled Serbia needing to be restored to its position of "equality," or more ominously to its "rightful place" within the federation.

The combination of leadership vacuum with the continuing and seemingly unending decline of the Yugoslav economy brought out in 1988 alone an estimated four to five million people to the streets to agitate against the hopelessness of their situation. Their pleas were heard by Milosevic who encouraged all manifestations of mass populism. His image as protector of the small, impoverished and downtrodden Serb, and champion of a "shackled" Serbia enabled Milosevic to manipulate the masses for his goal of a recentralized Yugoslavia.

His success was unprecedented. Using Kosovo and the inability of the Yugoslav government to quell the disturbances in the region, Milosevic argued for the need to change the 1974 Constitution to increase Serbia's power over its autonomous provinces as a necessary condition for restoring law and order in the region. His mass mobilization campaigns to pressure for changes culminated in the

[34] Dijana Plestina, "From 'Democratic Centralism' to Decentralized Democracy? Trials and Tribulations of Yugoslavia's Development," in *Yugoslavia in Transition: Choices and Constraints*, edited by John B. Allcock, John J. Horton and Marko Milivojevic, (New York and Oxford: Berg Publishers, 1991).

[35] In Belgrade, in the summer and fall of 1989, Milosevic was freely compared to a chameleon whose colors could easily change to accommodate the changing needs of the environment.

November 1988 *Bratstvo i Jedinstvo* ("Brotherhood and Unity") rally, the largest in Yugoslav postwar history, at which a million to a million-and-a-quarter Serbs amassed in Belgrade in support of Milosevic.

The willingness of the other federal units to acquiesce to what they saw as both inevitable and hopefully sufficient to appease Milosevic led to a restoration of Serbia's full powers over the two autonomous regions. Far from satisfying Milosevic, however, this was but a first step in the launching of his campaign for a recentralized Yugoslavia in which he would have a dominant role. Within three months, Milosevic had further engineered and secured the resignation of the leaderships of Vojvodina, Kosovo and Montenegro, replacing them with people who would be compatible, that is, obedient to him.

By early 1989, the cumulative effect of the failing economy had reduced the purchasing power of the average Yugoslav to the 1960 level as current monthly salaries, which plummeted to less than $50 for a factory worker and $150-$160 for professionals, were still falling.[36] With the official inflation rate at some 340%[37] and rapidly increasing, it was estimated that as much as two-thirds of the active labor force earned below the minimum necessary to provide for basic needs.[38]

One consequence of the above was the sharp increase in personal debt as growing numbers had to resort to bank loans to meet their daily expenses. This increasing individual indebtedness and pauperization of a large segment of the Yugoslav labor force, with no prospect of breaking the cycle, heightened frustration with the current regime. In that climate of uncertainty, the chauvinist rhetoric of the man who could "right" any variety of "wrongs"--a sort of latter-day Serbian Don Quixote of the masses--propelled Milosevic to the position of undisputed leader in Serbia and, in most Serb areas of Yugoslavia.

Yugoslavia's political crisis escalated through the winter and spring of 1989 with the Kosovo miners' strike in late February and early March. The moral and economic support given to the miners and their families by Slovenia and Croatia led, in turn, to a counterstrike by Serbs and Montenegrins in Kosovo and Serbia; it also led to the arrest of Azem Vllasi, the Kosovo leader ousted in Milosevic's October-to-January sweep of all anti-Milosevic forces in Kosovo, Montenegro and Vojvodina. A second miners' strike in March 1989 during which twenty-

[36] *Radio Free Europe* (RFE), Situation Report (SR), No. 6, July 6, 1988, p. 8.

[37] Calculated on the basis of the twelve-month increase, from February 1988 to February 1989.

[38] RFE, Vol. 14, No. 52, December 30, 1988.

four Albanians were killed,[39] along with the continuation of martial law restored an uneasy "peace" in Kosovo.

In Slovenia and Croatia, these events led to the formation of a few, at first hesitant, "groups" or movements for democratization led by individuals who saw in the Kosovo events a flagrant example of human rights violations perpetrated by the hard-line Communists. For these would-be democrats, Kosovo was one more proof of the need for establishing the "rule of law" guaranteed by a multi-party system and free and open elections. By fall 1989, many of their views had been taken up by the LC of Slovenia which on September 27 passed an amendment to its constitution proclaiming sovereignty over its affairs and, in case of conflict with the federation, its superiority.[40]

Fall 1989: The Slide into Chaos

The Slovenian constitutional amendments were the result of an agonizing debate which had begun in spring 1988 after the arrest of "Janez" Jansa, David Tasic, Ivan Borstner and Franci Zavrl on trumped up charges of military espionage.[41] Protest at the staged trial and the convictions which followed led to the creation of a genuine Slovenian grass roots movement for democracy and republic autonomy. Milosevic's campaign of "political differentiation" of the Vojvodina, Kosovo and Montenegro leaderships a few months later, and his further repression of Kosovo in March 1989, were all strongly protested in Slovenia. The Constitutional Amendments of September 1989 were thus a result of a natural evolution in the thinking of the Slovenian people, which the Slovenian LC had to accept or risk obsolescence.

For Milosevic, who was seeking an "enemy" to justify the need for a recentralized Yugoslavia, the constitutional amendments were "proof" of Slovenia's separatist "anti-Yugoslav" intentions. The argument of an internal enemy was particularly useful for domestic consumption, since by November 1989 the first sign of an organized (though still illegal)

[39] *Amandmani dele Jugoslaviju* [Amendments are Dividing Yugoslavia], special edition of *Borba* (Documents) (Belgrade, October 1987), p. 2.

[40] Actually, strengthening republic sovereignty was only one of the three key areas of change in the Slovenian constitution; the other two dealt with regulating human rights and reforming the economic system. *Vjesnik*, September 28, 1989.

[41] On May 31, 1988, Sergeant Major Ivan Borstner was arrested for allegedly passing military secrets to a journalist (Jansa), an editor (Tasic) and the managing editor (Zavrl) of the Slovenian student paper *Mladina*. The arrest of the above four, clearly aimed as a warning to the Slovenes to halt their process of democratization, led to mass protests in Slovenia, as well as to support for their release from individuals and organizations throughout Yugoslavia, the East bloc and the West. For more on this, see *Radio Free Europe*, Situation Report 6, July 6, 1988.

opposition to Milosevic began to appear in Serbia when the Serbian Socialist Youth Alliance declared itself in favor of a multi-party democracy. It was soon joined by Ljuba Tadic's Committee for the Defense of Freedom of Thought and Expression (*Odbor za obranu slobode misli i izrazavanja*)[42] and other groups whose membership was drawn largely from disaffected intellectuals, some of whom had previously supported Milosevic. The September visit of an international commission to Kosovo which reported gross violation of human rights, as well as charges that Vllasi's October trial was rigged, put Milosevic on the defensive. In addition, the much touted public loan program for the reconstruction of Serbia through the sale of bonds (*zajam Srbije*) was a clear failure. Of the projected one billion dollars, barely $25 million had been raised.[43]

To recoup from these failures, Milosevic used the Committee for the Return of Serbs and Montenegrins to Kosovo (*Odbor udruzenja za povratak Srba i Crnogoraca na Kosovo*), his front organization which had led "people's meetings of truth" in Vojvodina, Kosovo and Montenegro and toppled those leaderships, to organize a "meeting of truth" in Ljubljana. The much publicized meeting, however, was a fiasco; barely four dozen people--three dozen of whom were from the media--showed up. Having failed in his Ljubljana venture, Milosevic launched an economic boycott of Slovenia. This was a handy way to forfeit on Serbia's large debt to Slovenia, under the guise of a defense of Serbian rights which, according to Milosevic, had been violated by Slovenia's November emergency measures banning all public gatherings, thus pre-empting the so-called "meeting of truth."[44]

While according to the Yugoslav press, the country teetered on the brink of civil war, republic and regional communist parties were preparing for the congresses which were to be held in December. These

42 *Delo* (Ljubljana), November 13, 1989, and *Borba*, November 16, 1989.

43 Ramet, Sabrina, "Serbia's Slobodan Milosevic: A Profile," *Orbis*, Winter 1991.

44 The fear was of the violence that could be unleashed by an unruly mob (whose numbers according to the organizers were at first estimated at close to one million, then were revised to 100,000 or 150,000 and by November 17 were further revised to 10,000 to 20,000) on a "mission" to "bring the truth" even if, as one of the organizers stated in a television interview, it meant "cracking a few heads." Such fear may seem exaggerated when looked at from a distance, but in Yugoslavia in November 1989 it was real. After all, before the announced Ljubljana meeting, there had been the attempted destabilization of Macedonian and BiH leaderships (*Vecernji List*, August 11, 1989; *Vjesnik*, October 18 and 30, 1989); also, while the Slovenian parliament was still discussing its proposed Constitutional Amendments, Momir Bulatovic, party head of Montenegro, had stated (in front of television cameras) at a "*miting*" organized by the Montenegrin LC, that Slovenians "shouldn't reproach us, if we (Montenegrins and Serbs) ask for arms." (*Vjesnik*, September 29, 1989). The Slovenes were frightened enough to declare a state of emergency, thus making all public gatherings illegal.

congresses were called in preparation for the Fourteenth Extraordinary Party Congress, which after much debate and delay had finally been scheduled for January 20 to 22, 1990. It was with an eye to the Fourteenth Extraordinary Party Congress that Milosevic "lobbied" for the overthrow of the leaderships of Vojvodina, Montenegro and Kosovo in 1988-89. His (failed) attempts to destabilize Bosnia-Hercegovina, Croatia and, in late November 1989, Slovenia, were part of his positioning in anticipation for the Congress. For it was here that the political reforms, a prerequisite for the desperately needed reform of the Yugoslav economy, were to be decided upon. The decision to either recentralize, as Milosevic and his supporters wanted, or quicken the tentative steps toward democratization through further decentralization of power, as the Slovenians advocated, would be made at the Congress. With that decision, the future direction of Yugoslavia's development would be set.

Then to everyone's surprise, on December 12, the previously conservative Croatian LC (which had managed to stay out of the Serb-Slovenian nationalist debacle) repudiated the leading role of the party, declaring itself to be in favor of multi-party elections and choosing the liberal Ivica Racan for its party head.[45]

Over the following weeks, as the other republics held their party congresses, it became clear that the challenge of democracy sweeping across East Europe had, after all, been taken up in Yugoslavia as well. Only Serbia and its two autonomous regions, firmly under Milosevic's grip, remained recalcitrant. This was made clear in Serbia's November elections, described by Milosevic as "the most democratic elections held in Serbia thus far,"[46] which had renewed Milosevic's mandate for republic President with an impressive 86% of the popular vote--in an election which, it was subsequently discovered, brought out a record 107% of the population to the poll booths!

Economy

In the midst of these turbulent political events, the government of Ante Markovic heroically sought economic and moral support at home and abroad. Trips to the United States by both President Drnovsek and Prime Minister Markovic led to meetings with President Bush, with American business representatives and with the IMF.[47] In addition,

[45] *Vjesnik*, December 12-13, 1989.

[46] *Borba*, November 3, 1989, p. 3.

[47] See transcript of interview given to the (American) public broadcasting station PBS and reported in *Borba*, October 18, 1990.

meetings were held with EFTA representatives[48] and with the General Secretary of the OECD.[49] Foreign experts were brought in for consultation, and discussions with various groups of experts continued at home. Markovic also made an unprecedented effort to reach out and include the general population in the reform program, to make the government's actions intelligible to the lay person. His tireless and patient answering of questions in open television interviews, as well as in the press, won him a solid base of support in spite of the economic chaos in everyday life.

By December 1989, chaos was the only word to describe a situation in which inflation had reached 1.5% a day, or more than 2,500% for 1989. In the LDRs, all economic indicators had begun their downward spiral earlier and proceeded faster; only unemployment was increasing rapidly and in Kosovo had reached 60% by the end of the decade. The economic disparities between the developed and less developed had continued to increase; those between Slovenia and Kosovo now measured more than 1:8.[50]

At the height of this economic chaos and political uncertainty, Prime Minister Ante Markovic announced his economic program. On December 18 at 3:00 pm, a hushed and solemn country watched in astonishment as Markovic announced the full marketization of the Yugoslav economy, with its linchpin, the convertability of the dinar, pegged to the Deutsche mark and fixed for a six-month period at one dollar to twelve new dinars. Other measures, a tight fiscal policy, liberalization of foreign investment and of private property, freeing of 85% of prices, devaluation of the dinar and, most importantly, a refusal to bail out failing industries, were to ensure the implementation of the economic program.[51]

While Yugoslavia's economy was thus decisively reoriented to the market, some adjustments and compensations were made to give the LDRs an economic boost. In addition to the taking over of Serbia's one billion dollar debt, the federal government set aside $150 million for special training programs in the LDRs, and another $100 million dollars for social security and unemployment benefits in the poorest areas.[52] Yet, this was hardly enough to allay the fears of the LDRs that their specific problems were continuing to be marginalized.

48 *Borba*, October 17, 1989.

49 *Borba*, October 15, 1989.

50 SZZS, *Statisticki godisnjak Jugoslavije, 1989* [Statistical Yearbook of Yugoslavia, 1989] (Belgrade: Beogradski izdavacko-graficki zavod, August 1989), p. 419.

51 *Borba*, December 19, 1989.

52 Ibid.

In preparation for the Ninth Five-Year Plan, 1991-95, the criteria and measures for defining the LDRs were still being debated. While all agreed that the criteria of fixed assets, employment per thousand and their effect on GMP per capita be kept, the DRs wanted the measure of development set at two-thirds of the Yugoslav average, while the LDRs wanted it to be higher. It seemed that the measure that might be accepted would be 60% for GMP, 75% for fixed assets and 80% for employment in the social sector--a compromise which once again left everyone dissatisfied.[53]

In early 1990, the main concern of the LDRs over the upcoming marketization of the economy was focused on the ideological rationalization of economic inequalities that was sure to accompany it. An additional indication that the timing was not auspicious for the LDRs was the depletion in ranks of those who worked on the problem in research institutes, in the Development Fund and in the Federal Bureau for Social Planning. While many of the older experts had retired in the 1980s (Mihailovic, Mladenovic and others), their ranks had not been filled with younger people. And many of those who were still active had shifted their focus from regional development to general problems of the economy (among them Ocic, Sicherl, Baletic, Marendic, Kljusev and Jandric). This exodus reflected in large part a shift in government priority as commissioned studies and projects on regional development grew scarcer in the 1980s. At the same time, individual need for additional sources of income increased with the rising inflation, so that regional development experts, following the laws of supply and demand, rechannelled their work to more general areas.[54] Thus, by 1990 and 1991 there was a very distinct decrease of interest in issues of regional disparity and development, especially in the developed republics and at the center, in Belgrade.

End of a Decade, End of an Era

"*Fond je puko*"--"The Fund has busted." With those words Hasan Zolic began his update of the state of Yugoslavia's regional development in mid-August 1990.[55] It was a dramatic way to begin our talk--but the previous half year had been nothing short of dramatic.

First, the long anticipated Fourteenth Extraordinary Party Congress, which met on January 20, 1990, disbanded after a non-stop filibuster and blockade by Serbia compelled the Slovenian delegation

[53] Bozo Rusevan, Interview, Federal Bureau for Social Planning, Belgrade, January 5, 1990.

[54] Ibid.

[55] Hasan Zolic, Interview, Federal Bureau for Social Planning, Belgrade, August 12, 1990.

to walk out in protest. Milosevic's attempt at resuming the Congress without the Slovenes--thus shifting the balance of power in favor of the centralizers--was opposed by Croatia, which, backed by Bosnia-Hercegovina and supported by Macedonia, threatened to walk out as well. As a result, Milosevic backed down, and the Congress "recessed" for a two-week period--never to reconvene. The next day, *Borba*'s headline proclaimed in bold letters: *SKJ vise ne postoji*--The LCY no longer exists.

As winter gave way to spring, changes proceeded with bewildering speed. Though at a different pace in the different republics and regions, the leading role of the party was being abandoned as was its monopoly of power. Movements and groups were being legalized into opposition parties, and a number of these with representatives from all republics and regions were working for a peaceful solution to the Kosovo crisis. In Kosovo, martial law was lifted and Vllasi and his fourteen codefendants were freed. Then, in April and May, the first postwar free multi-party elections were held in two of Yugoslavia's federal units. The result in both Slovenia and Croatia was a defeat of the Communist parties in favor of nationalist parties which pledged to safeguard republic sovereignty and interests.[56]

On the economic front, the signs were encouraging as well. The inflation rate which for the month of December 1989 had reached 56% had, by the end of January 1990, fallen to 17.3%; by February it was down to 8.4%, in March it registered only 2.4% and by May and June it hovered around a low of 1%. In addition, foreign currency reserves had increased from $5.4 billion in December 1989 to some $7.4 billion by the end of June 1990. Industrial productivity had also increased and foreign loans had been secured to aid in the restructuring of the economy.

All these good signs, however, could in no way guarantee the success of the economic reform. For that was ultimately to depend on the restructuring of the economy, that is, on the closing of failing enterprises. Nevertheless, by summer 1990, Markovic's reform program had stabilized the economy and galvanized a degree of support and energy needed for the restructuring. The rest depended on the peaceful transition from communist power to a multi-party democratic rule.

Whether that would succeed remained somewhat uncertain, although almost everyone thought that ultimately "it must." After

56 While free, multi-party elections with equal media access to all constituted an important step toward liberalization and democratization, the nationalistic, often chauvinistic, pre-election rhetoric in both Slovenia and Croatia, and the lack of sensitivity of both the DEMOS coalition and even more of the Croatian Democratic Union toward the Serb minority further strained relations and provided fodder for the nationalist-chauvinist elements to agitate against dialogue and compromise.

all, communism had been overthrown in Eastern Europe, and even the Soviet Union was undergoing dramatic changes. The "direction of history" was on their side, most of the Yugoslavs kept repeating. There was, however, concern over the spread of democracy, over its extent and ultimately, over the cost in stability that it might entail. For despite the overall trend toward liberalization and democratization, Milosevic continued to fight the momentum.

On July 1, 1990, a referendum in Serbia eliminated the last vestiges of Kosovo's autonomy. The Kosovo Assembly protested and voted unanimously for its independence from Serbia and its incorporation as a seventh republic within the Yugoslav federation. The Serbian parliament retorted by suspending the Kosovo Assembly and Executive Council and, assuming full control of the region. Subsequently, the managers of radio and television stations were dismissed, Albanian language broadcasts were stopped and *Rilindija*, the main Kosovo newspaper, was closed down.

Elsewhere, tensions were mounting as well. In Croatia, a small group of Serbs, encouraged and supported by Milosevic and a rising number of other Serb ultranationalist leaders, defied a ban by the Croatian government and held a referendum on autonomy within Croatia. Their blockade at Knin of the main access road to the coast-line brought out the Croatian police as well as the Federal Army units to enforce "law and order."

While much of this was popularly dismissed as the work of "idiots" (*budale*) and "failures" (*propalice*), there was nevertheless a palpable increase in social tension and fear. The continuing provocations by these groups, like the one led by the dentist Milan Babic of Knin, no matter how small and unrepresentative, were making life more uncomfortable for all. Worse yet, they were leading to a rapid increase of uncertainty and suspicion and, more generally, to a climate in which escalation of "incidents" could easily lead to social disintegration.

It was in that atmosphere that Zolic's statement--*Fond je puko*--was made. By mid-August 1990, the Development Fund was still trying to collect the more than 20% of unpaid dues from the fiscal year ending in December 1989; for 1990, not one of the members had bothered to send in their full share of the money. The Fund was thus literally "busted;" for in a country where mistrust guided relations, and where the ethos of "*sauve qui peut*" had replaced that of "*Bratstvo i Jedinstvo*," the Federal Fund for Development, which ultimately relied for its functioning on the good will of the republics and regions had, de facto, ceased to exist.

6

Explanations Revisited: Summary and Conclusion

Introduction

This study has examined four decades of regional development in Yugoslavia in terms of articulation of goals, implementation of policies and their effects regarding the narrowing of regional inequalities. The focus has been, first, on the diverse Yugoslav explanations for the displacement of the goal of regional equalization through faster development of the LDRs; second, on the tinkering with regional development policies throughout the postwar period; and third, on the mixed results that the partial and haphazard policies produced. The main explanations for the regional development policies followed, as presented by Yugoslav academics, bureaucrats and politicians, have been examined and found inadequate. In general, although these Yugoslav accounts typically had some relevance to regional development in explaining either why the goal of regional equalization may have been temporarily displaced in one period, or why development of the LDRs was constrained in another, they do not explain why regional equalization, a proclaimed goal priority of vital importance for both ideological and pragmatic reasons in the socialist multi-ethnic-national Yugoslav federation, was *consistently displaced* and *subordinated* to other priorities and goals.

To conclude this study, this chapter will present an overview of the major approaches to and theories of regional development and discuss the Yugoslav alternatives to the ethnonational/political definition adopted by the regime in 1945. It will summarize Yugoslav explanations for the displacement of the goal of regional equalization as argued by Yugoslav decision-makers for the four decades of postwar development. Finally, it will show how although these were a constraining factor on regional development, it was *economic regionalism*, the primary pursuit of one's own region's economic interests, that fundamentally undermined the goal. The result was that after forty-five years of communist rule, inequalities between developed and less developed republics and regions in Yugoslavia had not only failed to narrow but, for all except Montenegro, had actually increased.

The Lack of a "Theoretical Basis" and the Problem of "Coherent Regional Development"

Academics, politicians and bureaucrats throughout Yugoslavia agreed that the major reason for the continuing economic disparity between the DRs and the LDRs, despite the many developmental measures taken by the regime, was that, in the words of Bosko Gluscevic, "at the broader level of theory there is no coherent plan of development."[1] As a result, they added, the measures passed were patch-up solutions that failed to provide a basis for the overall strategy of development, a prerequisite for the faster development of the LDRs and for the narrowing of economic inequalities between them and the DRs.

Given that so many respondents from all the republics and regions agreed on the necessity of a coherent plan of development, a number of questions arose concerning this gap between the Yugoslavs' stated need for a coherent development policy and the inability to arrive at one. To answer these questions we shall first briefly look at the neoclassical theory of regional development, its challenge in the 1950s and 1960s, the socialist approach to regional development and, finally, at the suggested Yugoslav models.

That the Yugoslavs had a difficult time arriving at a coherent model of regional development is not surprising given that, as a discipline, regional development is relatively new. It was only in the 1930s, with the onslaught of the depression and the general questioning of some of the cherished beliefs of the classical doctrine of capitalism, that the need for state intervention in the economy was slowly accepted, that regional inequalities within countries were acknowledged and that their development was seen as both a necessary and deliberate task of the regime, rather than as an automatic residual of development as a whole.[2]

[1] Bosko Gluscevic, Interview, Economics Institute, Titograd, Montenegro, June 15, 1983.

[2] J. Friedman, "Regional Planning as a Field of Study," in John Friedman and William Alonso (eds.) *Regional Development and Planning*, Cambridge: MIT Press, 1964, p. 59.

The neoclassical theory of regional development, according to which spontaneous mobility of labor to the DRs and of capital to the LDRs will result in faster development of the LDRs by increasing capital mobility and decreasing the labor pressure so that regional inequalities will have a tendency to decrease,[3] was concertedly challenged in the 1950s by Perroux, Myrdal and Hirschman. By showing that spontaneous development of market forces will further polarize the developed and less developed at the expense of the latter, these development theorists established the necessity of political intervention for decreasing regional inequalities.

As Myrdal pointed out, migration from the LDRs is selective, generally consisting of the able-bodied, more qualified population, resulting in a loss of potential for the LDRs, while capital is drawn to the DRs, where better conditions for development, among them infrastructure, skill and market, can ensure higher profits. The consequent unequal exchange between the DRs and LDRs results in a loss for the LDRs unless adequate compensatory measures are taken. Lacking these measures, the effect will be to increase the disparity between the developed and less developed, especially in the first phase of development, when the polarization effect is stronger than the trickle down. Whereas positive effects, such as the growth of raw materials and extractive industries, employment and general increase in skill level also occur in the LDRs, Hirschman notes that these are not strong enough in the early stages to overcome the negative effects of polarization, unless a conscious politics of development is undertaken.[4]

Although in socialist countries regional development was indirectly acknowledged from the beginning as an integral part of development as a whole,[5] the general lack of theories and knowledge of the processes of regional development, followed by the unidimensional character of the Stalinist "model" in a situation of low level of development overall, hampered the formation of a theory of regional development until the post-Stalin era.

[3] M. Kaldor, "A Model of Economic Growth," *Economic Journal*, Vol. 67, 1957, pp. 591-624, and J.E. Meade, *A Neo-Classical Theory of Economic Growth*, (London: Unwin University Books, 1962).

[4] Francois Perroux, *L'economie du XXieme siecle*, (Paris: Presses universitaires de France, 1964), Albert O. Hirschman, *The Strategy of Economic Development*, (New Haven: Yale University Press, 1958), p. 190, and Gunnar Myrdal, *Economic Theory and Underdeveloped Regions*, (London: G. Duckworth, 1957), pp. 26-29.

[5] Lenin first alludes, albeit indirectly, to the importance of regional development in *The Development of Capitalism in Russia*, [Moscow: Foreign Languages Publishing House, 1956] when he discusses the formation of economic regions and industrial centers, as well as the placement of industry and agriculture in relation to the internal market in Russia.

The development of Yugoslavia, which for historical reasons lagged behind that of Western Europe, was exacerbated by such factors as the large territorial inequalities in capital, skilled labor, modern work habits and social and economic institutions creating two different types of economies, a fairly modern industrialized one in the north and a more backward peasant-based one in the south.[6] The continuation of this situation in the interwar period, along with the effects of the laws of the market and the lack of any policy for regional development, resulted in a further increase in regional disparity.[7]

The chance for its reversal came with the ascendance to power of the CPY in 1945. Both socialist and pragmatic, the Yugoslav Communists set out to create a state in which, first, economic equality, a prerequisite for the creation of a socialist society as well as for political equality and therefore stability of the nation-state, would be achieved through economic equalization of the republics and regions; this was to enable the LDRs to develop faster than the DRs in order to catch up to them. Second, political equality, a prerequisite for stability in multi-ethnic-national Yugoslavia, was to be achieved through the federal form of rule.

Yugoslavia was peculiar in that it was a multi-ethnic-national country in which no single ethnic-national group was predominant, and the major ethnic-national groups largely corresponded to political boundaries and, therefore, to regional inequalities. According to the Yugoslavs, this meant that from the beginning regionalism was "historically determined and defined" in such a way that economic criteria took a secondary importance to the political criteria, facilitating certain economic irrationalities in investment decisions and inhibiting inter-republic mobility of labor and capital.[8] Yet, the official definition of republics and regions along ethnic-national and political/territorial boundaries did not go unchallenged.[9]

[6] For a general explanation see Alexander Gerschenkron, *Economic Backwardness in Historical Perspective*. (Cambridge: The Belknap Press of Harvard University, 1962).

[7] The difference in per capita industrial investment between 1918 and 1938 was such that Slovenia developed two times faster than Serbia, six times faster than Bosnia-Hercegovina (BiH) and almost twenty-five times faster than Montenegro. For more on this, see Nikola Cobeljic, Privreda Jugoslavije: rast, struktura i funkcionisanje, knjiga prva, [*The Economy of Yugoslavia: Growth, Structure and Functioning*, Volume I]. Belgrade: Savremena administracija i institut ze ekonomska istrazivanja," 1974.

[8] Nikola Cobeljic, Politika i metode privrednog razvoja Jugoslavije, 1947-1956. (*Politics and Methods of Economic Development of Yugoslavia, 1947-1956.*) Belgrade, 1959, and Cobeljic, 1974.

[9] While numerous alternate regionalizations have been offered in Yugoslavia, the three most influential ones will be examined here: they are that of Branko Kubovic, a Croat planner who gave the first comprehensive study of the problem in the 1950s; Kosta Mihailovic, a Serb economist who has studied the problem of regional inequality for

The first comprehensive alternative to the politically defined regionalization was that of Branko Kubovic, who divided Yugoslavia into 25 economic regions or units on the basis of shared characteristics and interests. Although the units were to be economically as complete as possible, their boundaries would be flexible to correspond to the potentially changing economic profile of the regions. For Kubovic, the essence of regional development consisted, first, in a versatile territorial division of labor within each economic region and, second, in the harmonious coordination of economic development among all territorial units.[10] In practice, this would have meant channeling new productive investments according to optimal economic relations within each economic unit, as well as deriving optimal use of all factors of production. This would have clearly disadvantaged the LDRs, which consequently opposed it.

According to Kosta Mihailovic, the preeminent theorist of regional development in Yugoslavia, a coherent politics of regional development that would encompass all regions with their mix of problems was never implemented in Yugoslavia either during the pre-Reform period or since the 1965 Reform. In both periods, regional development was characterized by a partial approach and faulty principles which focused on criteria and terms for disbursement of money, rather than on determining the degree of underdevelopment of the various republics and regions necessary for formulating the policies and obtaining the goals of regional development. Mihailovic rejected the official classification of four developed and four less developed republics and regions because, according to him, they did not correspond to reality.

more than 35 years and has been considered by many to be the most knowledgeable and influential authority on regional development in Yugoslavia; and Hasan Hadziomerovic, a Moslem economist from BiH who represent the view of the LDRs. There are a number of other alternate proposals for regional development which were still mentioned by some but no longer occupied a central importance such as the "Adriatic orientation" of the late Croatian economist Rudolf Bicanic, the alternate proposed by Kosta Mihailovic focusing on the main river routes of Sava-Danube-Morava-Vardar, or Milorad Lecic's concept of "Special Planning Zones," an agricultural variant of Francois Perroux's Theory of Growth Poles. Finally, there are those like Radmila Stojanovic or Nikola Kljusev whose general views are similar enough to the two poles represented by Mihailovic and Hadziomerovic that they shall not be examined independently here.
For more on these, see Rudolf Bicanic, *Economic Policy in Socialist Yugoslavia*, (Cambridge at the University Press, 1973.) Nikola Kljusev, Teorija i politika regionalnog razvoja, knjiga prva, [*Theory and Politics of Regional Development*] Niro, Belgrade, 1979.

10 Branko Kubovic, "Regionalni aspekt privrednog razvitka Jugoslavije," ["Regional Aspect of Economic Development of Yugoslavia] Zagreb: biblioteka Ekonomskog pregleda, 1961.

As an alternative, he offered a two-step process in which he first divided Yugoslavia into its 518 communes to examine the micro movement and magnitude of the territorial division of underdevelopment across all of Yugoslavia on the basis of the officially accepted development criteria of GMP, fixed assets and employment. This more detailed differentiation was the objective basis for determining who should receive and who should give to the Development Fund. The second step in the process was to reaggregate the communes into republics and regions. Here he offered a new classification to replace the two-tier developed/less developed categories. According to this classification, the republics and regions were divided into five levels of development. First was Slovenia, by far the most developed, having attained full industrial maturity. At the second level of development were Croatia and Vojvodina, both above the Yugoslav average on all criteria of development. In third and unique place was Serbia proper, a "backward" region at, or just below, the Yugoslav average. At the fourth level were Montenegro, Macedonia and BiH which are less developed. In fifth place, and at a great distance from the rest, was Kosovo, by all indicators of development a backward region.[11]

Mihailovic's approach to regionalization has been vociferously opposed by most in the developed and less developed regions. In the developed regions they noted that his is a fairly transparent nationalist attempt at ensuring that Serbia proper (no longer to be considered a developed republic) would be exempt from contributing to the Development Fund. In the less developed regions, the disaggregation into communes whereby only 20.3% of Yugoslavia's population would live in the LDRs, rather than the then current 36.5%,[12] would mean that financial intervention in the LDRs would be decreased by 48% to parallel the decrease in population.[13] Not surprisingly, the LDRs opposed Mihailovic's regionalization.

For Hasan Hadziomerovic, one of the half dozen most frequently mentioned experts on regional development in Yugoslavia and a

[11] For more on Mihailovic's views on regional development see K. Mihailovic, "Regionalni aspekt privrednog razvoja," ["Regional Aspect of Economic Development"] Ekonomska biblioteka 18. "Problemi regionalnog privrednog razvoja" ["Problems of Regional Economic Development"], Zbornik radova, Belgrade, 1982. "Drustveni ekonomski razvoj opstina SFRJ" ["Socio-Economic Development of the Communes of FSRJ"] Tom. 1, Ekonomika, Belgrade 1982. Ekonomska stvarnost Jugoslavije [*Economic Reality of Yugoslavia*], Belgrade: Ekonomika, 1982.

[12] Mihailovic, 1982, p. 130. By 1988,population in the LDRs had increased by 38.4% of Yugoslavia's total.

[13] In Kosovo, where it would be increased, there was less opposition to it among my respondents.

representative of the LDR's point of view, a coherent theory of regional development must begin with the definition of a region. Of the three possible choices in his typology, natural/geographic, historical/social and economic/geographic, Hadziomerovic chose the historical/social definition (the equivalent of what we would here call ethnonational/political), which represented the living space of an ethnonational group and, therefore according to him, its reality and identity. One of the main goals of the democratization process, according to Hadziomerovic, consists of the right of an ethnic-national group which belongs to a given space,

> . . to develop its own national economy and to decide on the most satisfactory direction of its inclusion into the inter-national (in the sense of between nations, i.e., republics and regions) division of labor. In a word, to be sovereign (on its territory), and that the territory itself as a result be considered a sovereign region.[14]

With this starting point, Hadziomerovic proceeded to the internal regionalization of the ethnonational space on the basis of democratic, social relations, concluding that the basic regional unit is the commune. To the criticism that disaggregation to the commune level would lead to autarchy in economic development,[15] Hadziomerovic answers that this need not (and must not) be the case, since in an effort to create the strongest possible economic base to ensure ethnic-national independence, sovereignty will impose a development of the ethnic-national economies in the direction of their most complete and rational economic development structure. As a result, according to Hadziomerovic, sovereignty will not lead to autarchic development of regions, but rather to a development optimum in which social and economic criteria are reconciled.

The reaction to both Mihailovic's and Hadziomerovic's attempts to articulate a "more coherent" policy of regional development was intense political debate. An example of the political nature of this debate is the following comment by Bozo Marendic, member of the Federal Economic Council, regarding Mihailovic's plan: "I don't like it. I've always been against it. It's a political trick . . . this way Serbia would gain the status of an LDR or at least lose the need to give to the

[14] Hasan Hadziomerovic, "Elementi ekonomske teorije regionalnog razvoja," ["Elements of Economic Theory of Regional Development"] Skopje, Macedonia: Makedonska akademija za naukite i umetnosti, 1980, p. 205, and Interview, Faculty of Economics, University of Sarajevo, BiH, June 9, 1983.

[15] For more of this criticism see the 1981 debate carried on in *Politika* between Kosta Mihailovic and Hasan Hadziomerovic.

LDRs . . . it's a very transparent trick."[16] Others, like Aca Bogunovic of the Planning Ministry of Croatia, rejected Mihailovic's proposal because of the parallelism to the days of the Central Investment Fund of the 1950s when investments were granted administratively by a centralized bureaucracy, supposedly on the basis of economic criteria, rationality and profit, in actuality more often on the basis of one's connections with Belgrade.[17] Similarly, in the Yugoslavia of the 1980s any step which could be interpreted as an attempt at recentralization of power (with the implication of an increase not only in federal but also in Serbian power) was flatly rejected.

The result of the inability to agree on a definition of a region was the acceptance of the historical/political definition as the determinant of economic development. Accordingly, the 1963 and 1974 Constitutions specified that the Socialist Federative Republic of Yugoslavia is a federation composed of six republics and two autonomous regions. It further stipulated that it was the duty of the developed republics and regions to aid in the development of the less developed (defined as BiH, Macedonia, Montenegro and Kosovo).[18]

Thus, by 1965 the question of regionalization had been finally decided and, with the creation of the Development Fund, institutionally confirmed in favor of the historical, national and political boundaries. The four LDRs were defined so that no LDR could be arbitrarily bumped off the list, as BiH had been between 1957 and 1961; nor could any be virtually passed over in terms of investment as Macedonia had been up to 1953; or, worse yet, be refused the status of an LDR, as Kosovo had been up to 1965. Furthermore, with the abolition of the General Investment Fund (GIF) and the creation of the Fund for Development of the LDRs, the *ad hoc* nature of investment distribution was to give way to regular, guaranteed and known sums. In addition to the very favorable credits for investments and supplementary resources for development of social services, priority in access to loans from the International Bank for Renewal and Development was granted to stimulate the development of the LDRs.

Furthermore, the Development Fund was also to encourage the exchange of knowledge and expertise by facilitating cooperation in both research and development as well as in production, through exchange of experts between the DRs and the LDRs. Finally, decision-making over investments allocated to the LDRs was now to reside with

[16] Bozo Marendic, Interview, Faculty of Economics, University of Zagreb, Zagreb, Croatia, September 27, 1983.

[17] Aca Bogunovic, Interview, Planning Ministry of Croatia, September 29, 1983.

[18] Constitution of the Socialist Federative Republic of Yugoslavia, Article 258.

the LDRs themselves, rather than with a centralized bureaucracy as it had in the period of the GIF. This was to permit a development orientation which would more directly benefit the LDRs, enabling them to replace the pre-Reform GIF-oriented development projects whose positive effects were so often felt much more in the developed regions. Thus, it appeared that by 1965 important prerequisites for coherent development of the LDRs had finally been created.

However, despite the Development Fund's potential for becoming a center for coordinating the cooperation of development efforts between the DRs and the LDRs, which could have led to coherent planning, the Fund remained primarily an agency for the transfer of resources, and another forum for interregional wrangling over their allocation. In a decentralized Yugoslavia where each republic and region was actively pursuing its own economic interests, it was too much to expect that the Development Fund could by itself overcome these centrifugal tendencies. As a result, this second, more indirect, attempt at coherent planning failed.

In sum, both the attempts to achieve greater coherence in regionalization as a prerequisite for coherence in development, as proposed by Mihailovic and Hadziomerovic in the 1950s, as well as the attempt to achieve a more coherent regional development policy through the 1965 Reform and the creation of the Development Fund, failed. This failure to attain coherence in regional planning was, in turn, usually bolstered by explanations of a series of regime crises which prevented them from actively pursuing the development of the LDRs. Thus the Yugoslavs themselves indirectly acknowledged that lack of coherence in regional development policy was not in itself an adequate explanation for the failure of regional equalization. A further explanation of the factors which made agreement on a coherent policy impossible is necessary. It is to a summary of these major explanations, given by the Yugoslavs to explain the failure to achieve the regional equalization through faster development of the LDRs in each of the four postwar decades of development, that we now turn.

1950s: Geopolitics, Economics and Ideology and Their Effect on Regional Development

Geopolitics

From its first days in power, the Yugoslav Communist regime professed as its goal the narrowing of economic inequalities between republics and regions. The strategy chosen to achieve this goal was the faster development of the LDRs within the context of overall development of Yugoslavia. Nevertheless, already in the first postwar decade, regional development was displaced as a priority. The reason, according to the Yugoslavs, is that the 1948 break with the Soviet Union and the Cominform, which both isolated Yugoslavia in the international arena and threatened its very survival, forced the CPY to abandon temporarily the goal of regional development, a prerequisite for the creation of a socialist society, for the goal of maximum growth of Yugoslavia as a whole to optimize self-sufficiency, a prerequisite for survival.

If the argument that an increase in international tension shifted the goal away from regional development, resulting in an increase in regional inequality, is valid, the opposite must also hold true. That is, a decrease in international tension should show a shift back towards an emphasis on regional development, and any subsequent increase and decrease in international tension should correlate with the shift away from, and back to, regional development. Yet, when we compare Yugoslav policy of the first two decades with the geopolitical climate of the time, we see that no such correlation exists.

Stalin's death in 1953 led almost immediately to a slow but steady *rapprochement* between the Soviet Union and Yugoslavia, culminating in the much photographed exchange visits of Khrushchev and Tito in 1955 and 1956. At the same time, Western (especially American) aid and soft loans, and the tacit understanding that the West for its own strategic reasons would guarantee Yugoslav independence, show that the relations with the West were also good. Furthermore, as one of the three founding members of the nonaligned movement in 1955, Yugoslavia had ended its international isolation and created for itself, relative to its size, a disproportionately large role in the international arena. Finally, investments in Bosnia-Hercegovina, strategically important for the defense of the country, decreased from their high of 24.7% in 1952 to 13.9% in 1957,[19] another indication that the Yugoslavs no longer viewed themselves as being under siege. Nevertheless, although the geopolitical threat had subsided by 1956, there was no shift in goal towards the faster development of the LDRs.

Similarly, following the Hungarian revolution in 1956, when Soviet-Yugoslav relations soured, no shift in Yugoslav development policy occurred. Finally, when the 1968 Soviet invasion of Czechoslovakia placed Yugoslavia on military alert, with Yugoslav democratization at its height and the geopolitical tension palpable, no

[19] Savezni Zavod za Statistiku [SZZS], Materialni i drustveni razvoj SFR Jugoslavije, 1947-1972, [*Material and Social Development of SFRJ*, 1947-72], Belgrade, 1973, pp. 227-228.

effect on the policy of regional development could be perceived. The above events provide additional support for the conclusion that the presence or absence of international tension has not been a determining factor in the policy of regional development.

Nevertheless, in one respect the Yugoslavs are justified in insisting that the break with the Soviet Union was important for the direction of Yugoslav development policy. As a unique event of major proportion, it had a conditioning impact on the young regime. Thus, the fear and sense of isolation that it engendered did not disappear immediately with the amelioration in their geopolitical situation. With a thousand-year history of various occupiers and the Cold War rhetoric of the 1950s, the threat of Stalin remained present in the psyche of many, even after the psychosis of the first few years had passed, and even when the international political situation had been normalized. As a result, Yugoslavia's expulsion from the Cominform and subsequent international vulnerability did result in a number of extreme measures. Collectivization and decollectivization, trials and purges and vigilance coexisted for a few years with the first elaboration of self-management. In terms of the developmental goals, a decisive shift occurred which relegated the development of the LDRs to a residual of the development of the country as a whole.

From that unique event, however, improvement in Yugoslavia's geopolitical situation was steady. Nevertheless, in spite of this improvement, policies regarding the development of the LDRs did not change. This suggests that there were other reasons why development of the LDRs was not pursued seriously before 1965. Before looking at these, however, let us examine the second explanation, by order of importance, given by the Yugoslavs to account for the displacement of regional equalization in the 1950s, that of economic scarcity.

Economic Scarcity

Yugoslavia's overall poverty and underdevelopment, exacerbated by the destruction caused in the war, argued the respondents, meant that the Yugoslav regime had to judiciously allocate its scarce resources to areas and sectors of the economy where they would give maximum return. This pressure for optimal development of the whole country further increased with Yugoslavia's geopolitical vulnerability following its break with the Soviet Union. As a result, the goal of the fastest possible development of Yugoslavia, with special emphasis on strategic defense industries, displaced all others, including that of faster development of the LDRs.

The economic argument, which focuses on the country's poverty and consequent lack of resources as a primary determinant of its development strategy, is given further weight in the case of Yugoslavia by the geopolitical situation and the threat to the viability of the nation-state. However, although this economic argument, especially in conjunction with the geopolitical one, has some validity, there are two important questions concerning the displacement of the development of the LDRs which must be answered. The first question is, given the scarcity of material resources, were these allocated according to criteria of economic rationality? Second, in light of the threatening geopolitical situation of the first years and the consequent shift in priorities, was there a change in policy and therefore a shift in resources towards the development of the LDRs with the removal of that threat?

As we have seen in the examination of the policies and their effects on regional development in the 1950s (as well as those of the 1960s and 1970s), both the per capita investments and the grants-in-aid allocated to the LDRs were consistently less than those allocated to the DRs. The reason given for the discrepancy in investment amounts between the DRs and the LDRs--most rational use of scarce resources--bears questioning; for among other reasons, this was the period which gave rise to the famous Yugoslav "political factories."

Furthermore, although economic scarcity along with geopolitical threat may further account for why faster development of the LDRs could not be pursued in the early years, by the 1950s Yugoslavia's economic condition had substantially improved. Ten years of development, large investments in production coupled with very low consumption, as well as the $1.2 billion in aid from the United States, had substantially ameliorated the economic condition of the country. Thus, the two major reasons cited by Yugoslav officials as explanations for the displacement of the goal of regional development in the 1950s, the geopolitical threat and the extreme paucity of resources, were no longer operating by the mid-1950s. Moreover, the Yugoslavs themselves were aware of changes in both of the above situations, as the shift in their economic policy exemplified; the halving of military investments in Bosnia-Hercegovina and the new emphasis on consumer-oriented production in the Second Five-Year Plan of 1957-62 demonstrated it.

In addition, the argument that it was necessary to invest more in the DRs than in the LDRs in order to maximize output does not hold. For throughout the 1950s, one LDR, Montenegro, received by far the most investment per capita, while the second most developed republic, Croatia, able to maximize output per investment, received barely its per capita share. Thus, economic rationality could not have been the determinant of the allocation of investments. Rather, the most plausible explanation for the non-rational and, in terms of the stated developmental goal, often irrational allocation of investments in the 1950s is that funds were disproportionately disbursed to those who had political clout, largely derived from the quality and quantity of their membership and participation in, and support of the CPY (Tables 2.8 and 2.9). Thus, Montenegro, Slovenia and, to a lesser extent, Serbia were able to obtain for themselves a disproportionately large share of investments and grants-in-aid (Tables 2.4 and 2.5), while Croatia, a highly developed republic, and Kosovo, the most underdeveloped region, were penalized for their inglorious wartime records. This indicates that, contrary to the Yugoslav claim, economic rationality was neither the only, nor even the main, determinant for the allocation of economic investments.

As a result, throughout the 1950s, despite the Yugoslav regime's proclaimed goal of narrowing regional economic inequality through faster development of the LDRs within the context of overall development of Yugoslavia, faster development of the LDRs was displaced as a goal with the result that the disparity between the DRs and the LDRs increased. Although the geopolitical situation, occasioned by the break with the Cominform and the scarcity of economic resources, *constrained* the CPY in its policy options towards the LDRs, especially in the first few years after the break with the Cominform, *it did not preclude them.* That the goal of faster development of the LDRs was de facto abandoned throughout the 1950s was neither a function of the geo-political hostilities nor of the scarcity of economic resources.

Ultimately, the decision to abandon the goal of economic growth with regional equalization in the 1950s was the result of conflicting economic interests of the republics and regions and of the political clout of some, which enabled them to enforce those interests. Thus, the development policy in pre-Reform Yugoslavia was determined neither by geopolitical hostilities, nor by economic scarcity, but by a political choice which allowed the economic interests of certain regions to dominate at the expense of genuine and significant development of the LDRs.

Ideology

A final explanation for the lack of regional equalization in the 1950s is based on an extrapolation of arguments and explanations made by the Yugoslavs which, depending on the respondents, either centered on or were derived from ideology as an explanatory factor. Because for the Yugoslavs the role of ideology was implicit, and therefore often remained either unarticulated or when articulated was often oblique, discussion of this "ideological explanation" must be placed in the context of a more general treatment of the role of ideology in Communist regimes.

One cannot talk about a Marxist-Leninist regime (or any other regime for that matter) without having some understanding of the ideology which has shaped it. For the political elite, what Lenin called the "vanguard," ideology provides the motivating force and defines the goal or task of the new regime and, to a large extent, the strategy or method for achieving the goal, thus affecting the direction which the dynamic of the regime takes.[20] Ideology fulfills the crucial cognitive function of providing to leaders and followers alike an identity and orientation for their life; and for all it provides the element which "grips the imagination," the necessary component which transforms the beliefs of the few into a mass-based political movement. It is argued here that the transformation of the society cannot be understood without understanding the viability of ideology for the political elite.

In the case of the Yugoslav Communist Party, faced with the overwhelming task of launching a development program and the uncertainty of where, how and what to start their development with, industry or agriculture, the CPY found the answer in their ideology. The importance for Marx and Engels of the proletariat and of industrialization, Lenin's emphasis on production and electrification, and Preobrazhensky's and later Stalin's reformulation of the socialist model of development, all were repeatedly invoked by the respondents as proof that industrialization was the only possible correct path to socialist development.

However, although ideology dictated that industrialization was the only path to socialist development, it was ideology as defined not only by Marx but also by Lenin, Preobrazhensky and Stalin; that is, Yugoslav socialist ideology was filtered through the Soviet experience. It is this *Soviet* version of socialist ideology, which continued well after the formal break with the Soviet Union and the abandonment of Soviet-type central planning, it is argued here, that skewed Yugoslav perceptions and policies, in the process further undermining the development of the LDRs.

[20] Since the focus here is on the effects of ideology rather than on its social determinants, there is no attempt to compare, evaluate, or apply the Marxist view of ideology as a cloak or mask for material interests, with the sociological explanation of ideology as a response to a loss of social orientation and psychological disequilibrium. For a good discussion of the latter see Clifford Geertz, "Ideology as Cultural System" in David E. Apter, *Ideology and Discontent*, (London: Free Press of Glencoe, 1964), pp. 47-65.

The Yugoslavs' virtually unanimous consensus that industrialization was the right path to development is striking for two reasons. First, only very rarely did Yugoslavs across ethnic, national, regional and functional lines agree on issues. Secondly, this consensus contradicted the following statement made by Momir Cecez concerning the 1947 debate in the Economic Council. Cecez, who was both secretary of the Economic Council when the First Five-Year Plan was being drawn up and a member of Kidric's Cabinet, testified that the problem of priorities in investment between agriculture and industry was one of the most important questions debated.

> To develop both industry and agriculture we needed twice the accumulation. In the Politburo there was disagreement over how much accumulation we have for investment and those supporting the Russian line said we didn't even have enough for the industrialization we wanted to pursue. We debated three days and three nights over this .... The question therefore was where to invest, in industry or in agriculture... and therefore we invested in industry and a little in the development of transportation.[21]

A number of observations need to be made regarding this statement. The first is that when the development strategy was being planned, the choice of priority between industry and agriculture was not a foregone conclusion; rather, it was hotly debated, with the development of agriculture having strong supporters in the top scholarly body. Second, industrialization was equated with the "Russian line" so that when industrialization won out as the strategy of development, it was, as mentioned earlier, industrialization of a specific (Soviet) type, one emphasizing development of capital-intensive heavy industry and producer goods, which was pursued. It is this equating of socialist ideology with Soviet ideology, and fairly close identification of socialist development with the Soviet model of development, even after the break with the Soviet Union, that resulted in policies supporting capital-intensive heavy industry, as opposed to either light industry or agriculture, which also undermined the development of the LDRs.

It is interesting to note that while respondents throughout Yugoslavia claimed that the basic model of development followed in the 1950s was correct, there had in fact been sharp disagreement in a top policy advising body, the Economic Council, and among top policy makers when the model was being formulated. These disagreements of

21 Momir Cecez, Interview at the Faculty of Economics, Sarajevo, BiH, June 9, 1983.

course would not have become public knowledge in 1947; and the structure of the Marxist-Leninist regime, as well as the imperatives of the independent Titoist regime, would work against them becoming widely known even later.

Moreover, as we know, once a policy is adopted a shift of public opinion in the direction of government policy tends to occur over time,[22] unless the policy effects are an unmitigated disaster. Additionally, there is the common propensity to rationalize one's past actions to oneself as well as to others. This would hold true for the middle-aged and older generation in Yugoslavia, who would have been the ones to pass the specific policies and to implement them. The younger postwar generation brought up with a revisionist view of the period might have had less tendency to question the "truisms." In time, the view of historical consensus over the early policy direction would take on an independent life. Thus, we can assume that many of the respondents genuinely believed, as indeed they seemed to, that there had been no disagreement over the model of development pursued in the early years.

Finally, the price of strong protest against government policy may have been too high in 1947-53; even in the early 1980s, it may have been counterproductive to the goals of those who would have had reason to criticize the early policy. In the quasi-Stalinist Yugoslavia of 1947 to 1950-52, the cost could have varied from prison and/or loss of job to direct or indirect economic sanctions. For the potential critics of 1982-83 it may still have been counterproductive. Perhaps a safer way to couch criticism of the early years was to state that while those policies were right for the time, they needed to be changed when the conditions changed--by the mid-1950s or early 1960s, or that they still had not changed enough in the 1980s. By supporting the early regime policies in retrospect, a critic could cultivate the image of sobriety, thoughtfulness and overall regime support, thus increasing the chances for leverage over current policies which needed change.

This interpretation would explain the large number of respondents who qualified their support of early policies with statements acknowledging that a better balance between agriculture and industry, as well as other branches of the economy, still needed to be made. It would also fit with the curious pattern that although all the respondents agreed that the development model of the 1950s was the right model for the time, almost all mentioned additional reasons why the model was followed; the manner in which they did so cast doubt on

22 See Murray J. Edelman, *The Symbolic Uses of Politics*, (Urbana: University of Illinois, 1964), John E. Mueller, *War, Presidents, and Public Opinion*, (New York: Wiley, 1973).

their belief in the Soviet model itself. Andrej Briski, aide to the Director for the Slovenian Development Fund, exemplified this ambivalent view:

> There were too little reserves in the Yugoslav economy for the development of industry and agriculture until the 1960s . . . even though more could have gone to agriculture especially after 1960 or 1965 . . . . There weren't enough means for the development of both branches . . . and there was the influence of the Soviet Model . . . that socialism is built on the industrial working class, etc., you know how it goes; there was also, on the side, some looking out for kulaks. Still today, there is overall too little development of agriculture, because the prejudice is still there.[23]

Given the development model adopted, the sector most sacrificed was agriculture, and it is on the treatment of agriculture that the consensus over the model of development followed in pre-Reform Yugoslavia broke down. The questions put to the respondents, which were devised to explore this issue, were the following: first, how much and for how long did agriculture have to be exploited to provide the accumulation for the build-up of industry? Second, why was agriculture discriminated against so much and for such a long time; was there influence of the Soviet model and/or fear of "kulaks?"

The answers can be divided into three main groups: those generally critical of the policies, about 25% of the respondents; those who thought totally along regime lines, about 15%; and a majority of 60% which was selectively critical but with an overall position of apologists. A number of more specific observations need to be brought out concerning the regime supporters. The first is that, with one exception, all were middle-level bureaucrats; and even the one exception was a former bureaucrat, newly-turned politician. The second is that they came from both the DRs and the LDRs, and third is that they all denied that either the Soviet model or the fear of "kulaks" influenced policy--or if they admitted to such a fear, then they also claimed it had dissipated by 1951-52. Finally, they all claimed that the agricultural policy followed was correct, and that the change in policy occurred at the right time, even though they placed that time variously as 1957, 1965, or 1970.

This curious consensus among bureaucrats from different republics and regions regarding the denial of influence of either the Soviet model or the fear of "kulaks" can, I believe, be explained by the following.

23 Andrej Briski, Interview, Slovenian Fund for Development of Less Developed Areas, Ljubljana, Slovenia, November 8, 1983.

First, the general explanation elucidated above, that the combination of rationalizing one's actions, accomodating a shift in opinion or beliefs over time and fearing sanctions, which held true for all respondents, was also true for bureaucrats. In addition, since bureaucrats were more directly involved in the formulation and implementation of the plans, they would have tended to support them more, both because their propensity to rationalize would be stronger (again because of their direct involvement) and because their socialization into the beliefs and norms of the system would have been greater because of their greater involvement with the system.

The difference between the other two groups, those who were highly critical and those selectively critical but with an overall apologist orientation, centered on the timing and extent of the stringency of agricultural policies, that is, on when the shift in agricultural policies should have occurred and when it did, and on what character it should have had and did take. The apologists saw the influence of the Soviet model of development ending by the early to mid-1950s, and they claimed that there was no fear of "kulaks" since the maximum land-holding of ten hectares prevented their formation. The critics on the other hand saw a continuing influence of the Soviet model in the mind-set of many decision-makers into the 1980s, including the fear that a successful peasantry would become a new "kulak" class. As Janko Gogic of the Economic Faculty of Titograd, Montenegro, put it: "This is the sickness of all socialist societies . . . this fear of getting rich."[24]

Finally, to the question, "Was there demand within or outside policy-making circles for the increased development of agriculture for either private or public sectors?", the answer depended on the respondent's age and proximity to power. Generally, the younger generation and those who had no positions during the years 1945-55 thought that there was no demand for increased investment in agriculture or that, if there was some, it came "from the side" (informally) and, therefore, was not important. This again backs up the claim that on the whole the younger generation believed the revisionist-consensual version of early policy formulation. Those who were older and had higher positions at the time testified that there were indeed demands for more investments in agriculture. These, according to Maurice Romano, member of the Presidency of the League of Communists of Macedonia, seemed to have come from two sources: first, from interested groups themselves, that is "from the communes

[24] Janko Gogic, Interview, Economics Faculty, Titograd, Montenegro, June 15, 1983.

which were sending in a lot of requests for money,"[25] and second, corroborating Cecez' statement about the Economic Council, from "scientific circles" (i.e., intellectuals or experts) who thought that a strategy of more equal development ought to have been followed. Thus, as Branko Horvat, the well-known Croatian economist and one of those who in the early days (1949-50) argued for increased investment in agriculture, has stated: "No one says that in the long run modernization doesn't come via industrialization; but it's a matter of how you start the process--and you don't start it by suppressing the only sector that works."[26]

Investment allocation between industry and agriculture was a "hot" issue, with opinions and interests divided along sectoral lines and perhaps, at least somewhat, along regional lines as well. Although a general agreement that industry should be the base for further development emerged, there was sharp disagreement over the balance between industry and agriculture, over how much, and for how long, accumulation had to come from agriculture. On this question there were sharply diverging opinions in the early 1980s, as there had been in the late 1940s and early 1950s. In the Yugoslavia of the 1980s these could be, and were, heard; and in the decentralized polity of the post-1965 period, they could have, and did have, a certain impact. In the Yugoslavia of 1950, however, before self-management had replaced Soviet-type central planning as the pivotal guide of the system, these could be heard in the "appropriate places" only. And even if experts in those circles argued for increased investment in agriculture, in the euphoric atmosphere and the centralized polity of the time, politicians/ideologues carried the day.

According to Ljubislav Markovic, member of the Krajger Commission for Economic Stabilization of Yugoslavia, and head of the committee for the social plan and development policy in Parliament, most of these metaphorical "graduates of the Russian school" [27] had only recently left behind their peasant past. For them, as Sulejman Kamenica of the Economic Institute of Sarajevo put it, agriculture stood for all that holds one back in the world, while "the factory was a concept, an idea."[28]

25 Maurice Romano, Interview, Republic Parliament and League of Communists of Yugoslavia (LCY) Building, Skopje, Macedonia, May 11, 1983.

26 Branko Horvat, Interview, Economic Institute of Zagreb, Croatia, October 6, 1983.

27 Ljubislav Markovic, Interview, Economics Faculty, Belgrade, Serbia, December 15, 1982.

28 Sulejman Kamenica, Interview, Economic Institute of Sarajevo, Bosnia-Hercegovina, June 8, 1983.

Finally, how do we explain that even in the republics and regions whose development was hurt by this policy (generally the LDRs, though it includes Vojvodina and is less true for Montenegro), respondents also agreed that the development model followed was the right one at the time?

This question brings us back to the importance of ideology in a socialist regime. For if in the LDRs and in the agricultural regions in general the Soviet model of development was accepted (even if not always welcomed), though it went against their short term economic interests, it was because of their belief in, and commitment to, a larger goal--the creation of the socialist society, for which the Soviet model of development was seen as the road map.

Giving credence to ideology, to the role of ideas in shaping policies, allows us to understand why an overwhelming majority of the respondents in the LDRs thought that, while the development model followed was suitable for the first few years of Yugoslav development, it should have changed by the mid- or late 1950s, rather than by 1965 or, as most saw it, even later. For, by the mid-1950s, both the geopolitical and the economic situation of Yugoslavia had vastly improved, while ideology, the motivating force in the first few years of the revolution, had declined in importance and was becoming increasingly eclipsed by the economic imperatives and interests of a few, who could keep the status quo by invoking this or that dogma. Nevertheless, with some inadequate changes, the policies were usually continued in the name of both self-management and socialism.

For the development of the LDRs, the above was disastrous. Overwhelmingly agricultural with a large unemployed and illiterate population, they were prevented from developing more rapidly by the systematic underpricing of their products. This was true not only for agriculture, resulting in the "squeezing" of the peasants, but also for their industry which tended to be of the extractive kind. As Ocic has shown, this underpricing of agriculture and raw materials, which followed the Soviet model of development, ensured that rapid industrial development with the fastest possible results (that is, in the DRs) could proceed apace. The result for the LDRs was that underdeveloped and already relegated to a position of dependency, their chances for bridging the economic disparity were further undermined.

1960s: Ethnonationalism and Economic Interests in a Changing Society

In the second decade of postwar development, the Yugoslav regime reaffirmed its goal of narrowing regional economic disparities and for the first time incorporated into the constitution the guarantee that it was the duty of the DRs to help in the development of the LDRs. Moreover, henceforth, development of the LDRs was to be ensured of a comprehensive treatment through a combination of measures, most importantly a Fund for Development which was to guarantee investment funds and grants-in-aid as well as an exchange of experts and expertise to help the LDRs in their developmental effort.

Nevertheless, despite these measures, by the end of the second decade of Yugoslav postwar development, economic disparities between the DRs and the LDRs as measured in terms of GMP per capita had once again increased. The explanation usually given by the Yugoslavs for the partial increase in economic inequality in the 1960s, despite both the Development Fund and other special measures designed to help the LDRs develop, and despite the decentralization which distributed power more equally among them, focuses on two related phenomena. Both of these, according to the respondents, were surprise developments that mandated adjustments in regional development policy. According to the Yugoslavs, attempts to resolve these two negative phenomena, the increase in ethnonationalism and the appearance of economic cycles, had to take priority, though they usually added that the goal of faster development of the LDRs was not short-changed in the process.

Ethnonationalism

Despite their "liberal" approach to the national question,[29] as Marxists, the Yugoslav Communists believed that ethnonationalism, that is, politicized ethnicity, a product of false consciousness of the bourgeois-capitalist stage of development, would be superceded almost automatically, with modernization and the establishment of the communist society, by a supranational (Yugoslav), and eventually international, proletarian consciousness. Thus, the CPY expected that, in time, the various nations would abandon willingly the narrow confines of ethnonationalism in favor of a common Yugoslav national identity. In the words of Slobodan Milic, Director of the Institute of Agricultural Economics in Belgrade, "After the war, the idea

29 "Liberal" in terms of forming a federation in which five of the six largest nations were granted republic status, recognition and, on paper at least, quasi-political sovereignty.

especially in Serbia and Montenegro was that Yugoslavia would be one country. . . that republics would be just a temporary thing."[30]

However, whereas for the central and regional party elites the issue of ethnonationalism was something which would be taken care of in the course of the development of the new Yugoslav socialist society, for the party rank and file and for the population at large, the traditionally deep-seated suspicion of and/or hostility toward foreign rule was partly assuaged by the federal solution which recognized most of the major ethnic groups as nations, granting them their own republics. Additionally, it was partly held in check by a still powerful and centralized CPY.

By the early 1960s, however, in the newly relaxed political climate, it became clear that the "National Question" had not been resolved. Neither the policy of *Jugoslovenstvo*, the attempt at cultural, historical and linguistic unitarism, nor the abandonment of this widely resented policy were able to attenuate ethnonationalism either among the party or among the general populace. In the prevailing atmosphere of open discussion over the direction of the economy and its implications on the polity, ethnonationalism was exacerbated when individual regions' interests were seen as being harmed by federal policies.

For the argument that ethnonationalism was, as some respondents claimed, responsible for the continuing regional economic inequality to be valid, the same ethnic-national group, or coalition of groups (at republic level), would have had to hold over a number of issues, when according to particular interests, one would have expected them to diverge. Diverge they did. The coalition of Serbia, Montenegro and Slovenia, which had held throughout the 1950s, fell apart over the issue of future direction of the Yugoslav economy and polity a few years later. In this case, Slovenia, Croatia and Vojvodina argued for decentralization of power in the polity and the introduction of the market in the economy, measures clearly meant to benefit their stronger economies.

By showing that despite the redistributive power of the centralized state of the 1950s, (except for Montenegro) "redistribution" had not benefitted the LDRs, the DRs were able to convince the LDRs that the Serbian argument of faster development of the LDRs within the centralized system was not convincing. Conversely, the DRs' argument that Serbian hegemonic tendencies were on the rise convinced both Bosnia-Hercegovina and Macedonia to cross over to the DRs on this issue and to vote for decentralization and the market. The price that

30 Slobodan Milic, Interview, Institute of Agricultural Economics, Belgrade, Serbia, September 8, 1983.

the LDRs exacted was the creation of a Development Fund to guarantee a consistent, predetermined amount of investment resources to aid in the narrowing of regional economic disparity. Thus, the shift in regional development policy in the mid-1960s was due to the convergence of ethnonationalism with regional economic interests, resulting in a realignment of actors who were then strong enough to pass the Economic Reform.

Furthermore, although the continuing Serb-Montenegrin alliance may indicate some support for the ethnic-national argument, it is argued here that while ethnic-national/cultural affinity may predispose these two toward each other, it is more often economic interests that create, maintain and break the alliance. This is corroborated by the divergence in the alliance in the 1980s over the issue of membership in the Development Fund. In this case, Montenegro, along with the other LDRs, bargained for continued membership in the Development Fund, while Serbia stood with the other DRs in negotiating the exclusion of all but Kosovo from the Development Fund.

The argument that ethnic-national alliances in Yugoslavia were in the final analysis based on economic interests rather than on cultural affinity is backed by socio-economic developments of the 1960s. The appearance of cycles in the Yugoslav economy of the early 1960s, which brought for the first time into the public arena a variety of economic interests, led to the first public formation of significant "interest groups" in postwar Yugoslavia. Although only a few respondents referred to the differences, stalemates and struggles of the 1960s in the context of the emergent "interest-group politics," used cautiously, the term is useful for understanding the changes in Yugoslav polity and society of the 1960s and beyond.[31]

Interest "Groups"

The autonomy of the groups and the restraint and accountability of the office holder, operating principles of a pluralistic polity, are the critical elements defining the presence, reliability and function of

[31]By the mid-1960s in an effort to gain more understanding of the changing nature of the Soviet system as well as to de-ideologize the study by putting it in a comparative perspective, Gordon Skilling, Frank Griffiths and other group theorists pointed to a new phenomenon in communist politics whereby policy on a given issue was the result of "interaction among conflicting tendencies of articulation," one of the signs of the pluralistic aspects of the system which would result in the narrowing of the gap between state and society. For more on the same see G. Skilling and F. Griffiths (eds.), *Interest Groups in Soviet Politics* (Princeton: Princeton University Press, 1971).

interest groups.[32] Were such groups present in Yugoslavia at any time in the past? Were they able to successfully lobby for their interests at the expense of the development of the LDRs? Can the interest group approach explain the continuing economic disparity between the DRs and the LDRs in Yugoslavia?

In the first period of CPY rule and up to the mid-1960s, while economic planning, resource allocation and commodity pricing were still determined by a centralized, ideologically defined state, articulation or manifestation of private interests was strictly limited by the state. Although that did not preclude a degree of reciprocity between the state and society, an example of which was the increase in consumerism in the late 1950s and the openness of the debates over the nationality question and over the direction of the economy in the early 1960s, that reciprocity was strictly dependent on the good will of the centralized state which remained largely independent of, and unaccountable to, society. And though the economic interests of certain republics and regions prevailed at the expense of others during this period, this was not the result of the successful articulation of demands by various social groups. Rather, political and bureaucratic elites of certain republics and regions were covertly able to influence policy in their interests by virtue of their access to and presence in the policy-making bodies at the federal center.

By the mid-1960s, however, the attempt of individual (republic and regional) members of the two "groups" to maximize their economic interests in the context of the debate over the Reform and the market had led to the creation of the Development Fund. Contrary to the intent of the federal decision-makers, the effect of the creation of the Development Fund was to further cement the particularized and now more clearly divergent "group" interests of the republics and regions into those of the developed regions, on the one side, and those of the less developed, on the other.

A number of important consequences followed for Yugoslav development in general, as well as more specifically for the development of the LDRs. At the general level of polity, the decentralization brought by the Reform created a "peripheralized

[32]For further elaboration of the above, as well as for a cogent and forceful criticism of the group approach to communist politics, see Andrew Janos, "Group Politics in Communist Society: A Second Look at the Pluralist Model," in Samuel P. Huntington and Clement H. Moore (eds.), *Authoritarian Politics in Modern Societ,y* (New York: Basic Books, 1970). Also; A. Janos, "Interest Groups and the Structure of Power: Critique and Comparisons," in *Studies in Comparative Communism*, Vol. XII, No. 1, Spring 1979.

federation"[33] or "confederation," in which the shift from federal to republic and regional centers resulted in the latter's virtual monopoly of power. The constitutional guarantee of equal representation of all federal units in both chambers of the federal legislature, and the requirement of unanimous consent on a substantial part of the federal legislation including changes in the constitution, effectively granted to republics and regions veto power over proposed federal legislation. Ironically, in the process, it enabled a minority to control/dominate the majority. Furthermore, the direct dependence of members of the top organs of both the federal government and the Communist Party on their regional organizations which elected them meant a decline in effectiveness of federal decision-makers. This occurred at the very time when the republics' and regions' power to veto legislation, which they perceived as impairing their short-term economic interests, created an increased need for a coordinating center. This led to a proliferation of particularized interests at regional levels and political immobilism at the federal center, as can be seen from the increasing amount of legislation that could not be agreed on and, therefore, was either not passed or was passed in greatly altered form and with great delay.

The devolution of power, thus, did not lead to an empowerment of workers and citizens[34] which would have led to real interest groups and true self-management; rather, it created regional and communal oligarchs. This in turn had two effects. The first is that the objectively different and often conflicting economic interests of the regions led to an increase in ethnonationalism with the consequent political and economic distortions of the system. The second was the attempt of regional elites to maintain and/or enhance their own power which frequently entailed their opposition to any reform of the system.[35] This limited the existence or viability of "interest groups" to those groups which could serve the local elite's purpose, thus severely limiting or even precluding the existence of "real," that is, independent, autonomous interest groups.

33 Vojislav Kosturica, "Transformation of Yugoslav Federalism from Decentralized to Peripheralized Federation," paper presented at the European Program of the Wilson Center, Smithsonian Institution, Washington, D.C., September 4-6, 1986.

34 Julie Mostov, "Regionalism and the Limits of Yugoslav Democracy," paper presented at the European Program of the Wilson Center, Smithsonian Institution, Washington, D.C., September 4-6, 1986.

35 This was reiterated time again in the interviews; it is also found in both earlier studies of the Yugoslav system such as that of Paul Shoup, 1968, and more recent Yugoslav and non-Yugoslav studies, among them Kosta Mihailovic, 1982; Ivan Simonovic, 1986; and Pedro Ramet, 1984.

This is not to say that "interest-group" activity was non-existent in Yugoslavia. Rooted in self-management, the pillar of Yugoslav socialism; indirectly guaranteed in the 1952, 1963 and 1974 Constitutions; and explicitly legitimized by Kardelj in 1977, "interest groups" were a fact of political life. Though always circumscribed, at times they exercised real power, for example regarding the decision to abandon the building of a nuclear plant near Zadar because of local opposition. However, most groups, such as trade unions, women's organizations, youth organizations and others, played the more traditional and marginal role of transmission belt for the regime. Furthermore, groups which strayed too far from this formula, like the *Praxis* group in the 1970s, risked losing their legitimacy, that is, being disbanded with some members imprisoned. One notable exception (in terms of being a vocal and powerful interest group) was the Veterans Organization whose power stemmed from the overlap and/or identity in membership of the Partisan veterans with the party/government/bureaucratic elite and made it one of the most influential groups in Yugoslavia.

In terms of regional development, the link between ethnonationalism and regional interests, especially economic ones, which by the mid-1960s had led to the passing of the Reform and the creation of the Development Fund as the best possible compromise, meant that the Development Fund's potential as coordinator in the development of the LDRs, and thus its potential as agent for "coherent" development, was undermined by the Fund's de facto status as the unofficial arena for articulation of regional economic interests.

To sum up, the sudden appearance of economic cycles in the early 1960s after a decade of unprecedented growth, and the obvious failure of the policy of *Jugoslovenstvo* as seen by the rise of ethnonationalism, brought to the fore the question of direction of Yugoslav polity and economy. The issue was settled in favor of decentralization. The resultant Reform, passed in 1965, was supposed to achieve maximization of economic rationality through the market, as well as political stability, by satisfying ethnonationalist aspirations through a devolution of power from the federation to the republics and regions. By taking power away from the federal center and giving it to the republics and regions, it was also thought by the LDRs that the equality among the republics and regions, would enable the LDRs to ensure the passing of measures necessary for enhancing their economic interests.

The result, however, was the opposite of what the LDRs had anticipated. That is, the market undermined the development of the LDRs since the result of its spontaneous operation was a gravitation of investments to the DRs. Furthermore, rather than increasing political stability, the devolution of power to the republics and regions further destabilized the federation because regional economic interests and ethnonationalism became even more intertwined. Since, on the one hand, major ethnic-national groups largely coincided with regional political boundaries, and economic interests of regions differed according to their varying levels of socio-economic development, while on the other, the increase in power of republics and regions at the expense of the federation enabled the former to pursue these often irreconcilable interests, a situation which could easily become explosive was created. Moreover, given the correspondence of regional economic interests with ethnic-national groups, the pursuit of regional economic interests tended to manifest itself in the rise of ethnonationalism as exemplified by, among others, the 1968 riots of Kosovo and the Slovenian Road Crisis.

Although the connections between economic interests and ethnonationalism are so complex that it is frequently difficult to separate them or to determine which is more important as a variable explaining "development," there is considerable evidence that economic interests were more often the cause, whose manifestation was ethnonationalism, and effect was the displacement of the goal of faster development of the LDRs and consequent increase in regional disparity. The argument that the rise of ethnonationalism was not responsible for the increase in regional disparity is underscored by the fact that no coalition based on ethnonationalism held across issues when economic interests were at stake. Thus, the resolution of the question of centralization vs. decentralization of the economy and polity split the alliance of Serbia, Slovenia and Montenegro; the issue of apportionment of the national GMP for credits and supplementary resources to the Development Fund split the DRs from the LDRs; and the issue of apportionment of the credits and supplementary resources from the Development Fund among the LDRs split the LDRs among themselves.

Nor were the DRs overwhelmingly concerned with the faster development of the LDRs when the development of the latter risked hurting their own economic interests. Thus, despite evidence that, as may have been expected, the market led to increased autarchy of development, "spontaneously" allocating a preponderant share of investment to the DRs, very little effort was undertaken to rechannel investments or to compensate the LDRs. As a result, throughout the entire postwar period, the LDRs continued to receive less investment per capita and fewer grants-in-aid, a situation that was not conducive to the narrowing of the economic inequalities between them and the DRs.

Thus, although the sharp downturn in the economy and the rise of ethnonationalism were serious domestic problems which thrust themselves into the limelight in the early 1960s, of themselves they would not have blocked the faster development of the LDRs for the entire decade. That they were able to do so was the result of the ability of the three most developed republics to ensure the passing of measures which would benefit their individual regional economic interests. Specifically, Slovenia, Croatia and Vojvodina's ability to convince the LDRs to vote for decentralization and the market by first "exposing" the threat of Serbian hegemony, then offering the Development Fund as a compensating economic measure for the market was, on the whole, more beneficial to the economies of the DRs than to those of the LDRs.

The relative increase in the political power which accrued to the LDRs as a result of the decentralization did not lead to a decrease in regional disparity, as this political power of the LDRs (with the exception of Montenegro) was not strong enough to compensate for the negative effects of the market. The subsequent withdrawal of the DRs from active participation in the development of the LDRs, leaving the latter to fend for themselves in a situation in which they could not effectively compete, undermined the possibility of accelerated development of the LDRs. The result was that on the whole, throughout this period as in the previous one, the disparity between the DRs and the LDRs failed to decrease.

1970s: Regional Interests, Economic and National

In the 1970s, Yugoslavia continued to grapple with domestic problems occasioned by the rise of ethnic-national tensions, the most serious one being the Croatian crisis of 1970-71. Once again, an economic issue, in this case Croatia's perception of being shortchanged in its foreign exchange allocation, as well as in the general capital disbursement, took on an ethnic-national manifestation. When this domestic crisis passed, the goal of regional development was not reinstated as a priority; instead, it was now displaced by the more overt, though still unacknowledged, pursuit of regional economic interests, facilitated by the 1965 Reform, subsequent amendments to the constitution, as well as by the ideological quasi-legitimation it received with Kardelj's "pursuit of self-managed interests."

As a result, even though both the Fifth and Sixth Five-Year Plans passed in the 1970s maintained as one of their main priorities the accelerated development of the LDRs, and the Constitution of 1974, like its predecessors, stipulated that it was the duty of the DRs to aid in the development of the LDRs, the economic disparity between the DRs and the LDRs once again failed to narrow. Further, the economic disparity between the most developed republic, Slovenia, and the least developed region, Kosovo, which by 1970 had increased to 1:6, had further increased by the end of the decade to 1:7.

The reasons given by the Yugoslavs for the continuing and generally increasing economic disparity in the 1970s span the range of explanations examined for the 1950s and 1960s. These are: ethnonationalism with particular reference to the Croatian crisis of 1970-71 and the later Kosovo crisis; overall economic decline and the need to maximize development of Yugoslavia as a whole; the increasing international competition and Yugoslavia's growing trade deficit; the shift in official ideology towards greater acceptance of inequality and partial encouragement of the pursuit of individual economic interests; and lastly, and most frequently either mentioned alone or in conjunction with other reasons, the lack of a "coherent plan" or "model" for the development of the LDRs.

What remains most striking about the Yugoslav recognition of these different factors as having contributed to the failure of regional equalization is the unacknowledged explanation, that of *economic regionalism*. Regional pursuit of economic interests, the implicit (and often explicit) link in the various explanations given by the Yugoslavs to account for continuing regional inequality, was alluded to by almost all the respondents throughout Yugoslavia; furthermore, as the following sample taken from interviews shows, it was stated overtly by many in the course of the interviews.

> Each republic is responsible for its own development and naturally they see things differently. It's not easy to harmonize interests in the same milieu . . . and it's so much more difficult in these different milieus we have in Yugoslavia.[36] Ivan Turcic, Professor of Economics at the University of Zagreb, Croatia.

> . . . different interests of developed and less developed. . . . The developed want to give the least possible or that what they give will be useful to them . . . All (republics and regions) have their own interests . . . and all are economically independent, and that's irreconcilable.[37] Misa Mitrovic, Planning Ministry of Vojvodina.

36 Ivan Turcic, Interview, Faculty of Economics, Zagreb, Croatia, September 27, 1983.
38 Misa Mitrovic, Interview, Republic Bureau for Social Planning, Novi Sad, Vojvodina, November 15, 1983.

Economic interests always coincide with republic interests.[38] Oskar Kovac, Professor of Economics, University of Belgrade and member of the inner groups of thirteen for Krajger's Commission for the Economic Stabilization of Yugoslavia.

The Fund for development was created so late because it was necessary to have consensus and that was difficult because of different interests.[39] Hasan Berisa, Director, Kosovo Planning Ministry.

The Fund for development is not a matter of Solidarity, but of everyone's interest.[40] Radovan Milanovic, Professor of Economics at University of Sarajevo, former Head of the Economics Institute in Sarajevo, member in the Executive Council of Bosnia-Hercegovina (1982-86).

Settlement (of issues) has to do with different interests and with money.[41] Ljubislav Markovic, former member of the Federal Executive Council, head of committee for social planning and development in the Federal Assembly and member of the inner group of thirteen for Krajger's Commission for the Economic Stabilization of Yugoslavia.

Since there are different levels of development, decisions will always have to be made by agreement . . . by a meeting of different interests.[42] Maurice Romano, member of the Presidency of The League of Communists of Macedonia, former ambassador to Chile, and republic delegate to the federal parliament.

Development of the LDRs is in the interests of all, as well as a matter of solidarity . . . LDRs differ among themselves. Behind the differences are interests and the desire for more means.[43] Andrej Briski, Assistant to the Director, Slovenian Planning Ministry.

38 Oskar Kovac, Interview, Faculty of Economics, Belgrade, Serbia, January 12, 1983.

39 Hasan Berisa, Interview, Kosovo Planning Ministry, Pristina, Kosovo, October 17, 1983.

40 Radovan Milanovic, Interview, Republic Parliament Building, Sarajevo, Bosnia-Hercegovina (BiH), June 10, 1983.

41 Ljubislav Markovic, Interview, Faculty of Economics, Belgrade, Serbia, December 15, 1982.

42 Maurice Romano, Interview, Republic Parliament and L.C.Y. Building, Skopje, Macedonia, May 11, 1983.

43 Andrej Briski, Interview, Slovenian Planning Ministry, Ljubljana, Slovenia, November 8, 1983.

You know, Yugoslavia is a very differentiated country . . .what's good for Slovenia and what they want, may not be good for Montenegro . . . . If a person doesn't represent the interest of his region, when he returns he won't have his position.[44] Budislav Soskic, Head of the Academy of Sciences of Montenegro, Professor of Economics at the University of Belgrade and member of the inner group of thirteen for Krajger's Commission for the Economic Stabilization of Yugoslavia.

We need a policy to solve the conflict in interests between those who have raw materials and those who produce secondary goods.[45] Klime Corbe, Head of the Federal Fund for the Development of the LDRs.

As these interview excerpts indicate, Yugoslav decision-makers recognized both the existence of various, often contradictory, economic interests and their regionally defined presence, despite the official unwillingness to acknowledge them. How can this unwillingness to recognize the impact of *economic regionalism* be accounted for when the cost of that unwillingness was failure to devise adequate policies for the faster development of the LDRs, resulting in repeated failure of their goal of regional equalization? In order to answer this question, we now turn to an examination of what for the Yugoslavs was the critical link between economic interests and the major ethnic-national groups inhabiting the republics and regions of Yugoslavia.

As mentioned earlier, when the Socialist Federative Republic of Yugoslavia was created, five of the six largest ethnic groups were recognized as nations,[46] and the six recognized nations had each been granted republic status, and with it quasi-political sovereignty. These eight political units, six republics with two additional regions attached to the republic of Serbia, thus became national homelands within a "supra-national" state. In the relatively close correspondence between ethnic group, nation and political boundary, political boundary was the framework within which increasingly from the mid-1960s and especially from the mid-1970s most of the political and economic power resided. At the federal level, coordination and harmonization (*usaglasavanje*) of views and interests were supposed to ensure that an overall Yugoslav policy emerged.

[44] Budislav Soskic, Interview, Academy of Sciences, Titograd, Montenegro, May 18, 1983.

[45] Klime Corbe, Interview, Federal Fund for Development of LDRs, Belgrade, Serbia, May 9, 1983.

[46] The Kosovo Albanians, who number three times the Montenegrins, were the exception who had neither the status of nation nor a separate republic within the Yugoslav federation.

However, given that both the historical background and the more recent social and economic differences between the republics and regions were so great, it was to be expected that both world views and material interests would differ, and that in the process, they would often give rise to sharp disagreements over policy formulation and implementation. The fact that these disagreements occurred between groups distinct in either ethnicity, national status or both and that, furthermore, these groups inhabited their own politically defined "homelands," that is, republics or regions, created the framework for a potentially adversarial relationship between the republics and regions.

Furthermore, the harmonization of interests that was supposed to take place through consensual decision-making was difficult to achieve, for whenever the goal of faster development of the LDRs collided with the maximization of one's own regional interests, the latter almost always won out.[47] Given that, with the republics' and regions' different levels of development, very few policies were equally beneficial to all, conflicts of regional interests were a constant that the regime had to negotiate. The result of this "negotiation" in the pre-Reform period, as we have seen, was legislation reflecting the economic interests of the politically stronger republics; thus, Slovenia and, to a lesser extent, Serbia were successful in getting policies passed which were beneficial to their development, while Montenegro was compensated through high investments and allocation of other grants. In the post-Reform decentralized Yugoslavia, when formally all the republics and regions had equal power, the LDRs still found it more difficult to maximize their economic interests. For despite the greater regional political equality, the laws of the market, in conjunction with the government withdrawal from allocative and other developmental responsibilities, meant that the LDRs' ability to compete effectively was undermined.

As a result, despite consistent proclamations and "good intentions" for regional equalization, pursuit of regional interests for the purpose of maximizing the development of one's own region displaced effective pursuit of faster development of the LDRs and, along with it, that of regional equalization. This conclusion is congruent with the findings of a study by Pedro Ramet, who examined the unlikely coexistence of stability and virulent crises in the multi-national Yugoslav "confederation."[48] Ramet, who studied twenty-one controversies and crises in Yugoslav inter-republican relations during the twenty-year

[47] The exception has been Kosovo, on whose critical need for development all agreed.
[48] Ramet, 1984, pp. 228-229.

period of 1963-83 and tested ten hypotheses derived from Kaplan's balance-of-power model, concluded that, "Throughout these crises the republics and autonomous provinces displayed autonomy of decision-making and willingness to realign in shifting coalitions according to perceived changes of interest." For our purpose it is not necessary to examine all the postulated hypotheses and their correlation with the crises. Suffice it to point out that Ramet's cross-tabulation of the ten hypotheses with the twenty-one controversies shows the strongest corroboration for the two hypotheses dealing with regional interests.

Specifically, the first hypothesis, which states that "federal units promote their own interests even when they conflict with the interests of the federal community," was fully confirmed in nineteen of the twenty-one crises and partially confirmed in the remaining two. The second hypothesis, that "federal units negotiate but provoke crises if necessary to protect their interests" was fully confirmed in sixteen cases and partially confirmed in another two. Although in the cases examined by Ramet these interests were not solely economic, they held for all cases where they were economic, except over aid to Kosovo on which all republics and regions agreed.[49]

The thesis of Ramet's work is thus congruent with the thesis being advanced here. This thesis is not that interests other than economic ones do not exist or that non-economic interests are not important to understand either Yugoslav politics in general, or more specifically, the politics of regional development. Rather, the thesis advanced here is that *economic regionalism*, that is, *the pursuit of one's own region's economic interests, explains better than any other factor the Yugoslav socialist regime's overall failure in narrowing regional economic inequalities.*

1980s: Economic Regionalism and the Disintegration of Yugoslavia

Despite the Yugoslavs' attempt at separating regional development from "politics," as the 1980s were to demonstrate, the two proved inseparable. The decade began with the riots in Kosovo where a high unemployment rate of 27.5%, in a climate of general underdevelopment and the increasing economic disparity between Kosovo and the other republics and regions, especially the developed ones, brought students to the streets. The brutal suppression of the student strikes turned the economic grievances into broader ethnonationalist ones for political

49 This coincides with information obtained in interviews held throughout Yugoslavia during 1982-83.

autonomy through republic status. Henceforth, for the Albanian Kosovars, Kosovo's economic underdevelopment remained linked to their ethnonational suppression by Serbia.

With the steadily declining economy through the 1980s, and an increasingly malfunctioning polity, the link between economic and ethnonational discrimination was increasingly hinted at by all. In regions where it coincided with an increase in economic inequality, as it did by then in all the LDRs except Montenegro, the linkage was particularly dangerous.

With a sharply deteriorating situation and the rise of Slobodan Milosevic in Serbia, concern for regional equalization through faster development of the LDRs dwindled. It, and most everything else, was soon superseded by Milosevic's unabashed exploitation of latent Serbian ethnonationalist sentiments. His initial linkage of ethnonationalism with economic mismanagement was soon broadened to include the claim of ethnonational oppression of Serbs in Kosovo. Economic impoverishment, a lack of leadership alternatives and an increasingly chaotic domestic situation aided Milosevic in mobilizing the Serbian masses against the "enemy." That enemy was first defined in 1988 as the Albanian "irredenta." Then, in late 1988, Slovenia was accused of economic exploitation of Serbia. Finally in 1990, charges of economic and political discrimination of Serbs living in Croatia were made against the Croatian government. When these were revised in early 1991 to include genocide of Serbs living in Croatia, the stage was set for the break-up of Yugoslavia.

Despite four decades of socialist effort at regional equalization through faster development of the LDRs, the Yugoslav regime failed to narrow economic inequalities between the developed and the less developed; this, despite relatively favorable domestic and international conditions. That is, the CPY came to power as leader of a movement that encompassed both national liberation and socialist revolution; thus, it was committed for both ideological and pragmatic reasons to the creation of a unified, egalitarian and socialist society. Furthermore, under the strong and stable leadership of Tito and a small cohesive elite at the head of a well-disciplined party, one would expect that regional equalization, the prerequisite for economic and, according to the Yugoslavs, for political equality, would have been followed forcefully from the beginning. As we have seen, such was not the case.

The reason in the pre-Reform Yugoslavia of 1945-65 is that when the federal center was strong enough to act as an agent of equalization, its regionally biased composition and subsequently biased representation of interests worked to the disadvantage of the development of the LDRs. Thus, regional equalization was not pursued forcefully from the beginning with the resultant opportunity cost for the LDRs.

In the post-Reform period of Yugoslav development, 1965-90, despite the relative equalization of political power, the center which had become far more representative of all republics and regions was also too fragmented to pursue policies of economic equalization. Furthermore, the possible benefits of the political equalization on the economies of the LDRs were now undermined by the effect of the market, which, in the absence of strong government interference, could not decrease the inequalities between the "haves" and the "have nots." Although political equalization of the republics and regions, the reliance on consensus in decision-making and the "ethnic key" factor acquired in this process, along with the additional "compensatory" measures of aid like the Development Fund and, later, preferential access to World Bank loans, did mitigate the negative effects of the market, without a more comprehensive approach to the problem and a concerted effort from the DRs they could not overcome them.

As a result, according to the original goal of regional economic equalization through faster development of the LDRs, the Yugoslavs' forty-five year effort at regional development has been a qualified failure. Of all the LDRs, only Montenegro, which throughout the postwar period secured far more than its share of resources, narrowed the gap with the DRs. For Macedonia the gap narrowed in employment, remained the same in fixed assets and increased in GMP per capita. Both Bosnia-Hercegovina and Kosovo fell further behind on all three counts (Table 5.3) and the gap in GMP per capita between the most developed republic, Slovenia, and the least developed region, Kosovo, had increased by 1990 to 1:8.

Although these results, which at first glance may appear quite disastrous, are mitigated by the fact that the LDRs had a respectable growth rate which moreover was slightly higher than that of the DRs (Table 6.2) and that it was their high birth rate which skewed the development picture, this is only part of the story. For even without the per capita factor, the growth rate in fixed assets, in employment and especially in GMP would have had to have been much higher in the LDRs than in the DRs, if the narrowing of inequalities was to have occurred.

As for the high population growth in the LDRs, although it made the narrowing of inequalities much more difficult to achieve, it is important to note that high birth rate which is perpetuated by underdevelopment is a problem which the regime failed to address. The failure to address this problem in the first twenty years, before political decentralization made a united policy from the center difficult to arrive at or implement, is one more indication of the lesser importance granted to the issue of regional development. It proved also to be a missed opportunity for which the regime was to pay a high cost. One consequence of the high birth rate in the LDRs, (especially high in Kosovo) was the increasing unemployment which, in conjunction with the declining economy in the 1980s, led to unrest. This was most evident in Kosovo, where the economic grievances of the unemployed, often educated, highly disaffected and mostly young people became politicized and took on an ethnonationalist turn.

Other regime policies which followed as a result of the Soviet influenced ideological blinders, such as the pursuit of capital-intensive industries, especially in the LDRs, along with the undermining of agriculture, the underpricing of raw materials and the push for rapid urbanization, led to waste of scarce resources and a skewed development at great cost to the Yugoslav economy as a whole. In the LDRs where investment planning was even more critical and where the economies were most dependent on production of raw materials and agriculture, the cost of sometimes misguided and other times uninterested development policies was that much higher.

One of the ways that the Yugoslavs dealt with this failure of their original goal, as defined in the early days when revolutionary zeal and *élan* were thought sufficient to attain the impossible, was through redefinition of that goal. That the goal of regional equalization had been redefined away from equalization in development between the DRs and the LDRs is seen in the shift of methods and goals of regional development policy which began in the mid-1970s and increased rapidly thereafter; it was also corroborated by the interviews. Thus, in the 1980s, there was increasing pressure for direct cooperation in projects between the DRs and the LDRs, replacing the disbursement of grants and loans to the LDRs through the Development Fund. Furthermore, respondants, especially those in the DRs and at the Federal level, consistently characterized as overly idealistic and "immature" the early goal of regional equalization and, *all* agreed that the goal of equalization was to be abandoned in favor of an agreement on specific criteria and indices by which to measure development levels and thus determine membership in the "club" of the LDRs. What was still lacking until the very end, however, was an agreement on what these threshold levels would be and thus, on who would continue to receive developement aid.

More than ten years after the question of criteria and threshold was first raised and almost a decade after the studies commissioned to determine the criteria and threshhold in all the republics and regions had been completed, three missed five-year plan deadlines later, the threshold of development had still not been agreed on. Even the prestigious Krajger Commission had been unable to reach a consensus concerning the threshold of development at the time of the presentation of its report in July, 1983. As a result, for the second time in a decade, the republics and regions were requested by the Federal Executive Council to submit proposals so that,

> . . . by the end of 1986, the Assembly of SFRY shall adopt a decision on the criteria, indices, and upper and lower limits for determining the level of economic development of the republics and autonomous provinces, on the basis of which it will be decided which republics and autonomous provinces are to be considered economically underdeveloped in the period after 1990.[50]

The decision was finally arrived at in late 1990. By then, however, payments to the Fund had effectively ceased to be made and, in the increasingly volatile political climate, regional development ceased to concern all but the less developed.

This continued inability to reach an agreement on the development threshold once again highlights the difficulty of reconciling the differing interests between republics and regions in the former Yugoslav federation, especially when those interests were economic. It also provides one more piece of evidence supporting the argument made throughout this study that enhancing, or at least safeguarding, one's own regional economic interests was the main priority of the republics and regions and, as such, accounts for the displacement of the goal of faster development of the LDRs for the purpose of regional equalization.

Pointing to these problems, however, does not diminish the progress that had been made in the development of the LDRs. Indeed, one of the striking aspects of the interviews was the degree to which all the respondents, even those of the LDRs as well as, more predictably, the ones in the DRs and at the federal level, had high praise for the general social transformation which had occurred in the LDRs over the past forty years.[51] Many began with statements like "You cannot imagine how much things have changed..." or "You could not have recognized this place from what it was thirty years ago." Often, at

50 The Development Plan of Yugoslavia, 1986-1990, Part Two, Section X, p. 96

51 This was much more true during the first phase of the interview process in 1982-83. From 1988 and on it was replaced by the fear that the growing Yugoslav economic crisis would wipe out all their gains.

this point the tone of voice was instinctively, almost imperceptibly, lowered in awe at the broad spectrum of changes that had occurred in the speaker's lifetime. Additionally there are, of course, the standard indicators of development which show in graphic form the magnitude and extent of this qualitative change (Table 6.1).

Nevertheless, although the LDRs acknowledged that a great deal was accomplished, they also noted that much still remained to be done, for the goal of equalization was more than ever out of reach (Table 5.3). As a result, fear that decreasing the pressure for resources would forever leave them hopelessly behind the DRs in development, kept the LDRs from doing so; it also made compromise more difficult to achieve. Simultaneously, the DRs insistance that their own growth rate had been declining and that continuing aid to the no-longer-so-less-developed LDRs would result in their own economic decline, as well as in the decline of the Yugoslav economy as a whole, made them increasingly intransigent as well. Thus, the fear of falling further behind ensured that both the DRs and the LDRs continued to first and foremost pursue their individual regional economic interests at the expense of both development of the LDRs as well as, in the long run, development of the Yugoslav economy as a whole.

Conclusion

This study has focused on the internal factors which have shaped the Yugoslav postwar policy regarding one--albeit, it is argued here, central--issue, that of regional economic disparity. The study found that despite favorable circumstances in terms of regime goal, capacity and commitment to regional equalization in a political situation of leadership continuity and regime stability, under both centralized and decentralized forms of rule, the goal of regional economic equalization proved to be elusive. The reason, as has been shown, is that despite generally "good intentions" and a relatively favorable domestic and international environment, when regional economic interests conflicted, as they did most often, the priority of enhancing one's own region's economic interests won out.

The Yugoslavs' refusal to explicitly acknowledge the pursuit of regional economic interests was a result of their fears that acknowledging regional economic rivalries could be tantamount to condoning them and that in the multi-ethnic-national Yugoslav federation these regional economic interests could then take on a more uncontrollable ethnonationalist and separatist direction. The specter of civil war and national disintegration continued to loom over the Yugoslav socialist regime throughout its forty-five years of rule. As a result, the regime consciously pursued what amounted to partial and haphazard politics of regional development, the unintended effect of which was to lead to an increase in regional economic inequalities. Although contrary to both the professed goal of the regime and, as evidence of positive regime measures has shown, to its intentions as well, these ad hoc policies were still seen as preferable to the feared alternative of socio-political disintegration.

"Because republic interests are too strong, there has been no commitment to regional development."[52] This statement by Nikola Kljusev, member of the sub-group for the study of regional development in the Krajger Commission, was reiterated in a less direct but no less clear manner by Nikola Stanic, Minister of Agriculture of Serbia, according to whom, "certain realities fly in the face of socialist illusions."[53] Thus, while the LDRs did receive aid in their developmental effort and while impressive results in their development did occur, as general indicators of development show and as all the respondents in DRs and LDRs pointed out, the disparity between the DRs and the LDRs, according to the official indicators of development, did not decrease. On the contrary, for all except Montenegro and in part for Macedonia, *economic inequality* as measured by social sector employment per thousand, GMP per capita and fixed assets per worker, the three indicators of development used by the Yugoslavs, actually *increased*.

To conclude, this study suggests that even for a socialist regime which for both ideological and pragmatic reasons may wish to pursue the goal of regional economic equalization, the prospect of equalization through faster development of the LDRs in both a centralized and a decentralized-type polity will be difficult to achieve. The centralized state may have the capacity to push through policies necessary for equalization; it may ultimately, however, lack the commitment. The federal elite, which will tend to be drawn predominantly from the regions supportive of the regime, will, even if unconsciously, tend to promote the interests of their regions at the expense of the others. Thus, regime capacity for equalization may be undermined by interests of the politically stronger.

With decentralization of power to constituent republics and regions, despite the increase in political equality, the economically weaker regions will, in the absence of a strong redistributive center, remain at a

[52] Nikola Kljusev, Interview, Faculty of Economics, Skopje, Macedonia. May 11, 1983.
[53] Nikola Stanic, Interview, Secreteriat of Agriculture, Belgrade, Serbia. August 27, 1983.

Table 6.1
Basic Indicators of Development

	Years	SFRJ	BiH	Montenegro	Croatia	Macedonia	Slovenia	Serbia Whole	Serbia Proper	(Serbia) Kosovo	(Serbia) Vojvodina
Population	1953 1988	100 100	16.7 18.8	2.5 2.7	23.2 19.9	7.7 8.9	8.8 8.2	41.1 41.5	26.3 24.8	4.8 8	10 8.7
GMP	1953 1988	100 100	14.4 12.8	1.8 2.0	26.7 25.4	5.2 5.6	14.3 16.7	37.63 37.5	25.4 25.0	2.2 2.2	10 10.3
GMP per capita	1953 1988	100 100	83 68	77 74	122 128	68 63	175 203	86 90	91 101	43 27	94 119
Average growth of GMP as a whole per capita	1956 1988	4.9 4	4.6 3.3	5 3.9	4.6 4.8	5.1 4.1	5.2 4.5	5.1 4.2	5.1 4.3	5.1 2.6	5.3 4.8
Fixed assets per worker	1952 1987*	100 100	82 94.9	46 136.6	101 109.9	69 74.2	122 133.7	106 82.0	112 91.0	89 91.8	95 101.6
Live births per 1,000	1947 1988*	26.1 15.1	35.1 15.3	28.9 15.8	22.4 12.8	35.0 18.5	22.4 14.2	25.1 15.6	23.1 12.6	38.5 29.1	24.4 11.5
Deaths per 1,000	1947 1988*	13.9 9	22.3 6.3	22.0 5.9	8.9 11.4	21.3 7.1	8.9 10.2	12.8 9.4	12.0 10.0	25.5 5.1	9.2 11.4

Infant deaths per 1,000 live births	1949 1988*	102. 24.5	125.6 16.1	41.0 15.6	112.0 12.4	136.1 44.7	81.3 11.4	107.1 30.9	91.2 21.6	133.0 51.8	129.7 11.0
Participation of women in total labor force (in percentage)	1952 1981	24.3 36.1	15.7 32.0	20.0 32.6	27.9 39.6	16.7 31.0	32.3 44.5	23.1 33.6	21.7 34.3	10.5 20.7	29.2 36.0
Illiterate population 8-10 years and over (in prcentage)	1948 1981	25.4 9.5	44.9 14.5	26.4 9.4	15.6 5.6	40.3 10.9	2.4 0.8	26.8 10.9	27.4 11.1	62.5 17.6	11.8 5.8
Households per radio subscriber	1947 1980	16.2 1.5	45.5 2.1	81.2 2.0	12.3 1.4	23.2 1.5	8.5 1.2	18.5 1.4	16.1 1.5	88.1 2.4	20.2 1.1
Inhabitants per doctor	1952 1987	2565 534	3314 680	4473 674	1947 477	4324 530	1704 496	2440 515	2104 440	8527 1092	2556 511
Percentage of births with medical assistance	1952 1979	38.7 86.9	16.9 84.1	25.9 91.9	59.6 98.9	23.3 79.5	97.1 99.6	36.2 82.1	28.0 94.3	9.3 51.3	83.7 99.4
Life Expectancy: Male Female	1952- 1954	56.9 59.3	52.6 54.8	58.4 59.9	59.1 63.2	54.9 55.1	63.0 68.1	57.1 58.8	59.1 61.1	48.6 45.3	58.3 62.1
Life Expectancy Male Female	1980- 1987	67.66 73.23	67.44 73.01	71.94 76.37	66.64 74.15	66.64 75.16	67.34 75.16	68.05 72.68	69.44 73.93	68.06 71.48	67.14 73.15

Based on 1987 Data

Sources: SZZS, Statisticki godisnjak Jugoslavije, 1982.
SZZS, Statisticki godisnjak Jugoslavije, 1989.

Table 6.2
Growth of GMP 1948-1988 (in 1972 prices)

	1948-1965		1966-1988	
	Index	Average Yearly Growth	Index	Average Yearly Growth
Yugoslavia	304	6.4	241	3.9
BiH	283	5.9	238	3.8
Montenegro	268	5.6	244	3.9
Macedonia	309	6.5	265	4.3
Kosovo	272	5.7	259	4.2
Croatia	322	6.7	231	3.7
Slovenia	318	6.6	257	4.2
Serbia	287	6.0	241	3.9
Vojvodina	319	6.7	227	3.6

Source: Evropski Centar za mir i razvoj, Belgrade 1991, p. 22.

disadvantage, as the effects of the market will tend to relegate them to a secondary, and less competitive, position. This is most likely to be true for multi-ethnic-national states, especially when the ethnic-national groups coincide with regional (political) boundaries. The result will be that in the absence of both state capacity and state commitment, *economic regionalism,* that is, pursuit of one's own regional economic interests will dominate and thus undermine the regional development of the less developed, despite ideological commitment, pragmatic considerations or sincere, though vague, notions of good intentions.

Appendix I: A Note on Methods

First, I want to clarify the aims and limits of this study. The title of the book is *Regional Development in Communist Yugoslavia: Success, Failure, and Consequences*.

Throughout Yugoslavia's postwar development there was considerable debate over the lack of an adequate or "coherent" theory of regional development[1]. The result of this lack, it was often claimed, was a faulty approach which focused on regions as politically defined rather than economically determined. Although this issue is examined in Chapter 6 inasmuch as it bears on Yugoslav accounts of the failings of regional development policy, *Regional* in this study refers to the formal political boundaries of republics and regions. This in no way indicates my own position on this issue. Rather, since the given framework was itself part of the politics of regional development in Yugoslavia, it made most sense to adopt it for this study; more practically, it was also the unit for which data was available. In addition, it is to be noted that *Regional Development* is the subject of this study, and not the overall economic development of Yugoslavia. The latter will be treated only as it pertains to regional development and its effects on the narrowing of regional inequalities.

The period examined is that of Communist rule (1945-1990) hence the *Communist Yugoslavia* of the title. However, since 1945-1947 marked the reconstruction period, the study begins with the promulgation of the First Five-year Plan in 1947.

Failure, because according to the regime's own criteria, fixed assets per worker, social sector employment and GMP per capita, the goal of regional equalization through faster development of the less developed republics and the region of Kosovo (LDRs) failed.

Success, because even though the regime did not meet its original goal of equalizing development levels between republics and regions through faster

[1]Although the term *regional development* connotes the development of both republics and autonomous regions,and these are usually referred to seperately, there are frequent references to "*region*" alone. It is implicitly understood that, within the context, the broader meaning of *region*, that is, republic or autonomous region is then employed.

development of the LDRs, nevertheless, development in the LDRs did occur (Table 6.1 and 6.2).

It, however, was not enough to mitigate the haphazard and partial policy of development of the LDRs. The consequence was the growing gap between the republics and regions which, in the multi-ethnic-national Yugoslav federation, took on a political significance with disastrous *consequences* for all.

Second, issues concerning definition, criteria and evaluation of regional disparity have been handled in the following way. I have taken the regime's own definition of equality to examine how it changed over time, from equality as sameness to equality as equal opportunity and examined the effects of the changed definition on the development of the LDRs. I have also taken the regime's own criteria for measuring regional inequality both in terms of *effort,* fixed assets per worker, and *effect*, as measured by social sector employment per thousand and GMP per capita. Thus, the evaluation of the regime's performance is based on its own criteria, rather than on any potential personal bias.

The research for this study was begun in the fall of 1982 when Yugoslavia was a communist country; and even though it was a relatively open communist country, nevertheless certain peculiarities common to one-party states had to be confronted. Consequently, the *research method* devised had to take into account the more restricted access to sources of information and, more importantly still, the interviewing technique had to elicit information which might be more deeply hidden in what the decision-makers had to say. In other words, because of the correspondence of regional political boundaries with ethnic-national groups and the resulting fear of openly discussing regional development because of its inflammatory potential, it was anticipated that decision-makers might avoid such issues because they were afraid that they might "get into trouble" if they expressed their opinion or "divulged" "compromising" information. Other reasons for anticipating less than full and open discussion were the possibilities that their information could be used by others within or outside their region either personally against them or against the interests of their region; or that by presenting a view of a factionalized Yugoslav federation, they could be inadvertently undermining the image and therefore the interests of the country to outsiders, especially those who, in the words of a number of respondents, "may wish to see the Yugoslav experiment fail."[2]

The first major point of potential controversy centers on the *definition* of equality. First, does equality presuppose the *same* regional configuration in

[2] There was some fear or concern of the above for about two thirds of those interviewed in 1982-83. In the later years the number declined sharply.

urbanization, social services, income and other such indicators, or can it mean the *equivalent* configuration based on the regional division of labor? The obvious problem with the latter definition is who decides what is "equivalent." Second, is equality to be measured by "*effort*," that is by government spending in the LDRs, or by "*effect*," or impact of that spending? One complicating factor here is "efficiency," both a cause and an effect of the developmental level and in turn dependent on, among other things, the structure of investment. Third, is the thrust of equalization to be directed at *productive forces* or at the *social services*?

Closely tied to these conceptual issues concerning the definition of equality is the *selection of criteria* to *measure* regional inequality or the equalization process. Does one look at GMP per capita, employment, longevity, number of hospital beds, increase in output of electricity? Although long lists are useful for giving a composite picture, a selection must necessarily take place.

The third difficulty is the choice of appropriate *statistical measures* to evaluate regional data. The importance of this can be illustrated by the following simple example. If we look at disparity in GMP per capita between the most and least developed in Yugoslavia, Slovenia and Kosovo respectively, we see that during the forty-year period from 1950 to 1990 it increased from 1:3 to more than 1:8. Accordingly, one might conclude that regional inequality increased sharply in the forty-five year period of Communist rule. Yet, if we measure the dispersion among the LDRs and compare the GMP of each to the Yugoslav average, the picture is not so bleak. For some the disparity has decreased; for others it has increased in certain respects. For example, in terms of per capita GMP, employment and fixed assets the disparity between Kosovo and all other republics and regions has increased, though the increase was largely due to the high population growth, despite Kosovo's respectable record of economic growth.

The fourth conceptual issue centers on the *standard of evaluation* by which to judge regional equalization. Although the choice of standard of evaluation is potentially the most subjective aspect of the methodology, accepted criteria derived from the literature on development or from the regime's own criteria of development can insure against the researcher's idiosyncratic or biased choice.

Given the anticipated reluctance on the part of respondents to address the questions fully and openly, a principal research objective was to obtain as much documented information as possible. For that, objective indicators of commitment in terms of investment and investment per capita in the development of the LDRs, as well as other development-oriented measures, were examined as were the indicators of the development level achieved, the "hard data" obtained from statistical bulletins and the statistical index which illustrate the results of the above. In addition, both semi-classified and published documents obtained in such places as the ministries, banks, research institutes and the Development Fund at both republic/regional and federal levels were used, sometimes directly to illustrate the discrepancy between general claims and specific policies promulgated or implemented, other times indirectly to clarify the politics of decision-making surrounding regional development.[3] Of course, secondary sources, articles and books written over the forty-five year period on regional development or pertaining to it, such as debates on agriculture vs. industry as a strategy for development or on development of the economy as a whole, were consulted to increase understanding of the problem of regional development.

The main part of the research and the most significant in terms of making a contribution to an understanding of regional development in Yugoslavia, and in a broader sense to Yugoslav decision-making, consisted of in-depth interviews with 105 Yugoslav decision-makers involved in regional development. The first group of people interviewed were selected on the basis of a list of those accorded the most prominence in the literature on Yugoslav regional development. In addition, the list of influentials was expanded on the basis of names consistently cited in the course of the interviews.

A second line of selection of interviewees was based on the formal positions held in the bureaucracies, political bodies and research centers. Here an individual was targeted first according to the position held irrespective of expertise; and second and parallel to each main official, one or two subordinates were sought-out whose expertise level and willingness to impart information were often significantly greater. The tactic of separate interviews of both the official "expert" or head of the group, as well as of one or two subordinates, was important since the top bureaucratic and political positions were held by political appointees for a term of four or eight years on the basis of the Yugoslav nationality "key." Thus, the group was as likely to be made up of people who had neither the knowledge nor the commitment to regional development that the subordinates, usually there for the long haul and possessing expertise as well as interest and commitment to the problem, tended to have.

The majority of the people interviewed can be grouped into three categories: (a) *academics and other intellectuals* in universities and research institutes who wrote on the problem of regional disparity;[4] (b) *bureaucrats* who staffed the work groups of the planning ministries and who formulated the short-, medium- and long-term development plans for regional development; and (c) *politicians* who, through a complex and often convoluted process of consensus building, were responsible for the final formulation and, along with

[3] At the request of the correspondents, not all of these classified and semi-classified sources are listed in the bibliography.

[4] Of the respondents, about one-half can be classified as academics and intellectuals, one third as bureaucrats and the remaining as politicians at the time of the interviews.

local bureaucrats, for the eventual implementation of the policies adopted. Additionally, a number of individuals outside these groups whose position and/or expertise in such diverse fields as banking, journalism, the industrial or agricultural industries and the chamber of commerce made them particularly suitable for providing additional insight into certain facets of regional development, were also interviewed.

The interviews averaged two to three hours each and many were followed up by a number of meetings over a ten-year period. They were conducted in all six republics and two autonomous regions of the former SFR of Yugoslavia as well as at the federal level in Belgrade. The major practical problems encountered were, first, ensuring that a meeting with all the targeted individuals took place; second, ensuring that the meeting would last longer than the perfunctory forty minutes that Yugoslav courtesy mandated; third, with bureaucrats and politicians, that it would occur on a one-to-one basis without the inhibiting presence of note-taking secretaries or subordinates. All of the main targeted people were interviewed, all of the interviews were of sufficient length for substantive issues to be raised, and all interviews were eventually conducted on a one-to-one basis.

Another practical difficulty confronted in this research project was how to elicit explanation and bring out the knowledge and experience which for a variety of political reasons the respondents did not generally want to divulge. Thus, the style or tone of the interview was as important as the questions pursued, and it was essential to establish an atmosphere of trust. In addition to ensuring that the interviews were held on a one-to-one basis, I eschewed the use of a tape recorder, instead taking a few notes and transcribing them in long form immediately at the end of each interview. This facilitated an informal exchange of information, more like a conversation than an interview, which became more pronounced as my own research progressed, and my already overall favorable position as "one of ours, interested in understanding and explaining to the outside what we are trying to do,"[5] was enhanced by the knowledge and information which I acquired in the various republics and regions. In the quasi-confederal Yugoslavia this information was as scarce and therefore as interesting to my respondents as theirs was to me. This free exchange was further facilitated by the fact that with my Yugoslav passport, I did not need to obtain special permission to go to the various government institutions; more importantly still, my respondents did not have to report that our conversation took place. The result was often an uninhibited exchange which frequently led to disclosure of confidential information, which, although at the request of some respondents is not used here directly, nevertheless contributed greatly both to the general understanding of the Yugoslavs'

[5] My American redentials (U.C. Berkeley and/or America) and "sympathetic to our situation" (Canada-Yugoslavia exchange fellowship gave added legitimacy).

perspectives on regional development as well as to the critical assessment of this perspective and of the politics and policy-making pertaining regional development.

A final note on research method concerns the actual questions put to the respondents. Two types of questions were used throughout the interviews. First, a series of six questions was asked, each consisting of two or three parts, whose main purpose was to bring out perceptions of respondents concerning the policies of regional development and their effects; these were compared across functional lines and regional boundaries.[6] In addition to these more formal questions (listed in Appendix II), numerous other questions tailored to the person interviewed were interjected. The purpose of these was to gain more insight into specific issues, events or time periods about which that individual had first-hand knowledge or experience. Approximately half of those interviewed were asked both sets of questions. In a number of cases individually tailored questions were far better suited to the person being interviewed given the information that they could provide. This was true for almost all respondents after the initial interview, as well as for those interviewed in 1988, 1989, 1990, 1991 and 1992. In a few cases the stilted, two to three line "*regimski* " answers to the formal questions made it clear that there was no point in pursuing specific questions.[7]

"Inequality," in the final analysis, is what this study is about. For at the very core of Yugoslav discussions of regional economic development was their understanding and perceptions of economic inequality between republics and regions in Yugoslavia and the mixed picture it presented: where and why it increased and the reason for the mixed results despite the state's claimed forty-five year effort at equalization.

[6] The list of the six questions is provided in Appendix II.

[7] In all cases where this happened during 1982-83 the respondents were either lower level bureaucrats clearly afraid lest they "divulge" something or entry-level but aspiring, politicians.

Appendix II: Formal Interview Questions

The following questions, consisting of the more formal part of the interview, were asked of the the Yugoslav decision-makers. In addition to these, specific questions tailored to the person interviewed were also asked. The latter are not dealt with here.

1. (a) What have been the main goals, achievements and shortcomings in terms of development of the LDRs? (b) Was the goal really pursued from the beginning or was it given secondary importance because of the "difficult objective situation" that Yugoslavia found itself in?

2. (a) Why was industry preferred over agriculture for the development of Yugoslavia? Was there influence of the Soviet Model...or fear of the "kulaks"? (b) Was there any demand either within or outside the policy making circles for the increased development of agriculture?

3. What made the development of the LDRs a more important issue in the 1960s than in the early years? Why the change in course in 1965 (creation of the Fund for Development)? Who was for and who against this change? Was it a "gift" from the "top" or a response to increased dissatisfaction?

4. How do you judge the result of industrial investments to date in terms of efficiency and success for the development of the LDRs?

5. Given the fact that development of the LDRs is an important goal for political and ideological reasons, what do you think is the best way of achieving it?

6. Has the economic disparity between the DRs and the LDRs narrowed or increased, and if the latter, why?
   A. "Bad" politics of development
   B. Politics are good, but poorly implemented
   C. Inevitability of development, i.e. Kuznetz's inverted curve

Appendix III

Names and Positions of Interviewed Yugoslav Decision-Makers for Regional Development, by Republic or Region

Federal

Bazler-Madzar, Marta. Economics Institute.*
June 3, 1983.

Bjelica, Petar. Director of Institute for Industrial Research.
September 10 and 13, 1983.

Boderoga, Nedo. Yugoslav Chamber of Commerce, in charge of regional development and thus of the joint ventures between the DRs and the LDRs; secretary of the working group for regional development led by Jovo Kepdija. Past positions: president of a commune in Sarajevo, delegate to the Federal Assembly for BiH, director of a work organization.
October 12, 1983.

Buric, Rasa. Economist UNDP, Belgrade.
October 11, 1983.

Cemovic, Momcilo. Federal Fund for the Crediting Faster Development of the Insufficiently Developed Republics and the Autonomous Provinces, director.
January 6, 1990. June 21, 1991. May 25, 1992.

* The above institutes marked by asteriks were de-federalized in 1972, at which point they automatically became republic institutes (and banks). However, because the views expressed and positions taken consistently reflected a broader (than Serbian regional) view, which coincided with the fact that all respondents had begun working in institutes while they were still federal or just after the de-federalization, I have placed them in the federal category.

Corbe, Klime. Federal Fund for the Crediting Faster Development of the Insufficiently Developed Republics and the Autonomous Provinces, director. Past position: member of the Presidency of the LCY.
May 9 and 10, 1983.

Djilas, Milovan. One of Tito's most trusted war-time associates, Djilas was the first to warn of the impending degeneration of the Yugoslav revolution and of its leadership into a "New Class." The party expulsion and arrest of "one of their own," made him the first and best known post-war communist dissident of his time.
At his home in Belgrade. August 17 and 18, 1988. January 6, 1990. May 25, 1992.

Gajevic, Misa. Federal Bureau of Statistics.
September 3, 1983.

Inkovic, Milica. Federal Bureau of Statistics.
September 3, 1983.

Jandric, Misa. Federal Bureau for Social Planning, member of a group of four for regional development.
August 30 and September 13, 1983. August 12, 1990.

Kepdija, Jovo. Federal Bureau for Social Planning, in charge of the section for regional development. (His mandate ran out in the course of 1983 and his new position, still at the Federal Bureau for Social Planning, was that of director of Industrial Development.) Past positions: Chef du Cabinet of the Prime Minister, First President of the State Planning Commission of Yugoslavia.
September 13 and 21, 1983.

Kovacevic, Zivorad. Yugoslav Ambassador to the United States, Washington, D.C.
July 26, 1989.

Lecic, Milorad. Institute for Agricultural Economics,* the Institute which is the mandator for the World Bank, for agricultural development of all Yugoslavia; for 32 years was in charge of the development of hilly and mountainous regions for agricultural development. Past positions: inspector on the State Control Commission, 1946-51.
September 6 and 7, 1983.

Mandic, Nedeljko. Federal Executive Council, member without portfolio representative from BiH. Federal Representative of the inter-republic committee for the development of the LDRs, attached to the Federal Executive Council.
September 7, 1983.

Marinkovic, Dragutin. Head of Cabinet of the Federal Executive Council. September 7, 1983.

Markovic, Ljubislav. Federal Assembly member, and member of the congressional committee for development of the LDRs in the Federal Assembly (in the Chamber of Republics and Provinces); member of the inner group of Krajger's Commission for Economic Stabilization; member of the Presidency of the Socialist Alliance; professor Faculty of Political Science, University of Belgrade. Past positions: Markovic has held numerous positions in the Party and the government, both republic (Serbia) and Federal, among them secretary of the CPY committee and member of Bureau for administration of districts (Srez), 1944-47; director of the Party School CK of Serbia, 1954-55; member of the constitutional commission, 1969-74; member of the Federal Executive Council, 1969-74; Serbian representative in the Federal Chamber of Republics and Regions, 1974-78 and 1978-83.
October 10, 11, November 11 and December 15, 1982. January 28, 29, February 16, 17, April 20, 27, May 30, July 23,and September 20, 1983. July 12, 1988.

Medenica, Spasoje. Federal Executive Council, member without portfolio. Past positions: Vice-president of the republic Executive Council of Montenegro, President of the inter-republic committee for social planning and development.[1] Past position: general director for policy and planning of development in the Federal Bureau for Social Planning, section for economic-technical cooperation.
September 20, 1983.

Milic, Slobodan. Institute for Agricultural Economics, director. September 8, 1983.

Miljkovic, Dusan. Statistical Bureau, Beograd. January 3, 1990. May 25, 1992.

Mladenovic, Mihailo. Federal Bureau for Social Planning, section for regional development.[2] Member of sub-group for studying development of the

[1] The committee is comprised of one representative from each of the republics and regions, and Medenica, the federal representative. It is, in Medenica's words, the "filter between the FEC and the Assembly; that's where compromises are sought." That is, all eight take their positions - plus the person who represented the proposal, Mladenovic (from Federal Bureau for Social Planning, section on regional development) who may want to defend it.

[2] Mladenovic worked in the section for development of the LDRs from 1955 when the sector for development of the LDRs was first created; along with Kosta Mihailovic, he was the person most consistently referred to as the expert on regional development throughout Yugoslavia. He is also the person who actually wrote the section on "The Regional Aspect of Yugoslav Development" for Krajger's 1983 program of Economic

LDRs, ex officio member of committee on regional development in the Federal Executive Council. Past Position: professor of economics at the University of Belgrade.
March 3, July 25 and August 19, 1983.

Mrkic, Branislav. Fund for the Development of the LDRs, aide to the director, and delegate from Serbia. Past position: aide to director of Republic Bureau for Social Planning of Serbia, 1968-79.
August 20 and 28, 1983.

Nikolic, Mica. Federal Bureau for Statistics. Past positions: Head of Industrial Statistics, 1954-72; director of Economic Statistics, 1958-72; Advisor to Institute of Statistics, 1972-82. At the time of the 1983 interview, Nikolic had just left the Statistics Bureau for the Economic Institute because a new director had come to power at the Bureau for Statistics, who "changed the manner of work, and even the goals." Not a Party member.
Mid-September, 1983. August 12, 1990.

Othman, Khalil. UNDP, Head of the Delegation, Belgrade.
October 11, 1983.

Radovanovic, Jovan. Journalist, BORBA, Belgrade.
November 10, 11, 12, 18 and 22, 1983.
August 16, 1988. August 24 and November 16 to 19, 1989. January 20 and 21, 1990. August 12, 1991. May 23 to 25, 1992.

Rusevan, Bozo. Federal Bureau for Social Planning, Belgrade.
January 5 and August 12, 1990.

Spasic, Slobodan. Fund for the Development of the LDRs, member of the directing committee of 24.
May 9 and August 20, 1983. November 16, 1990.

Skerlavaj, Andrej. President of Commission for International Relations in Parliament.
August 4, 1988.

Vajgl, Ivo. Porte Parole for Secretary of Foreign Affairs, International Press Center, Belgrade.
July 11, 1988.

Vujanic, Nenad. Agrobanka,* Belgrade. (Before decentralization in 1972, this was the Federal Bank through which most of the investment for agriculture

Stabilization of Yugoslavia; the group then added Part I, and omitted his section on the conception of the transformation of the Development Fund and the evaluation of development of the LDRs to date. Not a Party member.

was channeled; after 1972 it became the bank for Serbia proper [without the autonomous provinces] for the development of agriculture.]
August 27, 1983. August 3, 1988.

Vukmanovic-Tempo, Svetozar. One of Tito's chief lieutenants in the Partisan Resistance movement and leader of the legendary uprising in Bosnia-Hercegovina. Vukmanovic-Tempo held the post of Chairman of the Federal Planning Commission from 1952 to 1956 (de facto from 1950 when Boris Kidric became ill). In that position, he was responsible for industrial development.
January 23, 1990.

Zolic, Hasan. Federal Bureau for Social Planning, Belgrade. In charge of the section for development of the LDRs.
November 16 and 17, 1989. January 5 and August 12, 1990.

Slovenia

Bajt, Alexander. Economics Institute, director, professor of Economics at the Faculty of Law, University of Ljubljana. Member of the inner group (of 13) of Krajger's Commission.
November 9, 1983. August 3, 1988.

Bole, Veljko. Economic Institute, Ljubljana.
July 22, 1989.

Briski, Andrej. Republic Bureau for Social Planning, Slovenia, assistant to the director. Responsible for regional development within Slovenia and also for inter-republic cooperation. In 1983, he had worked there for 20 years. Past positions: Republic Bureau for Urbanization, high-school teacher.
November 8, 1983.

Ferfila, Bogomil. Economist and Political Scientist, Faculty of Sociology, Political Science and Journalism, University of Ljubljana, Slovenia.
August 4, 1988. January 9, 1990.

Kukar, Stanka. Institute of Economic Research, Ljubljana.
January 9, 1990. May 29, 1992.

Pockar, Gregor. Faculty of Economics, University of Ljubljana. Member of the broader group (of 35-40) that worked in Krajger's Commission for the Economic Stabilization of Yugoslavia.
November 9, 1983.

Repe, Bozo. Historian, Ljubljana.
January 9, 1990.

Rus, Veljko. Institute for Sociology, director. Interviewed at the Sociological Meetings 1983, first meetings allowed to be held in a decade, Portoroz, Slovenia, November 9-12, 1983.
November 9 and 10, 1983.

Sicherl, Pavel. Faculty of Law (Economics section) of the University of Ljubljana. Past positions: ten years (1964-74) at the Federal Economics Institute in Belgrade under Branko Horvat as his deputy; previously worked at the Federal Bureau for Social Planning.
November 7, 1983. January 10, 1990.

Suklje, Borut. Member of the Republic Executive Council, Ljubljana.
August 4, 1988.

Croatia

Bicanic, Ivo. Economist, Faculty of Philosophy, Zagreb, Croatia.
November 13, 1989. May 21 and June 1, 1992.

Bogunovic, Aleksander. Faculty of Economics, University of Zagreb (half-time) and Republic Bureau for Social Planning, Croatia (half-time), section on regional development. (In 1983 he had worked there for sixteen years, including the six years spent at Horvat's Institute in Belgrade.)
September 29, 1983. June 1, 1992.

Crkvenac, Mato. Republic Bureau for Social Planning, director since 1978; member of the Republic Executive Council; member of the inter-republic committee for the development of the LDRs attached to the Federal Executive Council, headed by Spasoje Medenica (see Federal); Chair of the Commission on Development and Planning in Croatia; and assistant professor at the Faculty of Economics, University of Zagreb.
September 30, 1983.

Dapcevic-Kucar, Savka. Croatian Prime Minister and head of the Party from 1966 until the December 1971 purge of the leaders of the "Croatian Spring." Since the fall of communism she has reemerged as the leader of one of the opposition parties in Croatia, the Croatian National Party (*Hrvatska Narodna Stranka*).
May 27, 1992.

Grdesic, Ivan. Faculty of Political Science, University of Zagreb.
June 20, 21, 30 and 31, 1991. May 21, 22, 28, 29 and 30, 1992.

Horvat, Branko. Faculty of Law, University of Zagreb, and Economic Institute of Zagreb. Was head of the Federal Economic Institute in Belgrade.

September 26 and October 3 and 6, 1983.

Korosic, Marjan. University of Zagreb and Economics Institute, Zagreb. Member of the Federal Economics Council, i.e., one of the four Croatian representatives on the economic advisory body of the Federal Executive Council.
September 29 and October 4, 1983. July 8, 1988.

Lang, Rikard. Economic Institute, Zagreb.
September 26 and 29, 1983.

Marendic, Bozo. Economic Institute, Zagreb; has worked on individual republic projects for the long-term development of Macedonia, Serbia, Montenegro, Vojvodina, Kosovo, Croatia; member of the republic commission for the development of the less developed areas of Croatia. Past position: assistant to Branko Horvat at the Economic Institute, Belgrade.
September 27, 1983.

Pajic, Zeljko. Republic Bureau for Social Planning (Croatia), replacement for the general director; previously was in charge of the sector for regional development for Croatia.
December 18, 1989. August 13, 1990.

Stipetic, Vladimir. Faculty of Economics, University of Zagreb; director of the Lexographic Bureau.
October 5, 1983.

Supek, Rudi. Sociologist, regime critic, former head of the Association of Yugoslav Sociologists (purged in 1975) and co-founder and head of the philosophical-sociological journal PRAXIS censored in 1975.
November 21, 1983. July 6, 1988. November 7, 1989.

Tomac, Zdravko, Vice-President of Croatia, Professor of Political Science, University of Zagreb.
May 28 and 29, 1992.

Turcic, Ivan. Economic Institute, Zagreb and Faculty of Economics, University of Zagreb. Past position: Head of the sector for Regional Development in the Republic Planning Bureau of Croatia, 1963-66)
September 27, 1983.

Vojnic, Dragomir. Head of Federal Economic Council and Director of Economic Institute, Economic Institute, Zagreb.
July 8, 1988.

Vojvodina

Korbatfinski, Viktor. Republic Bureau for Social Planning, Vojvodina. In 1983, he had worked there for 25 years.
November 15, 1983.

Korica, Sinisa. Member of the Executive Council of Vojvodina, President of the Planning Commission of Vojvodina and member of the inter-republic committee for the development of the LDRs, attached to the Federal Executive Council headed by Spasoje Medenica (see Federal).
November 16, 1983.

Mitrovic, Misa. Republic Bureau for Social Planning, Vojvodina, director.
November 15, 1983.

Poroski, Milan. Center for Information and Propaganda, Novi Sad.
August 9, 1988.

Radivojevic, Rados. Marxist Center, Novi Sad.
August 10, 1988.

Serbia

Beric, Branislav. Economic Institute.
September 13, 1983.

Berkovic, Eva. Economic Institute.
September 17, 1983.

Kovac, Oskar. Faculty of Economics, Belgrade. Member of the the inner group of 13 of the Krajger Commission. Past position: Republic Planning Bureau (Serbia).
January 12, 1983.

Macura, Milos. Economic Institute.
September 17, 1983.

Marsenic, Dragutin. Faculty of Economics, Belgrade. Past position: Secretary of the Economic Council of Yugoslavia, member of the President's cabinet, 1963-69.
January 17, 18, 21 and August 24, 1983.

Mihailovic, Kosta. Economics Institute, director. The preeminent Yugoslav expert on Regional Development.
January 12, 20, February 14, March 3 and September 7, 1983. July 14, 1988.

Mladenovic, Radmila. Invest Banka; has worked there since 1962 when it was still an all-Yugoslav Investment Bank, section on crediting.
August 19, 1983.

Nekarada, Radmila. Economics Institute (Sociologist).
September 13, 1983. July 14, 1988.

Ocic, Ceslav. Economic Institute.
June 3, 1983. August 9 and 16, 1988. November 17, 1989.

Pecujlic, Miloslav. Faculty of Law (Sociologist).
June, 1983.

Peic, Lazo. Faculty of Economics, Belgrade.
January 24, 1983.

Radic, Mihailo. Faculty of Economics, Belgrade.
March 4, 1983.

Ristic, B. Faculty of Economics, Belgrade.
February 18, 1983.

Saljic, M. Republic Bureau for Social Planning, Serbia, section on regional development. Past position: Trepce mine (lead & zinc), Kosovo, assistant to the financial director.
September 16, 1983.

Stanic, Nikola. President for the Committee for Agriculture (i.e. Secretary of Agriculture), Serbia. Past positions: deputy director of Republic Planning Bureau, Serbia (agriculture). Member of Republic Assembly, Serbia.
August 27, 1983.

Zunkovic, Demetar. Faculty of Law of the University of Belgrade, section for International Affairs.
September 1, 1983.

Kosovo

Alicir, Lindita. Journalist, Pristina, Kosovo.
October 16, 1983.

Basota, Noori. Faculty of Economics, University of Pristina.
October 18, 1983.

Berisa, Hasan. Republic Bureau for Social Planning, Kosovo, director. Member of the inter-republic committee for the development of the LDRs

attached to the Federal Executive Council, led by Spasoje Medenica (see Federal). Past positions: led the program for coordinated metal industries of Kosovo (2 years); SIZ for employment (7 years).
October 16 and 17, 1983.

Berlajolli, Sami. Cooperative Bank of Kosovo, advisor in the sector for Planning and Analysis (i.e., the sector which allocates the Development Fund money for investments). Past position: director of the Bureau of Statistics, Kosovo, 1970-74. (Director of Plan for Regional Development of Kosovo.)
October 18, 1983.

Bljakaj, Rama. Republic Bureau for Social Planning, Kosovo, assistant to the director, and head of section for development of less developed areas of Kosovo.
October 17, 1983.

Gerguri, Gani. Journalist, Pristina, Kosovo.
October 16, 1983.

Janicjevic, Ljubislav. Republic Chamber of Commerce, Kosovo.
October 17, 1983.

Limani, Musa. Faculty of Economics, University of Pristina. Member of the Federal Economic Council. Past position: member of the Kosovo Executive Council, 1970-75.
October 18 and 19, 1983.

Sahmanovic, Zuki. Radio-Television, Pristina.
October 16 and 18, 1983.

Zejnulaku, Josuf. Director of Ferro-Nickel. Member of the broader group of the Krajger Commission. Past positions: under-secretary for road building in Kosovo, director of Bureau for Economic Development of Pristina, Vice-President of Chamber of Economy.
October 18, 1983.

A medical doctor, an engineer, a student--all requested anonymity, Pec.
October, 1989.

Bosnia-Hercegovina

Cecez, Momir. Faculty of Economics, Sarajevo. Head of Learned Society (section) of Economists of Yugoslavia. Past positions: director of the Institute of Economics, Secretary of the Economy for BiH, director of *Jablanka*, worked for the Economic Council of SFRJ in Boris Kidric's cabinet (1947-52), has worked on a number of U.N. projects for LDCs.

June 9, 1983.

Director of Republic Bureau for Social Planning, BiH. Past positions: director of the Bureau for Social Planning for the city of Mostar, president of a commune.
June 10, 1983.

Duric, Nenad. Republic Bureau for Social Planning, BiH, section for regional development. Past position: Institute for Urbanization.
June 10, 1983.

Gavranovic, Suha. Republic Bureau for Social Planning, BiH, coordinator of the group for development of the LDRs.
June 10, 1983.

Hadziomerovic, Hasan. Faculty of Economics, University of Sarajevo, and Economics Institute, member of the Academy of Arts and Sciences, BiH.
June 9, 1983.

Kamenica, Sulejman. Economics Institute, development of the less developed areas of BiH.
June 8, 9 and 10, 1983.

Maksimovic, Slobodan. Director, Economic Institute, Sarajevo.
July 28, 1988.

Milanovic, Radovan. Member of the Republic Executive Council, BiH, and professor at the Faculty of Economics. Past position: director of the Economics Institute, 1975-83.
June 10, 1983, and July 18, 1988.

Montenegro

Gluscevic, Bosko. Economics Institute, head of the group for development of the LDRs in the Krajger Commission (resigned before completion). Past positions: eight years in federal Government, Ambassador to France, Italy and Great Britain.
June 14 and 15, 1983. July 18, 1988.

Gogic, Janko. Faculty of Economics, University of Titograd.
June 15, 1983.

Ivanovic, Marija. Economics Institute. Past positions: at the republic level, head of the economic sector; head of the financial sector in a firm.
June 16, 1983.

Sisevic, Bozidar. Economics Institute and Faculty of Economics, University of Titograd.
June 15, 16 and September 7, 1983. July 18, 1988.

Soskic, Budislav. Head of the Academy of Sciences of Montenegro, member of the inner group of 13 of Krajger's Commission, head of the group on unemployment and professor at the Economics Faculty in Belgrade.
January 11 and June 15, 1983.

Vukcevic, Risto. Economics Faculty, Titograd.
June 15 and 16, 1983.

Macedonia

Andrejevski, Uros. Socialist Alliance of Macedonia, president. Past positions: once republic delegate and twice delegate to the Federal Assembly, member of the inter-republic committee for development of LDRs, at 17 (1943) he became deputy minister of labor in Macedonia; at age 15 he had received the highest medal of Macedonia, "certificate of service," the youngest person in Macedonia to have received it.
May 12 and 24, 1983.

Kljusev, Nikola. Economics Faculty, University of Kiril and Metodija, Skopje.
May 11, 1983.

Malinovski, Cane. Republic Bureau for Social Planning, aide to the director.
May 11, 1983.

Popovski, Nadjenko. Republic Bureau for Social Planning, Macedonia, director. Member of the inter-republic committee for the development of the LDRs attached to the Federal Executive Council, headed by Spasoje Medenica (see Federal).
May 11, 1983.

Romano, Maurice. Member of Republic Presidency of the League of Communists of Macedonia. Past positions: Macedonian delegate to Federal Assembly (eight years), vice-premier of government of Macedonia, Ambassador to Chile, Professor at the faculty of Economics; at the republic level, Minister of Finance (eight years) and Minister of Trade (four years).
May 11, 1983.

Veljkovic, Dusko. Faculty of Economics, President of the Committee for Regional Development.
May 11 and July 19, 1983.

Zelenkov, Branko. Institute of Economics, Skopje, director. May 26, 1983.

Selected Bibliography

Apter, David E. *Ideology and Discontent*. London: Free Press of Glencoe, 1964.

Bahry, Donna and Nechemias, Carol. "Half Full or Half Empty?: The Debate over Soviet Regional Equality." *Slavic Review*. 1982, pp. 366-383.

Banac, Ivo. *The National Question in Yugoslavia*. Ithaca: Cornell University Press, 1984.

Baskin, Mark. "Crisis in Kosovo," *Problems of Communism*, March-April, 1983.

Begic, Kasim. *Jugoslovenski "sjever" i "jug." (Yugoslav "North" and "South")*. Sarajevo: Nisro "Oslobodenje," 1989.

Bicanic, Rudolf. "The Economics of Socialism in a Developed Country." *Foreign Affairs*, July 1966.

_______. *Economic Policy In Socialist Yugoslavia*. Cambridge, Mass.: Cambridge University Press, 1973.

Bilandzic, Dusan. *Geneza ideje o ustavu iz 1974: Prijepori oko politickog sistema, (Genesis of the Idea on the 1974 Constitution: Arguments over the Political System)*. Zagreb: Centar za idejno-teorijski Rad GK SKH, Zagreb.

Bombelles, Joseph T. *Economic Development of Communist Yugoslavia, 1947-1964*. Stanford: Hoover Institution of War, Revolution and Peace, Stanford University Press, 1968.

_______. "Federal Aid to the Less Developed Areas of Yugoslavia." *East Europe Politics and Society*. Vol. 5, no. 3. Fall, 1991.

Brass, Paul R. *Ethnicity and Nationalism*. New Delhi: Sage Publications, 1991

Brown, A. and Gray, J., eds. *Political Culture and Political Change in Communist States*. 2nd edition. New York: Holmes and Meier Publishers, 1979.

Burg, Steven L. *Conflict and Cohesion in Socialist Yugoslavia*. Princeton: Princeton University Press, 1983.

Burkett, John P. *The Effects of Economic Reform in Yugoslavia*. Berkeley: Institute of International Studies, University of California, 1983.

_______. "Stabilization Measures in Yugoslavia: An Assessment of the Proposal of Yugoslavia's Commission for Problems of Economic Stabilization," U.S. Congress, Joint Economic Committee, *East European Economies, Slow Growth in the 1980s*, Vol. 3 Washington, D.C., 1986.

Burkett and Skero. "Inter-Regional Economic Integration in Yugoslavia, 1963-84." Unpublished paper presented at the European Program of the Wilson Center, Smithsonian Institution, Washington, D.C., September 4, 1986.

Burks, R.V. *The Dynamics of Communism in Eastern Europe*. Princeton: Princeton University Press, 1961.

Cecez, Momir. *Neki aspekti efikasnosti drustvenih sredstava u privredno nedovojno razvijenim podrucjima*. (*Some Aspects of Efficacy of Social Means in the Economically Insufficiently Developed Regions*). Skopje: Makedonska Akademija na naukite i umetnosti, 1980.

Cobeljic, Nikola. *Privreda Jugoslavije: rast struktura i funkcionisanje, knjiga prva*. (*The Economy of Yugoslavia: Growth, Structure and Functioning, Volume I*). Belgrade: Savremena administracija i institut za ekonomska istrazivanja, 1974.

_______. *Privreda Jugoslavije: rast struktura i funkcionisanje, knjiga druga*. (*The Economy of Yugoslavia: Growth, Structure and Functioning, Volume II*). Belgrade: Savremena administracija i institut za ekonomska istrazivanja, 1974.

_______. *Politika i metode privrednog razvoja Jugoslavije, 1947-1956*. (*Politics and Method of Economic Development of Yugoslavia, 1947-1956*). Belgrade, 1959.

Colanovic, Branko. *Razvoj nerazvijenih pokrajina Jugoslavije*. (*Development of the Underdeveloped Areas of Yugoslavia*). Belgrade: Medunarodna Politika, 1966, no. 9.

Comisso, Ellen Turkish. *Workers' Control Under Plan and Market*. New Haven & London: Yale University Press, 1979.

______. "Yugoslavia in the 1970s: Self-Management and Bargaining." *Journal of Comparative Economics*, 4:192-208.

The Constitution of the Socialist Federal Republic of Yugoslavia. Belgrade: 1974.

Darski, Josef. "Reformism and Nationalism: Two Responses to the Crisis of Communist Power in Yugoslavia," *Uncaptive Minds*, Vol. 11, No. 2, March-April, 1989.

Dolenc, Marjan and Pleskovic, Boris. "Regional Development in a Socialist, Developing and Multinational Country: The Case of Yugoslavia." *International Regional Science Review.* 7:1-24.

Drustveni plan razvoja Jugoslavije od 1947 do 1952 godine. (Social Plan of Economic Development of Yugoslavia for the Period 1947 to 1952). Sluzbeni List FNRJ no. 36/47.

Drustveni plan privrednog razvoja Jugoslavije od 1961 do 1965 godine. (Social Plan of Economic Development of Yugoslavia for the Period 1961 to 1965). Sluzbeni List FNRJ, no. 53, 1961.

Drustveni plan razvoja Jugoslavije od 1966 do 1970 godine. (Social Plan of Economic Development of Yugoslavia for the Period 1966 to 1970). Sluzbeni List FNRJ, no. 28, 1966.

Drustveni plan razvoja Jugoslavije za period od 1971 do 1975 godine. (Social Plan of Development of Yugoslavia for the Period 1971 to 1975). Sluzbeni List FNRJ, no. 33/35, 1971.

Drustveni plan razvoja Jugoslavije za razdoblje od 1976 do 1980. (Social Plan of Economic Development of Yugoslavia for the Period 1976 to 1980).

Drustveni plan razvoja Jugoslavije za razdoblje od 1981 do 1985. (Social Plan of Economic Development of Yugoslavia for the Period 1981 to 1985).

The Development Plan of Yugoslavia, 1986-1990. Belgrade: Jugoslovenski pregled, 1986.

Economist, 16, Belgrade, 1963, no. 1.

Edelman, Murray J. *The Symbolic Uses of Politics.* Urbana: University of Illinois, 1964.

Ekonomska Misao, Vol. VIII, No. 3, December 1975. Vol. XVI, No. 2, June 1983, No. 3, September 1983.

Evropski Centar za mir i razvoj (ECMR) [European Center for Peace and Development] *Fond Federacije za kreditiranje brzeg razvoja privredno nedovoljno razvijenih republika i pokrajina 1965-1990: iskustva i rezultati.* (Federal Fund for the Crediting for Faster Development of the Economically Insufficiently Developed Republics and Regions 1965-1990: Experience and Results) Belgrade, 1991.

Fond Federacije za kreditiranje brzeg razvoja privredno nedovoljno razvijenih republika i autonomnih pokrajina, (Fond Federacije). *Priliv, plasman i utrosak sredstava fonda za period 1966-1970.* Podaci iz zavrsnih racuna fonda za posmatrane godine. (*Influx, Placement and Expenditure of the Fund for the Period 1966-70.* Data from the completed accounts of the fund for the years 1966-70). Belgrade: 1971

_______. *Dokumentacija, o prilivu, plasmanu i utrosku sredstava fonda u periodu od 1.I 1971. do 31.XII 1975. godine.* (*Documentation on Influx, Placement and Expenditure of the Means of the Fund for the Period January 1, 1971, to December 31, 1975*). Belgrade: May, 1976 .

_______. *O priticanju i usmerivanju sredstava fonda u periodu od 1976 do 1980 godine.* (*On the Flow and Direction of Means of the Fund for the Period from 1976 to 1980*). Belgrade: May, 1981.

_______. *U funkciji ostvarivanja dogovorene politike razvoja privredno nedovoljno razvijenih republika i SAP Kosovo u razdoblju 1976 do 1980 godine.* (*In the Function for Implementing the Agreed upon Policies of Development of the Insufficiently Developed Republics and the Region of Kosovo for the period 1976 to 1980*). Belgrade: October, 1981.

_______. *Sistemske osnove i zakonski propisi kojima se regulise privredni razvoj nedovoljno razvijenih republika i autonomne pokrajine Kosovo.* (*Systemic Foundations and Legal Statutes Regulating the Economic Development of the Insufficiently Developed Republics and Autonomous Region of Kosovo*). Belgrade: August, 1982 .

_______. *Statut fonda federacije za kreditiranje brzeg razvoja privredno nedovoljno razvijenih republika i autonomnih pokrajina.* (*Statute of the Federal Fund for the Crediting of Faster Development of the Economically Insufficiently Developed Republics and Autonomous Regions*). Belgrade: February, 1983 .

_______. *Razvoj privredno nedovoljno razvijenih podrucja u Jugoslavije.* (*Development of the Insufficiently Developed Regions in Yugoslavia*). Belgrade: Srbostampa, 1986.

Francis, E.K. *Interethnic Relations*. New York: Elsevier Scientific Publications, 1976.

Friedman, John and Alonso, William., eds. *Regional Development and Planning*. Cambridge: MIT Press, 1964.

Geertz, Clifford. "Ideology as a Cultural System." In *Ideology and Discontent*, edited by David Apter. London: The Free Press of Glencoe, 1964.

_______, ed. *Old Societies and New States*. New York: The Free Press of Glencoe, 1963.

Gerschenkron, Alexander. *Economic Backwardness in Historical Perspective*. Cambridge: The Belknap Press of Harvard University Press, 1962.

Gluscevic, Bosko. "U istoriji popravni ispit ne postoji." (In History There Is No Make-Up Exam). *Interview*, Fall 1982.

Gusija, Ismet. *Prirodni izvori i privredni razvoj SAP Kosova*. (*Economic Sources and Economic Development of the SAP of Kosovo*). Pristina: Jedinstvo, 1982.

Hadziomerovic, Hasan. "Jedan model regionalizacije primenjen na projeckciji privrednog razvoja BiH." (One Model of Regionalization Applied to the Projection of the Economic Development of BiH). *Ekonomist*, no. 1-2, 1965.

_______. *Elementi ekonomske teorije regionalnog razvoja*. (*Elements of Economic Theory of Regional Development*). Skopje: Makedonska akademija za naukite i umetnosti, 1980.

Hirschman, Albert O. *The Strategy of Economic Development*. New Haven: Yale University Press, 1958.

Hobsbawm, Eric. *Nations and Nationalism Since 1790*. New York: Cambridge University Press, 1990

Hoffman, George W. and Neal, Fred Warner. *Yugoslavia and the New Communism*. New York: Twentieth Century Fund, 1962.

Horvat, Branko. *Analiza privredne situacije*. (*Analysis of the Economic Situation*). Belgrade: Institut Ekonomskih Nauka, 1969.

_______. *Analiza privrednih kretanja i prijedlozi za ekonomsku politiku*. (*Analysis of Economic Mobility and Suggestions for Economic Policy*). Belgrade: Institut Ekonomskih Nauka, 1969.

_______. *Privredni sistem i ekonomska politika Jugoslavije. (The Economic System and the Political Economy of Yugoslavia)*. Belgrade: Institut Ekonomskih Nauka, 1970.

_______. *Business Cycles In Yugoslavia.* White Plains: International Arts and Sciences Press, 1971.

_______. *The Yugoslav Economic System.* White Plains: International Arts and Sciences Press, 1976.

Ivanovic, Marija. *Finansiranje razvoja nerazvijenih podrucja Jugoslavije. (Financing the Development of Underdeveloped Areas of Yugoslavia)*. Titograd: Institut za drustveno-ekonomska istrazivanja, 1978.

Janos, Andrew. "Interest Groups and the Structure of Power: Critique and Comparisons." *Studies in Comparative Communism,* 11, No. 1, Spring 1979.

_______. "Group Politics in Communist Society: A Second Look at the Pluralist Model." In *Authoritarian Politics in Modern Society,* edited by Samuel P. Huntington and Clement H. Moore. New York: Basic Books, 1970.

Jowitt, Kenneth. "Inclusion and Mobilization in European Leninist Regimes." *World Politics,* 28. October, 1975.

Kaldor, N. "A Model of Economic Growth." *Economic Journal,* 67: 591-624.

Kardelj, Edvard. *Pravci razvoja politickog sistema socialistickog samoupravljanja. (Directions of the Development of the Political System of Social Self-Management)*. Belgrade: Komunist, 1978.

Keller, James G. *The Politics of Nationalism and Ethnicity.* New York: St. Martin's Press, 1971.

Kidric, Boris. *Privredni problemi FNRJ. (Economic Problems of FSRY)*. Belgrade: Kultura, 1948.

Kljusev, Nikola. *Teorija i politika regionalnog razvoja, knjiga prva. (Theory and Politics of Regional Development, book one)*. Belgrade: Niro, 1979.

Komisija saveznih drustvenih saveta za probleme ekonomske stabilizacije, Dokumenti komisije, knjiga 4: regionalni aspekti razvoja Jugoslavije. (Documents of the Commission, book 4: Regional Aspect of the Development of Yugoslavia). Belgrade: Centar za radnicko samoupravljanje, 1983.

Kommunist No 7, July 1953.

_______. February 28, 1958.

_______. Supplement, May 10, 1962.

Korosic, Marijan. *Ekonomske nejednakosti u jugoslavenskoj privredi.* (*Economic Inequalities in the Yugoslav Economy.*) Zagreb: Biblioteka Znanstvenih Radova, 1983.

Kosturica, Vojislav. "Transformation of Yugoslav Federalism from Decentralized to Peripheralized Federation." Paper presented at The European Program of the Wilson Center, Smithsonian Institution, Washington, D.C., September 4-6, 1986.

Kubovic, Branko. *Regionalni aspekt privrednog razvitka Jugoslavije.* (*Regional Aspect of the Economic Development of Yugoslavia*). Zagreb: Biblioteka Ekonomskog Pregleda, 1961.

Lenin, Vladimir I. *Development of Capitalism in Russia.* Moscow: Foreign Languages Publishing House, 1956.

Limani, Musa. *Investicije i privredni razvoj socijalisticke autonomne pokrajine Kosovo.* (*Investments and Economic Development in the Socialist Autonomous Region of Kosovo*). Pristina: Biblioteka-Posebno izdanje.

Madzar, Ljubomir. "The Economy of Yugoslavia: Structure, Growth Record and Institutional Framework," in *Yugoslavia in Transition: Choices and Constraints,* edited by John B. Allcock, John J. Horton and Marko Milivojevic New York and Oxford: Berg Publishers Limited, 1991.

Markovic, Ljubisav. *Ekonomija Jugoslavije.* (*The Economy of Yugoslavia.*) Belgrade: Naucna Knjiga, 1979.

Marsenic, Dragutin V. *Ekonomska struktura i privredni rast Jugoslavije.* (*Economic Structure and Economic Growth of Yugoslavia*). Belgrade: Savremena administracije, 1982.

Martin, Christopher and Tyson, Laura D'Andrea. "Can Titoism Survive Tito: Economic Problems and Policy Choices Confronting Tito's Successors." In *Yugoslavia in the 1980s,* edited by Pedro Ramet. Boulder: Westview Press, 1985.

Meade, J. E. *A Neo-Classical Theory of Economic Growth.* London: Unwin University Books, 1962.

Mihailovic, Kosta. "The Dynamics of Structural Changes as a Context for the Growth Pole Theory." Belgrade: Centre for Regional Development, 1975.

______. "*Drustveni ekonomski razvoj opstina SFRJ.*" (Socio-Economic Development of the Communes of FRSJ). vol. 1. Belgrade: Ekonomika, 1982.

______. *Ekonomska stvarnost Jugoslavije.* (*Economic Reality of Yugoslavia*). Belgrade: Ekonomika, 1982.

______. "Problemi regionalnog privrednog razvoja." (Problems of Regional Economic Development). Belgrade: Zbornik radova, 1982.

______. "Privredna Kriza Jugoslavije: uzroci i moguci uzlaz." (Yugoslav Economic Crisis: Reasons and Possible Exits). Ekonomska Misao, Godina XVI, Belgrade, June 1983.

______. "Regionalni aspekt privrednog razvoja." (Regional Aspect of Economic Development). Belgrade: Ekonomska biblioteka.

Mihailovic, K., Inkovic, P., Srebcic, B. "Les déséquilibres régionaux en Europe." Bruxelles: Centre European de coordination de recherche et de documentation en Sciences Sociales.

Milenkovitch, Deborah D. *Plan and Market in Yugoslav Economic Thought.* New Haven: Yale University Press, 1971.

Mladenovic, Mihailo. "Neki rezultati razvoja privredno nedovoljno razvijenih republika i pokrajine Kosovo 1971-74." (Some Results of the Development of the Insuffieciently Developed Republics and the Region of Kosovo, 1971-74). *Jugoslovenski Pregled* Godina XIX, 1975-76.

______. "Razvoj privredno nedovoljno razvijenih republika i pokrajine Kosovo." (Development of the Economically Insufficiently Developed Republics and the Region of Kosovo). *Jugoslavenski Pregled* 9, 1981.

Moore, John H. "Industrial Production in Yugoslavia, 1952-72." U.S. Congress, Joint Economic Committee. *East European Economics, Post Helsinki.* Government Printing Office: August 25, 1977.

Mostov, Julie. "Regionalism and the Limits of Yugoslav Democracy." Paper presented at The European Program of the Wilson Center, Smithsonian Institution, September 4-6, 1986.

Mueller, John E. *War, Presidents, and Public Opinion.* New York: Wiley, 1973.

Myrdal, Gunnar. *Economic Theory and Underdeveloped Regions.* London: G. Duckworth, 1957.

Neuberger, Egon. "The Yugoslav Investment Auctions." *Quarterly Journal of Economics.* Fall 1959, pp. 88-115.

Ocic, Caslav. *Nacionalna ravnopravnost i regionalni razvoj. (National Equality and Regional Development).* Belgrade: Institut Ekonomskih Nauka, 1986.

_______. *Razvijenost Jugoslavenskih republika i pokrajina od 1950 do 1984. (Development of Yugoslav Republics and Regions from 1950-1984).* Belgrade: Institut Ekonomskih Nuaka, 1986.

OECD Economic Surveys: Yugoslavia (Paris OECD, 1987).

Perroux, Francois. *L'economie du XX eme siecle.* Paris: Presses universitaires de France, 1964.

Pjanic, Zoran. *Samoupravni privredni sistem. (The Self-managed Economic System).* Belgrade: Radnicka Stampa, 1983.

Plestina, Dijana. "From 'Democratic Centralism' to Decentralized Democracy? Trials and Tribulations of Yugoslavia's Development," in *Yugoslavia in Transition: Choices and Constraints,* edited by John B. Allcock, John J. Horton and Marko Milivojevic. New York and Oxford: Berg Publishers Limited, 1991.

Politika i resultati razvoja nedovljno razvijenih podrucja u Jugoslaviji. [translation] Belgrade: Biblioteka Skupstine SFRJ, 1977.

Radio Free Europe, 5, no. 58, November 1980.

_______. Situation Report (SR), No. 6, July 6, 1988.

_______. SR, No. 10, November 11, 1988.

_______. Vol. 14, No. 52, December 30, 1988.

Ramet, Pedro. *Nationalism and Federalism in Yugoslavia, 1963-1983.* Bloomington: Indiana University Press, 1984.

Ramet, Sabrina P. "Serbia's Slobodan Milosevic: A profile." *Orbis,* Winter 1991.

Rothschild, Joseph. *Ethnopolitics: A Conceptual Framework.* New York: Columbia University Press, 1981.

Rubinstein, Alvin Z. *Yugoslavia and the Nonaligned World.* Princeton: Princeton University Press, 1970.

Rusinow, Dennison. "Anatomy of a Student Revolt." I, II in *American Universities Fieldstaff Report*, Southeast Europe Series, 5, 4 and 5. Hanover, N.H.: American Universities Fieldstaff, 1968.

_______. *The Yugoslav Experiment 1948-1974.* Berkeley: University of California Press, 1977.

_______. "National Policy and 'National Question.'" *Yugoslavia in the 1980s.* edited by Pedro Ramet. Boulder: Westview Press, 1990

Sacks, Steven. "Divizionalization in Large Yugoslav Enterprises." *Journal of Comparative Economics*, 4:209-25.

Savezni Zavod za Drustveno Planiranje (SZDP), *Ostvarivanje politike brzeg razvoja privredno nedovoljno razvijenih republika i SAP Kosovo. Sa prikazom regionalnog razvoja.* (*Implementation of the Politics of Faster Development of the Insufficiently Developed Republics and the Autonomous Province of Kosovo. With a Survey of Regional Development*). Belgrade: 1965.

_______. *Razvoj Jugoslavije 1947-1981* [*Development of Yugoslavia 1947-1981*]. Belgrade: May, 1982.

_______. *Analiza* [*Analysis*]. Belgrade: November 3, 1988.

SZZS i SZDP, *Razvoj Jugoslavije 1947-1981.* [*Development of Yugoslavia 1947-1981*]. Belgrade: May, 1982.

_______. *Kriza i reforme, Drustveno-ekonomski razvoj Jugoslavije u periodu 1970-1989 godine.* Belgrade: Izdavacki centar Komunist, 1989.

Savezni Zavod za Statistiku (SZZS), *Jugoslavija 1945-1964, Statisticki pregled.* (*Yugoslavia, 1945-1964), Statistical Overview*). Belgrade 1965.

_______. *Materialni i drustveni razvoj SFR Jugoslavije 1947-1972.* (*Economic and Social Development of FSRY 1947-1972*] Belgrade, 1973.

_______. (SZZS) *i Savezni zavod za drustveno planiranje (SZDP), Razvoj Jugoslavije 1947-1981.* (*Development of Yugoslavia, 1947-1981*). Belgrade, 1982.

_______. *Statisticki godisnjak Jugoslavije, 1983. (Statistical Yearbook of Yugoslavia, 1983)*. Belgrade: Beogradski izdavacko-graficki zavod, August, 1983.

_______. *Jugoslavija 1945-1985, Statisticki prikaz (Yugoslavia 1945-1985, Statistical Overview)* Belgrade, 1986.

_______. *Statisticki godisnjak Jugoslavije, 1989 (Statistical Yearbook of Yugoslavia, 1989)*. Belgrade: Beogradski izdavacko-graficki zavod, August, 1989.

Schrenk, M., Ardalan, C., and El Tatawy, N. A. *Yugoslavia: Self-management Socialism and the Challenges of Development*. A World Bank Country Economic Report. Baltimore: The Johns Hopkins University Press, 1979.

Seton-Watson, Hugh. *Eastern Europe Between the Wars 1918-1941*. 3rd edition, Hamden: Archon Books, 1962.

Schapiro, Leonard and Lewis, John Wilson. "The Roles of the Monolithic Party under the Totalitarian Leader."

Schapiro, Leonard. *Totalitarianism*. New York: Praeger, 1972.

Shoup, Paul. *Communism and the Yugoslav National Question*. New York: Columbia University Press, 1968.

_______. ed. *Problems of Balkan Security: Southeastern Europe in the 1990s* Washington: The Wilson Center Press, 1990

Simonovic, Ivan. "The Impact of Self Management on Federal V.S. Regional Relations in Yugoslavia." Paper presented at The European Program of the Wilson Center, Smithsonian Institution, September 4-6, 1986.

Singleton, Fred. *Twentieth Century Yugoslavia*. New York: Columbia University Press, 1976.

Sirc, Ljubo. *The Yugoslav Economy Under Self-Management*. New York: St. Martin's Press, 1979.

Skilling, H. Gordon and Griffiths, Franklyn, eds. *Interest Groups in Soviet Politics*. Princeton: Princeton University Press, 1971.

Tito, Josip Broz. *Borba za novi svet. (Struggle for a New World)*. Collected and edited speeches of Josip Broz Tito. Belgrade: Preskliping, 1982.

Todorovic et al., *Ekonomska politika FNRJ*. (*Economic Policy of SFRJ*). Belgrade: Rad, 1958.

Tomasevich, Jozo. *Peasants, Politics and Economic Change in Yugoslavia.* Stanford: Stanford University Press, 1955

Tomc, Gregor. "Social Stratification and National Formation in Post-War Yugoslavia." Paper presented at The European Program of the Wilson Center, Smithsonian Institution, Washington, D.C., September 4-6, 1986.

Tyson, Laura D'Andrea. "Investment Allocation: A Comparison of the Reform Experiences of Hungary and Yugoslavia." *Journal of Comparative Economics*, 7:288-303.

_______. *The Yugoslav Economic System and Its Performance in the 1970s.* Berkeley: Institute of International Studies, University of California, 1980.

_______. "The Yugoslav Economy in the 1970s: A Survey of Recent Developments and Future Prospects." U.S. Congress, Joint Economic Committee, *East European Economies Post-Helsinki.* Government Printing Office: August 25, 1977.

Ulam, Adam B. *Titoism and the Cominform.* Westport: Greenwood Press, 1952.

Ustav Socialisticke Federativne Republike Jugoslavije, 1963 godine, "Osnovna Nacela." (Constitution of FSRY, 1963, "Basic Tenets"). Belgrade, 1971.

Vinski, Ivo. Fiksni fondovi Jugoslavije: njenih republika i pokrajina od. 1953 do. 1973. (*Fixed Assets of Yugoslavia: Its republics and regions from 1953 to 1973*). Belgrade: Ekonomika, 1978.

_______. "Regional Growth of Fixed Assets in Yugoslavia, 1946-1980." *Regional Science Association Papers,* 11:127-151.

Vujicic, Danilo. *Udruzivanje sredstava za investicije u nasoj privredi.* (*Association of Means for Investment in Our Economy*). Belgrade: Privredni pregled, 1981.

Waterston, Albert. *Planning in Yugoslavia: Organization and Implementation.* Baltimore: The Johns Hopkins University Press, 1962.

Zerjavic, Vladimir. *Gubici stanovnistva Jugoslavije u drugom svjetskom ratu. (Losses of Yugoslav Population in the Second World War)*. Belgrade: Jugoslavensko Viktimoslosko Drustvo, 1989.

Newspapers

Borba.

Delo

NIN

Politika

Sluzbeni list SFRJ

Vecernji List

Vjesnik

Index

About the Book and Author

The brutal war now raging in what was Yugoslavia, the author argues, is fueled not merely by interethnic hatred but also by longstanding disparities in economic well-being among republics and regions. The Communist leadership, having stated its intention when it took power to eliminate economic disparities, nonetheless failed to confront the conflict of interests that distorted the country's economic policy—and thus never worked out a coherent strategy for regional development. Interregional tensions were inflamed by the failure to close the gap between wealthy and poor areas, directly contributing to the breakup of the country.

Basing her argument on longitudinal data and on in-depth interviews with Yugoslav leaders at federal and regional levels (Milovan Djilas, Svetozar Vukmanovic-Tempo, Bosko Gluscevic, Hasan Zolic, and several dozen others), Dijana Pleština examines and assesses the economic inequalities as well as the effects that the leadership's regional policies had on them. She shows that despite the mandate for equalization that was part of socialist doctrine, Yugoslav leaders were at first unwilling, and later unable, to formulate policies that would enhance the economic well-being of the poorest regions. Instead, they adopted a strategy of "top-down" growth, which enhanced the further development of the wealthier regions. Later, partially in an effort to placate the disadvantaged, they shifted funds to some of the less-developed regions. Rather than promoting equality, such ad hoc "solutions" fostered competition for scarce resources and intensified political cleavages.

Pleština also looks at how the devolution of decisionmaking from central to regional levels, designed to increase government legitimacy and efficiency, actually provided an opportunity for regional leaders to build independent power bases. This trend, in conjunction with the economic slump of the 1980s, further eroded the unity of the federation.

Dijana Pleština is assistant professor of political science at the College of Wooster.

www.ingramcontent.com/pod-product-compliance
Lightning Source LLC
LaVergne TN
LVHW011125300926
849160LV00008B/512
9780367300906